UN/POPULAR CULTURE

SUNY Series, Identities in the Classroom
Deborah P. Britzman and Janet L. Miller, editors

UN/POPULAR CULTURE

*LESBIAN WRITING
AFTER THE SEX WARS*

Kathleen Martindale

STATE UNIVERSITY OF NEW YORK PRESS

Selection from Diane DiMassa, *Hothead Paisan: Homicidal Lesbian Terrorist* Pittsburgh: Cleis Press, 1993) reprinted by kind permission of Giant Ass. Publishing, P.O. Box 214, New Haven, CT 06502.

Published by
State University of New York Press, Albany

© 1997 State University of New York

All rights reserved

Printed in the United States of America

No part of this book may be used or reproduced in any manner whatsoever without written permission. No part of this book may be stored in a retrieval system or transmitted in any form or by any means including electronic, electrostatic, magnetic tape, mechanical, photocopying, recording, or otherwise without the prior permission in writing of the publisher.

For information, address State University of New York Press,
State University Plaza, Albany, NY 12246

Production by Marilyn P. Semerad
Marketing by Terry Abad Swierzowski

Library of Congress Cataloging-in-Publication Data
Martindale, Kathleen, 1947-1995
　　Un/popular culture : lesbian writing after the sex wars / Kathleen Martindale.
　　　　p.　cm. — (SUNY series, identities in the classroom)
　　Includes bibliographical references and index.
　　ISBN 0-7914-3289-0 (hc : alk. paper). — ISBN 0-7914-3290-4 (pbk. : alk. paper)
　　1. Lesbians' writings, American—History and criticism.
2. Homosexuality and literature—United States—History—20th century. 3. Lesbians' writings, American—Study and teaching.
4. Lesbians in literature. 5. Sex in literature. I. Title.
II. Series.
PS153.L46M37 1977
810.9'9206643—dc21
　　　　　　　　　　　　　　　　　　　　　　　　　　96-47153
　　　　　　　　　　　　　　　　　　　　　　　　　　　CIP

10 9 8 7 6 5 4 3 2 1

CONTENTS

Foreword — vii

Acknowledgments — xi

Chapter 1
    The Making of an Un/popular Culture:
    From Lesbian Feminism to Lesbian Postmodernism — 1

Chapter 2
    Paper Lesbians and Theory Queens — 33

Chapter 3
    Back to the Future with *Dykes To Watch Out For*
    and *Hothead Paisan* — 55

Chapter 4
    Toward a Butch-Femme Reading Practice:
    Reading Joan Nestle — 77

Chapter 5
    Sarah Schulman: Urban Lesbian Radicals
    in a Postmodern Mainstream — 103

Chapter 6
    Que(e)rying Pedagogy: Teaching the Un/popular Cultures — 137

Notes — 161

Bibliography — 195

Index — 213

FOREWORD

At stake throughout this text is a pedagogy made from argument. The belief is that on the way to the making of insight one must pass through the hesitations of the argument. Here, the particular arguments caught in their own acts are those of the literary, which is to say, those fictions made from the stuff of communities. The surprise is that the author does not settle the arguments, but works the arguments to unsettle. Readers are invited to grapple with the author's restless consideration: a setting in motion the commotion that is caught off guard within surprising terms of "the unpopular."

When Kathleen Martindale decided on her text's title, she offered readers the means for an ironic trespass through conceptual geographies and identities that argue with the entanglements of disciplines, communities, and of course a book series called "Identities in the Classroom." First, the disorder of the discipline. In the case of disrupting disciplinary borders, Martindale's reach might best be called anti-disciplinary, a method that is akin to what Freud called, when he watched his grandson at play, the game of "fort/da," or the here/gone of a certain reading practice. Our author moves in and out of academic analysis, the stray conversation, and the coincident anecdote. Along the way we pass through the contemporary arguments of literary theory, cultural studies, pedagogical theory, and psychoanalytic inquiry as these play out on the grounds of Lesbian and Gay studies. Occasionally we are asked to stop and ponder strange epistemological formations that point elsewhere. And in all of these actions, readers may consider what makes this text possible: Martindale's own love of learning and love for the complications of language.

Such a volatile combination of theory, wishes, and desire returns in the figure of the paper lesbian, a sort of textual golem who, when called upon and when given life through the author's word, simultaneously interferes and transforms the state of textual and sexual affairs at issue in this text. The state of these affairs is also a state of emergency: the paper lesbian is, after all, an invention called upon for the curious task of commenting on her own design and hence of commenting upon the curious encounter between the wishes of the designer and the desires of the reader. Martindale might call this meeting "community."

We mention that the border of the book series is also trespassed here. Questions of identities in the classroom must take a detour into what supposes the classroom, into what supposes knowledge, and into what supposes identity. From these suppositions we might infer something about the illusiveness of identity and classroom. Readers are offered a rigorous consideration of the stuff of pedagogy as it unravels in university classrooms, in the conference presentation, in the academic argument, in the teacher's rehashing of disturbing events. The drama of the classroom, after all, is played out on larger stages; and the reader passes through the characters of theoretical disputes, the strange work of ignoring texts, the constraints of institutional histories, and most centrally, Martindale's own intellectual biography. The biography as well is one that is made from ironic trespass: of finding ideas in the wrong places, of studying the breakdowns of meaning, of making curiosity from the unpopular, of sifting through reading practices that find the caustic stakes of discontentment.

As we learn in chapter 1, the staging of the polemic is troubled by the very practices of narration. We find not just a story, but a style of telling that is uniquely Martindale. By chapter 2, the text becomes crowded with new imagined communities: comic book heros haunt academic conferences, theory takes a detour into the happenstance of its own citational anxiety. Two forms of comic strips return in chapter 3 where the stakes between what Martindale calls, "the violently surreal of *Hothead Paisan* [meets] the gentle realism of *Dykes To Watch Out For.*" More than genre is at stake when perversity meets diversity but in juxtaposing two ends of this cultural spectrum, Martindale is able to reach what is uncanny for both in cultural politics. Bodily style and the aesthetics of gender are considered in chapter 4. Rather than secure the meanings of Butch and Femme, Martindale surprises with an epistemology of the gift the author Joan Nestle offers. In so doing, Martindale offers readers the gift of a new reading. A different lesbian generation and a different imagined geography is offered in chapter 5, through the work of Sarah Schulman. The reading is archeological and in dusting off the characters, the sense of time at stake in this fiction is not so much the demands of continuity but a consideration of what happens when the demands of the detour pass through the demands of continuity. The questions raised throughout this text return in the form of a reply in the last chapter on pedagogy. And then the texts of the previous chapters return to crowd that singular site of the classroom. The textual practices Martindale offers in reading the particular hesitations of teaching and learning suggest after all that there may be no difference between reading the work of fiction and reading the dream of pedagogy. We become responsible in the reply.

From all of this, we might surmise something about the labile qualities of "the unpopular." We are speaking here of the question of community, of the community that takes its form in question. For throughout this text what is unpopular has to do with the complexities of the arguments within a culture-how these arguments are read, ignored, reconstituted- and, with what happens when this clamorous inside meets a rather hostile outside. The figure of the paper lesbian can then transform into a kaleidoscopic lens upon which to view not just its own formations but the distortions of something larger than itself: the fort/da of representation. Again, our borders are trespassed for the dynamic qualities of "the unpopular" are unstable, unreliable, and contradictory. Canonical debates on the suitability or the properness of the literary figure are of no help here. For after all, this antimony, this improperness is the stuff of pedagogy. This text decided to reside in the curious fault lines of many communities to comment on the marginalities of the center, the marginalities of the margin.

In reading through the acknowledgments, readers will get a sense of the range of Martindale's intellectual communities and friendships. And in reading through the text, one may sense Martindale's restless curiosity and the gift of her signature she leaves behind on a field of study. As Martindale acknowledges in the text's opening gesture, the event of completing this manuscript was also, for Martindale and those she loved, the event of her breast cancer. It is my sadness, and of course, the collective sadness of many others, to report that in the late Fall of 1994, her breast cancer reoccurred and on February 17, 1995, Kathleen Martindale died.

DEBORAH P. BRITZMAN

ACKNOWLEDGMENTS

This book took a longer time to write and finish than it should have because I have been fighting breast cancer since January 1992. Both before and after the first diagnosis and surgery, I have been particularly grateful to the organizers of conferences and panels in Canada, the United States, and Europe who invited me to give papers and presentations on lesbian subjects even when it was controversial for them to be associated with me or this work.

To Liana Borghi, now of the University of Florence, go many debts of gratitude. Liana took over from Elizabeth Meese of Alabama in organizing a small international conference of feminist and lesbian academics and critics in Florence in July, 1989, where I gave the earliest version of what became my chapter on the work of Joan Nestle. I am also indebted to the feminist and lesbian academics who, as officials of the English Institute, Harvard University, supported the first lesbian session in August, 1990, where I announced my intention to write a book about lesbian popular culture, and gave the presentation which became my chapter on *Hothead Paisan* and *Dykes To Watch Out For*. I want to thank the Italian, Scottish, and English feminist academics who organized the Glasgow conference, "Feminist Theory: An International Debate," in July, 1991, where I gave a paper on the relationship between Joan Nestle's *A Restricted Country* and feminist discussions of subject positioning. That paper was published first in Italian by La Tartaruga in 1993 under the title "L'in-discreto soggetto lesbica si rifiuta de negoziare," in the collection *Questioni di teoria Femminista,* edited by Paola Bono. Julia Creet and Fahdi Abou-Rihan worked very hard and long at organizing the Queer Sites conference at the University of Toronto in May 1993, where I gave an early version of what became my chapter "Paper Lesbians and Theory Queens." An anonymous reviewer for Series Q of Duke Press wrote very interesting comments about my argument in "Paper Lesbians and Theory Queens." The *Journal of*

Curriculum Theorizing, organizers of the Bergamo Conference on curriculum theorizing, asked Deborah Britzman and me to do a session on queer pedagogy at their annual conference in October 1993. My Bergamo presentation became the final chapter of this book, and another version of the chapter is being published in *Radical Interventions: Identity, Politics, and Differences in Educational Praxis,* edited by Suzanne de Castell and Mary Bryson for their book in the SUNY series, Identities in the Classroom. I am also grateful to Liana Borghi, who as organizer of a two-part workshop entitled "The Apple Pie Amazon," brought about the first public session on American lesbian writers at the European Association for American Studies in Luxembourg in March, 1994. Though the audience in the lovely European Parliament Building where I gave a paper on the novels of Sarah Schulman which became chapter five of this book was hostile and homophobic, our workshop felt like a historic breakthrough. In one of the many ways Liana encourges feminist and lesbian studies in Italy, she invited me to give two presentations about my book in general and about queer pedagogy in particular in April 1994 to the Italian lesbians of the Amando(r)la group who meet weekly at the L'Imaggine Gallery in Florence.

I also want to thank Julia Creet, Richard Dellamora, Paul Leonard, and Bob Wallace, members of a small but keen Lesbian and Gay Theory Discussion Group in Toronto that met with me between 1991 and 1992. These friends and colleagues read early versions of my book proposal and offered many thoughtful written and oral responses, asking questions and making comments that helped me to rethink and rework the proposal. My feminist colleague and friend, the translator and literary critic Barbara Godard, also read and commented about the proposal and several early chapter versions as well as all my publications in my tenure file.

Many gay and lesbian academics in Europe, Canada, and the United States later lent support to my tenure file as the first out lesbian in the English department at York University by commenting favorably on earlier pieces of writing in feminist or lesbian studies. Moreover they wrote glowing reports about my work in response to the grant application I submitted to the Social Sciences and Humanities Research Council of Canada to get money to finish this book. Particularly generous were the remarks of Liana Borghi, Teresa de Lauretis, Richard Dellamora, Katie King, Elizabeth Meese, Catharine Stimpson, and Bob Wallace. The Canadian Social Sciences and Humanities Research Council gave me a generous three-year long research grant which allowed me to complete the research for this book, and to buy a new computer and laser printer on which to produce the manuscript.

In my sabbatical year, 1993–1994, I was able to spend time at the inspiring Lesbian History Archive in Park Slope, Brooklyn, New York, where my research on lesbian pop culture, especially lesbian cartoons and queer zines, was very much helped by Polly Thistlewaite and Joan Nestle. I also enjoyed discussing current developments in lesbian and gay studies, partiularly the notion of a generational paradigm shift with Martin Duberman, Director of the Center for Lesbian and Gay Studies at the City University of New York; Jeff Escoffier, and Ruth-Ann Robson.

For several years of less formal but lengthy spoken exchanges about the relationship between psychoanalysis and feminist and lesbian pedagogy I am grateful to Alice Pitt of the Ontario Institute for Studies in Education. My greatest intellectual debt since October 1992 is to my friend and colleague at York University, Deborah P. Britzman. Before Bill Germano at Routledge and Ken Wissoker at Duke expressed a desire to publish this book, Deborah read early versions of the book proposal and urged me to send it to the series she and Janet Miller edit, Identities in the Classroom, at SUNY Press. From 1993 on, Deborah read early versions of every chapter, as well as my discussion of lesbian theory, "What Makes Lesbianism Thinkable?: Lesbian Theory from Adrienne Rich to Queer Theory," which became a chapter in *Feminist Issues*, a collection of essays edited by my colleague Nancy Mandell which was published by Prentice-Hall in Toronto in October 1994. Each conversation with Deborah gave me new books to read about imagined communities, the practice of everyday life and queer pedagogy, but talking with her made me realize how to rewrite each chapter.

Belief in my work by three other lesbians sustained me in various ways throughout what sometimes seemed the endless amount of time I took to finish this book. My ex-student and friend Susan Shea researched lesbian fashion practices in libraries in Toronto; another friend, Melissa Caplan, read and copyedited the entire manuscript in its final version in Kingston, Ontario in August, 1994, before correcting the endnotes and the bibliography. From beginning to end, as librarian extraordinaire, critic without portfolio, and reader of every presentation and every version of every chapter, my lover Melody Burton kept me and this book alive.

Every day I thank you.

CHAPTER 1

THE MAKING OF AN UN/POPULAR CULTURE:

FROM LESBIAN FEMINISM TO LESBIAN POSTMODERNISM

Recent work in lesbian and gay studies recycles the same story about how the American feminist sex wars over sexual representation in the early 1980s created lesbian category trouble, broke up the feminist cultural consensus, realigned lesbians with gay men and then brought forth the newest kid on the block: lesbian postmodernism. Penelope Engelbrecht was the first to use the term, in her 1990 article, "'Lifting Belly is a Language': The Postmodern Lesbian Subject."[1] In 1994, a critical collection of essays using and refusing the term appeared under the editorship of Laura Doan; the title, *The Lesbian Postmodern*, beginning as it does with the definite article, is, ironically enough, most unpostmodern. While the most insightful analyses of the sex wars and their aftermath, such as B. Ruby Rich's "Feminism and Sexuality in the 1980s," Catharine R. Stimpson's "Nancy Reagan Wears a Hat: Feminism and Its Cultural Consensus," and Arlene Stein's "Sisters and Queers: the Decentering of Lesbian Feminism," suggest that the story in its broad outlines is correct, what is becoming the received version fails to do justice to the theoretical complexity and the contradictions of lesbian-feminism. In particular, it occludes the part that social and especially cultural differences played in stirring up lesbian category trouble and in instigating a new phase of lesbian creative and critical expression. What fascinates me is the part of the story that hasn't been given much attention; namely, how lesbian-feminism became an un/popular culture. How lesbian-feminism changed from being a political vanguard into a cultural neo-avant-garde is the subject of this book.

The simplest version of the transformation of the category "lesbian" goes like this: thesis—lesbian-feminism—antithesis—the feminist sex wars—synthesis—lesbian postmodernism. The chain reaction is summed up in one recent and typically provocative title, a collection of essays edited by Arlene Stein—*Sisters, Sexperts, Queers: Beyond the Lesbian Nation*.[2] It's a story, a myth of origins[3] about a generational changing of the guards, marking and almost always celebrating a shift from the alleged inclusivity of the boast that "any woman can be a lesbian" to the much more exclusive and unabashed elitism of lesbian (cultural, theoretical, and most of all, sexual) chic. The project of accessibility shifted to a more disturbing one of excessibility.

THEORIZING ACCESSIBILITY TO EXCESSIBILITY

Three intellectual events shaped this shift: the publication in 1980 of the powerful polemical essay by the poet-critic Adrienne Rich, "Compulsory Heterosexuality and Lesbian Existence," which theorized lesbianism as not only inside but central to feminism; the sex wars within feminism from 1982 on, which displaced lesbianism either above or below feminism as a set of sex-cultural practices not necessarily bounded by the realm of "the political"; and then, from the late 1980s on, the emergence of lesbian postmodernism, which destabilized, disjoined, and deconstructed the relationship between lesbianism and feminism. In the process, both lost their coherence, uniqueness, and authenticity. The new hybrid, however, has achieved a greater degree of theoretical and cultural prestige—as a sexy new avant-garde at a time too "post" to believe in the possibility or usefulness of either lesbianism or feminism.

Rich's text shows lesbian and feminist theoretical practices at a moment of consolidation and legitimation. If one article has achieved canonical status both in the literature of women's studies and lesbian and gay studies, it is this classic. Still widely anthologized, Rich wrote her poetic polemic with women's studies students and faculty as her intended audience. She wrote to change minds: to decrease heterosexism in the women's movement and its scholarship, and to build bridges between heterosexual and lesbian feminists.[4] Rich successfully used the ideological work of 1970s feminist culture which had transformed the image of lesbians from sexual outlaws to respectable citizens. Her chief stroke of brilliance in this rhetorical takeover was to make lesbianism inherently natural, womanly, and feminist.

Legitimizing lesbianism this way is tricky. Obviously, it requires rewriting all the myths, popular and scholarly, about ugly man-hating lesbians. Less obviously, it requires rewriting the twentieth-century history of relationships among feminists, lesbians, and gay men. Given the revolutionary task she set herself, it's not surprising that Rich's argument is frequently contradictory, unsupported by evidence, or simply incredible at key points. Rich argues that lesbianism is a choice and, therefore, any woman can become a lesbian. Lesbians are made, not born. In making this choice, women aren't choosing a sexuality so much as they are choosing to reject patriarchy. Heterosexuality isn't a choice for women but collaboration with the enemy in the interests of survival. While any resisting woman is entitled to take a spot on the "lesbian continuum," the patriarchy will try to destroy her if she does so. Therefore, feminists make the best lesbians; lesbian/feminism is industrial strength feminism (unlike earlier pre-feminist lesbians who were sex-crazed and therefore not really political). If all women became lesbians, the patriarchy would crumble.

"Compulsory Heterosexuality and Lesbian Existence" exemplifies what Katie King calls an "origin story," an interested tale about the relationship between lesbianism and feminism.[5] Since Rich wants to unite the two, to make lesbianism feminism's "magical sign," she sometimes forges the link visually as well as rhetorically—"lesbian/feminism."[6] Throughout this account—another interested tale—of shifts in the relationship between these terms, I will use the typography that the theorist or writer under discussion used. My own standard will be the simple juxtapositioning. Since there is no standard form, usage varies, probably reflecting the relationship the writer imagines as existing between lesbianism and feminism. For theorists and others who are lesbian and feminist but not "lesbian feminist," I will use the term "feminist lesbian."

The tensions between feminism and lesbianism are suppressed by Adrienne Rich because she sought to unify them. Her position builds from a view typical of lesbians active in the 1970s who saw lesbianism as a solution to the problems of female heterosexuality.[7] Because of what she forced underground, Rich's article is probably much more often cited for the memorable phrases she introduced into feminist culture than read as an extended argument. While the latter part of the title is often forgotten or misquoted, perhaps because Rich's argument about the all-encompassing, transhistorical and transcultural nature of "lesbian existence" has been largely discredited by historians, the first and most shocking part of the title, the notion of "compulsory heterosexuality," has become a cornerstone of feminist and lesbian theorizing.

Rich's insight that heterosexuality should be considered by all women as an institution, a frequently violent and always coercive social construction, rather than as a natural state, has had some acceptance in other academic disciplines such as literature, psychology, sociology, and cultural studies, and has even made its way into the larger world outside the academy. For many feminist readers, who typically encounter this text as the token lesbian reading in an otherwise heterosexist women's studies syllabus, Rich *is* lesbian theory. Lesbian theorists, however, have largely rejected her arguments. It's important to recall that the most significant and most immediate critiques of Rich anticipate the sex wars and their aftermath.

Feminist scholars responded in various ways to Rich's controversial essay and, in fact, the debate about it remains ongoing. One of the most important responses to Rich, by the socialist-feminist lesbian Ann Ferguson, is crucial in understanding the directions that lesbian theorizing took during and after the sex wars, and the role that theorizing played in the break-up of what Catharine Stimpson called the North American feminist "cultural consensus."[8] Ironically, though Ferguson has the better and more historically grounded argument, and later theorists have largely followed her lead by applying her methodology and asking similar questions about lesbian identity, her response has been forgotten while Rich's polemic has been canonized.

Rich's article holds this pride of place because it creates an appealing myth of the lesbian/feminist as a present-day freedom fighter against patriarchy who has a mystical connection to all the heroic women who have ever lived. In its scope and imaginative grandeur, Rich's article is a manifesto of lesbian modernism. Sharing the bonds of women-identification with non-lesbians rather than isolated as a pervert because she performs deviant sex acts, Rich's lesbian is a romantic though respectable figure. Naturalizing the lesbian, freeing her to float free from historical impurities and taints, linking her oppression to the oppression of all women, Rich makes lesbianism intelligible and seductive in normative heterosexual terms. That is, she desexualizes lesbianism.

In the *Signs* 1981 issue, Ferguson includes a section in the "Viewpoint" essay, "On 'Compulsory Heterosexuality and Lesbian Existence': Defining the Issues." Entitled "Patriarchy, Sexual Identity, and the Sexual Revolution," Ferguson's critique is a response to Rich that pricks the romantic bubble by finding Rich's vision ahistoric, exclusionary, and utopian.[9] Unconvinced by Rich's totalizing claims that compulsory heterosexuality is the motor driving patriarchy and the lesbian continuum is the nestling place for all women, Ferguson questions Rich's definitional strategies and her broadly inclusive claims about lesbian identity. She does this by setting out five different definitions of lesbian identity, including Rich's and her own, that reflect changes in ways of being sexual and thinking about sexual identity.

The major difference between Rich and Ferguson is that Ferguson reestablishes the importance of the creation of "an explicit lesbian identity connected to genital sexuality," though she admits that no one definition fits all cases.[10] The question of lesbian identity must remain open-ended, demanding self-conscious reflexivity and a grounding in material and cultural specificities. Ferguson's is a far narrower and less romantic view of lesbianism, one not so easily assimilable into heterosexual feminism. Unlike Rich, Ferguson neither overlooks the significant political differences that divide women nor puts the lesbian into the vanguard position. At two places in her counter-argument, Ferguson asks who is excluded from or devalued by Rich's redefinition of lesbian existence. In contrast to Rich, Ferguson observes:

> any definitional strategy which seeks to drop the sexual component of "lesbian" in favor of an emotional commitment to, or preference for, women tends to lead feminists to downplay the historical importance of the movement for sexual liberation. The negative results of that movement...do not justify dismissal of the real advances that were made for women, not the least being the possibility of a lesbian identity in the sexual sense of the term.[11]

In its rejection of the political vanguardism of lesbian-feminism and acknowledgement of sexual diversity within the lesbian community, Ferguson's essay prefigures not only the sex wars, but the emergence of lesbianism in a postmodern mode.

FROM THE SEX WARS TO THE TEXT WARS

Every scholar who has discussed this period agrees that "The Scholar and The Feminist IX" conference in April, 1982 at Barnard College in New York on the subject "Towards a Politics of Sexuality" marked the official outbreak of the sex wars. These were disputes about the meanings of lesbian life in large American cities in the 1970s, although they also troubled lesbian and feminist communities in urban areas elsewhere. To illustrate, here are two versions of what they involved.

Janice G. Raymond has a celebratory but sorrowful view of a lesbian feminist paradise lost:

> There was a time when this movement called lesbian feminism had a passion, principles, and politics. Without romanticizing that period as the golden age of lesbian feminism, I would like to recall for us what that movement was and what it stood for. This movement was the strongest challenge to hetero-reality that feminism embodied. It challenged the worldview that women exist for men and primarily in relation to them. It challenged the history of women as primarily revealed in the family ...It challenged that seemingly eternal truth that "Thou as a woman must bond with a man," forever seeking our lost halves in the complementarity of hetero-relations. It even challenged the definition of feminism itself as the equality of women with men. Instead, it made real a vision of the equality of women with our Selves. It defined equality as being equal to those women who have been for women, those who have lived for women's freedom and those who have died for it; those who have fought for women and survived by women's strength; those who have loved women and who have realized that without the consciousness and conviction that women are primary in each other's lives, nothing else is in perspective. This movement worked on behalf of all women. ...But then something happened. Women—often other lesbians—began to define things differently.[12]

By contrast, Joan Nestle has a very critical view of what lesbian-feminism suppressed:

> We Lesbians from the fifties made a mistake in the early seventies: we allowed our lives to be trivialized and reinterpreted by feminists who did not share our culture. The slogan "Lesbianism is the practice and feminism is the theory" was a good rallying cry, but it cheated our history. The early writings need to be reexamined to see why so many of us dedicated ourselves to understanding the homophobia of straight feminists rather than the life-realities of Lesbian women "who were not feminists" (an empty phrase which comes too easily to the

lips). Why did we expect and need Lesbians of earlier generations and differing backgrounds to call their struggle by our name? I am afraid of the answer because I shared both worlds and know how respectable feminism made me feel, how less dirty, less ugly, less butch and femme. But the pain and anger at hearing so much of my past judged unacceptable have begun to surface.[13]

These visions are compelling polemics. They show how the sex wars divided lesbian from lesbian and led to the proliferation of lesbianisms and the legitimating of other sexual minorities who have more tenuous connections to feminism. The breakdown of the grand narrative of sexuality which offered two flavors—heterosexual and lesbian—ushered in the new age of postmodern sexuality, with its twin offer to end the policing of sexual boundaries and expand the variety of sexual expressions.

But this is getting ahead of the narrative. What were the sex wars about? The immediate catalyst was the picketing and leafletting at the conference by what Lillian Faderman called "cultural feminists"[14] (this descriptor is generally used derogatorily, but Faderman's usage is neutral to positive) who were offended by the presence of lesbian sex radicals at a feminist event. By attempting to stop the conference, since they regarded the radicals' presence as part of the backlash against feminism, the demonstrators made it legendary. The fate of feminism itself seemed to hang in the hands of those who were there or wrote analyses of it. Since the sex wars were largely fought by (white, American) intellectuals over books and ideas and then were rehashed in more books and scholarly articles, the whole affair might seem like a tempest in a teapot. Perhaps, as it recedes from view, that will be the way feminist history will regard it. Looked at from the vantage point of another decade, however, this highly cerebral and ironically disembodied struggle set the terms and the agenda for contemporary feminist and lesbian discourses on sexuality and sexual representation.

Scholars differ about the extent to which this was almost entirely a lesbian dispute over unconventional sexual practices such as sadomasochism, public sex, the use and production of pornography, and butch-femme role-playing. Lesbian social historian Lillian Faderman, in her study of twentieth-century lesbianism, *Odd Girls and Twilight Lovers: A History of Lesbian Life in Twentieth-Century America*, is of two minds about this. In one of the most concise analyses, Faderman claims that "the lesbian sex wars of the 1980s between those lesbians who were cultural feminists and those who were sex radicals reflected the conflicting perceptions of the basic meaning of femaleness and lesbianism with which women have long struggled."[15] If she's right, then the issue is a large one, with a potential for involving a very large number of women, even though the number of actual combatants who argued publicly was small.

Though in the quotation just cited she indicates that the sex wars engaged profound issues, the thesis driving most of Faderman's chapter about them suggests something quite different—the sex wars were a momentary blip. They weren't about the naturalness or constructedness of lesbian sexuality, relationships with heterosexual feminism, or representational politics. They were about what lesbians do in bed. Faderman concludes, based on her interview data, that the attempt by lesbian sex radicals to change lesbians' sexual behavior largely failed because lesbians, like other women, share the same female socialization which emphasizes tenderness, love, romance, and sexual safety above the pleasures and dangers of adventuring on the fringes, let alone outside the borders of sexual respectability.[16]

If the sex wars are looked at less concretely, however, the immediate outcome was not what Faderman reports—the cultural feminists, or the "lesbian essentialists," as she names them, won the battle and the sex radicals, or "lesbian existentialists," lost.[17] Looked at in larger terms, the sex wars are only the latest round in a two hundred year long struggle over the boundaries between normalcy and sexual deviance, in which feminists have tended to play the role of regulators as well as the regulated.[18] Critiquing feminism's historic role as sexual regulator drives lesbian sex radical and anthropologist Gayle Rubin's article, "Thinking Sex: Notes for a Radical Theory of the Politics of Sexuality," the most cited and important piece in the influential anthology of papers from the Barnard conference, *Pleasure and Danger*. If Adrienne Rich's essay, "Compulsory Heterosexuality and Lesbian Existence," is the first contemporary classic of lesbian culture, then Gayle Rubin's article is the second. Using a Foucauldian analysis of modern sexual history, Rubin argues that the sex wars should be studied as a symbolic contest between feminists and sex radicals over a stratified and unitary sexual system.

Like Rich before her, Rubin is a powerful polemicist who is trying to legitimize and naturalize her preferred form of lesbian identity, namely lesbian sado-masochism. Unlike Rich, who tried to valorize hers by blurring the boundaries between heterosexuality and lesbianism, Rubin privileges hers by attacking the very notion of sexual hierarchy.[19] Calling lesbian-feminists on their habit of legitimizing themselves by demonizing the sexual practices of other sexual minorities, Rubin knocked lesbian-feminism off the throne of transcendental signifier and the pedestal of sexual purity. Now that some historical distance has been put on the most inflammatory aspects of these rhetorical battles, this part of Rubin's argument has come to be regarded as more significant than her sexual libertarianism.[20]

While Lillian Faderman regards the adoption or rejection of kinky sexual practices for lesbians as a blip in the pattern of female sexual socialization, Rubin treats the sex wars as a crucial moment in the history of sexuality. The sex wars, like the period in the late eighteenth century when homosexuality was "invented," were a time of "sexual ethnogenesis," in which new sexual minorities were created and communities forged.[21] For those living through it, this moment is hard to comprehend because anything having to do with sex is highly mystified in western culture. Sex wars and moral panics are "often fought at oblique angles, aimed at phony targets, conducted with misplaced passions, and are highly, intensely symbolic" because they are territorial conflicts over sexual and ethical values.[22]

For many feminists, Rubin's article makes uncomfortable reading. Not only does she resexualize lesbians, removing the halo of respectability that 1970s feminism had worked so hard to create, she also unties feminism as a theory of gender oppression from lesbianism as a sexual identity and practice. By prying apart the categories of gender and sexuality, Rubin laid the theoretical groundwork for a new disciplinary formation, lesbian studies, which parallels but does not overlap with women's studies.

Rubin makes a compelling argument that feminism should no longer be seen as the "privileged site of a theory of sexuality"[23] and that it is of limited usefulness for lesbians and other sexual minorities:

> Feminist conceptual tools were developed to detect and analyze gender-based hierarchies. To the extent that these overlap with erotic stratifications, feminist theory has some explanatory power. But as issues become less those of gender and more those of sexuality, feminist analysis becomes irrelevant and often misleading. Feminist thought simply lacks angles of vision which can encompass the social organization of sexuality. The criteria of relevance in feminist thought do not allow it to see or assess critical power relations in the area of sexuality.[24]

Whereas, in her earlier and equally influential essay, "The Traffic in Women," she had suggested that the concept of a "sex/gender system" allowed the best ways of understanding the structural links between sex and gender, Rubin here repudiates her previous work.[25] "Thinking Sex" helped to rupture the fragile theoretical unity between heterosexual and lesbian feminists. By providing the theoretical foundations and justifications for another "gay/straight" split within feminism, Rubin's essay should be seen as the opening round in a still ongoing legitimation crisis over sexuality.

In retrospect, because of the insightful deconstructive analyses offered first by B. Ruby Rich to feminist and lesbian audiences in 1986 and then by Catharine Stimpson to literary critics in 1988, it has become clearer that the sex wars were primarily intramural disputes or "family romances." Taken to a higher interpretive ground, "sex" was something of a pretext. Critics like Ruby Rich and Stimpson refigured the sex wars neither as catfights nor conspiracies but as infights over the meanings of feminist and lesbian sexual and cultural practices. In Ruby Rich's case they are competing romanticisms, and in Stimpson's they concern differing theories of representation.

While sexual issues provided the conflagration point, questions of style, particularly with respect to cultural as well as sexual respectability and visibility, were profoundly divisive. Stimpson locates the emergence of a new feminist subculture at an earlier and less controversial Barnard conference, the 1979 session on "The Future of Difference." What she terms "feminist postmodernism" (and she may have been the first to use the phrase) is a mix of "revisionary psychoanalyisis, European poststructuralism, and feminism."[26] As a result, feminists and lesbians had to choose: be pure but old-fashioned, or become trendy but difficult. In effect, the sex wars became the text wars. If you didn't keep up with your reading, you couldn't play.[27] Though the sex wars burnt themselves and most of their combatants out some time ago, by the time they subsided in the late 1980s it had become apparent that the antagonists were so opposed on questions of representation, subjectivity, and culture as to be mutually unintelligible.

More and more, the sex wars seem like the first round of feminist cultural wars. One side, which included most lesbian-feminist critics and academics, many of the latter associated with women's studies, had the numbers and the other, a much smaller grouping of lesbian intellectuals who considered themselves poststructuralists or materialist feminists, had the greater institutional prestige and cultural capital. Notwithstanding, feminist lesbian critics such as Catharine Stimpson, Teresa de Lauretis, Sue-Ellen Case, and Elizabeth Meese,[28] who have written candidly and lucidly about the implications and consequences—theoretical, literary, and political—of the cultural conflicts within American feminist and lesbian communities as a first step to breaking the stalemate and moving the discussion forward, have not been very successful. Academic feminism still continues to ignore or otherwise marginalize lesbian postmodernist culture, and lesbian postmodernists have largely given up on women's studies in favor of lesbian and gay studies or queer theory.

LESBIAN POSTMODERNISM: CATEGORY TROUBLE OR TROUBLING CATEGORY?

Not everyone has found the makeover cause for rejoicing. The dissenters include lesbians who are skeptical about claiming that deep links exist between sexual identities and postmodernism as an aesthetic or a philosophical critique;[29] lesbians who are critical of postmodernism for political reasons,[30] and lesbians who dismiss the sexy new avant-garde as "lifestyle lesbians."[31] Though I too use the apparently unstoppable narrative of lesbian postmodernism, I subject it to a symptomatic reading: From lesbian category troubling to troubled category, what is enabled and what made more difficult under the aegis of this new un/popular culture?

It's important to acknowledge that the category "lesbian" was in trouble both before and after the sex wars for cultural and political reasons that were only loosely linked to those debates. One of the chief reasons "lesbian" is a troubled category is that as a name and a notion it's so limited and limiting. The lesbian philosopher Marilyn Frye has ruefully analyzed its baffling etymology, its negating ontology, and its implicit ethnocentrism.[32] When the word is uninflected, it can be taken to mean white, euroamerican, and middle-class.[33] Because it seems disembodied and euphemistic, some of those it names reject "lesbian" as not only racially and culturally exclusive, but as inappropriately cerebral, preferring instead the more visceral and down to earth "dyke" or "queer."[34] While one solution to such category trouble is to choose a name to fit the occasion, whatever will keep its critical edge critical, the dis-ease around the category underscores the cultural and political reality that there is no such thing as a monolithic or international lesbian culture.

"Lesbian" was a category in trouble for cultural reasons well before the outbreak of the sex wars in 1982. As early as 1974, the experimental lesbian novelist Bertha Harris complained about lesbian-feminist attempts to make lesbians and lesbian literature "palatable and 'speakable'...universally acceptable and welcome."[35] Lamenting that literary lesbian-feminists and those who preferred to read their banal writing had successfully assimilated themselves into ordinary people, she feared that they had lost the chance of becoming great—as monsters. "Lesbians, instead, might have been great, as some literature is: unassimilable, awesome, dangerous, outrageous, different: *distinguished.*"[36] As early as 1978, for different reasons but with a similar iconoclastic bravado, Monique Wittig stunned academics at the Modern Language Association (MLA) annual conference by declaring that lesbians are not women.[37] Then as well as now, such claims disturbed many lesbians. Those who want to pass as "women" or to be assimilated as the girls next door still reject the claims of a Harris or a Wittig as queer and incomprehensible.

By the beginning of the 1990s, when lesbian-feminism was thought by some feminists and lesbians to have gone the way of the dodo, observers of American feminist communities voiced yet other reasons why the category of the lesbian was in trouble. Some were delighted, others were perplexed or worried. Was the category "lesbian" empty or ineffective as a descriptive or discursive tool, on the one hand, or too totalizing, on the other?[38] If lesbianism, by the mid-1980s, had lost the political aura it had just barely managed to achieve as feminism's "magical sign," what had a decade's worth of theoretical elaboration turned it into? In a little over ten years, lesbianism may have refigured itself from being the "rage of all women condensed to the point of explosion," to its lust.[39] In 1992, Michael Warner fantasized that Judith Butler's anti-figuration might be that a "lesbian is the incoherence of gender binarism and heterosexuality condensed to the point of parody."[40] By the 1990s, the lesbian had imploded into a subject position, a performance, a space, a metaphor, or an instability in the system of signification.[41] As a consequence of this theoretical efflorescence, all of it undertaken during the longest period of economic depression and political reaction in the western world since the 1930s, it's unclear whether "lesbian" should be understood now primarily in political, sexual, or cultural terms. "Lesbian" has gone from something any and all women supposedly could be, to a politicized sexual identity, to something wild and recherché that perhaps only an outlaw elite with the right clothes, sex toys, and reading lists could fantasize being. Currently, the category is undergoing a shift as dramatic, as seismic, and as controversial in terms of its potential cultural and political consequences as the one attributed to the nineteenth-century sexologists. Though this shift as yet directly involves only a minority of a minority, its manifestations and consequences will be of interest not only to lesbians but to all those following the debates about postmodernism, feminism, and the development of lesbian and gay studies.

THE MAKING OF AN UN/POPULAR CULTURE

As a shaper of how both lesbians and other people thought about lesbians, lesbian-feminism has played a contradictory and important mediating role in the making of this un/popular culture. Lesbian-feminism was successful, to a degree, in removing the stigma attached to lesbianism as a clinical category of psychopathology that seemed as exotic and vaguely un-American as it was erotic. Lesbian-feminists promoted themselves as the respectable deviants who may have had sex less often than other groups, but did so more high-mindedly and with greater revolutionary impact. And, while lesbian-feminism was never exactly popular as a political subculture—the most common adjective used to describe adherents was "strident"—there was something vaguely warm and fuzzy about its countercultural populism. Though obviously (and unfortunately) not every woman, it turned out, *wanted* to be a lesbian, there was that welcoming invitation extended to all women to claim a place on "the lesbian continuum." Culturally speaking, however, the continuum had the same affectations and limitations it largely shared and inherited from the new left and hippie countercultures: an uncritical soft spot for amateurish, accessible, and affirmative cultural expressions such as folk music, social realism, and veneration for all things natural. Not surprisingly, the cultural legacy of lesbian-feminism seems restricted to softball and Holly Near. (In fact, an unapologetic disdain for "women's music" and preference for almost anything else, whether opera, jazz, or dance music, may have been the first cultural marker of the emergence of lesbian postmodernism.)

As a stance toward culture, lesbian-feminism was and is suspicious, tending to reject high culture as elitist, popular or mass culture as mindless, and both as sexist and misogynist. Hence, lesbian-feminists have largely been uninterested in theorizing culture except as an obstacle or a tool for individual and social transformation. Lesbians writing as lesbians have until quite recently made few interventions about lesbian investments in mainstream or mass culture. (One powerful exception to this general rule is Patricia White's "Female Spectator, Lesbian Specter: The Haunting.")[42] In a recent and fairly inclusive overview of critical approaches to cultural studies entitled, *An Introductory Guide to Cultural Theory and Popular Culture,* by John Storey, it's revealing but not surprising that in his informed and sympathetic chapter on feminist work, there is no mention of either lesbian-feminism or lesbian-feminist work in these areas.[43]

The writing produced by or preferred by lesbian-feminists, such as the coming out story, the romance, and various forms of didactic fiction, from the detective story to speculative fiction, was designed to convey subversive ideas in realist modes that were affirming of lesbian lives as well as formally and linguistically accessible. Lesbian-feminism as a stance toward art and culture was suspicious about or opposed to what it perceived as artistic or formal innovation, unnecessarily difficult or challenging modes of expression, and anything that smacked of critical, negative, or nihilistic attitudes toward lesbians. Because aesthetically, lesbian-feminism rejects not just lesbian postmodernism but lesbian modernism as well, lesbians who loved art or music that was considered difficult, challenging, or elitist were regarded with suspicion or outright contempt.[44]

I term lesbian theorizing and other cultural productions in a postmodern mode an "un/popular culture" not only because the highly contested terms "lesbian" and "culture" are charged with unpopularity, especially in the current American context, but because it's apparently difficult to think "lesbian" in the same frame with respect to "culture"—of any sort. That lesbians *have* a culture is itself an unpopular idea, partially because any way you look at it, how "lesbian" modifies "culture" is contentious. For example, according to the subject headings in library online catalogues and various databases, "lesbian culture" and "lesbian intellectuals" do not exist. If you look for them, you will be informed that "no entries [are to be] found." Citations to scholarly writing about lesbianism are largely relegated to the *Social Sciences Citation Index*, in the areas of deviancy and psychopathology. Unlike our (white) gay brothers, we have yet to make much of a dent in the more culturally oriented *Arts and Humanities Citation Index*. If you look for lesbians in a recent and supposedly comprehensive reference work about contemporary literary and cultural theory published and promoted by the MLA, Donald G. Marshall's *Contemporary Critical Theory*, which their promotional material calls a "concise bibliographic overview of major critical theories and theorists" from Adorno to Wimsatt—yes, Wimsatt—you will find none.[45]

Before looking at the ways the words complicate each other when juxtaposed, let's take each term separately, starting with "culture," which as Raymond Williams in *Keywords* reminds readers, is one of the two or three most complicated words in English.[46] Culture isn't an object to be described but is rather, as Williams treats it, a process word for the activity of tending. Culture connotes approximation as well as self-fashioning. In consideration of both connotations, I will use the concept in this materialist sense throughout this book, but in addition, I will attempt to hear its always gendered, raced, and sexed inflections.

Culture originally referred to the concrete tending or honoring with worship of things and animals and was then extended and abstracted to refer to the development, especially the higher development—that is, intellectual, spiritual and artistic tending—of human beings. Awareness that culture is a "contested, temporal, and emergent" term[47] is implied in the second main line of usage, the ethnographic and anthropological, in which the word refers to particular and changing ways of life of different peoples during different periods. Williams places the class associations in the foreground and hints at the racial and imperialist ones which became more obvious to progressives from the eighteenth century onward. He argues that the central question underlying disputes over the concept is how material and symbolic productions are to be related. Though he ends by noting the blatant hostility which began to be directed at the concept of culture and related words such as "aesthete," "aesthetic," and "intellectual" in English during the Victorian era, he fails to connect this disdain to "culture's" gendered or sexual connotations.

Several years later, in a lengthy and provocative review of the *Cultural Studies* anthology edited by Lawrence Grossberg, Cary Nelson, and Paula Treichler, Fredric Jameson also ignored the gender of culture, but used psychoanalytic insights to develop and deepen Williams's Marxist observations about the fear, loathing, and even violence that "culture" inspires. Like Freud's view of civilization as an achievement that not only requires renunciation of instinctual life but recognizes that "others" refuse to do this, Jameson's perspective makes "culture" a site of aggression. Jameson accordingly stresses that cultural studies "will also entail its quotient of the libidinal, will release violent waves of affect—narcissistic wounds, feelings of envy and inferiority, the intermittent repugnance for the others' groups."[48] While Jameson, like Williams, can hardly imagine women's let alone lesbians' contributions to the study or production of culture, his insight deserves consideration. Because of the stress he places on unmasking culture as an always relational and violent objectification of and fantasy about the Other, an "objective mirage that arises out of the relationship between at least two groups,"[49] his remarks are suggestive for theorizing the intrications and detours between culture and lesbians, whether as imagined, contested, or ignored, by lesbians as well as non-lesbians.

As Danae Clark summarizes, in the relationship between lesbians and culture, lesbian subjects have been positioned with respect to hegemonic cultural practices by a "history of struggle, invisibility and ambivalence."[50] As if by way of providing evidence, Camille Paglia says, unselfconsciously and unironically, "[t]he lesbian aesthete does not exist."[51] Hence, and not unsurprisingly, the more self-conscious and visible lesbians become, the more contentious (and fantastic) will their relationships with culture appear to be. If cultural studies is always in some sense a border dispute in which no one owns the real thing, then the claims and counter-claims by lesbian-feminists, feminist lesbians, and lesbians who are not feminists about who is policing whom or regulating ingress and egress from lesbian cultures and identities are not only unresolvable but construct the conditions of possibility for forming and reforming our imagined communities. Groups and cultural formations, moreover, such as "the lesbian-feminist" or "the lesbian postmodern," are imaginary, as Jameson, who alludes to the work of Mary Douglas, Benedict Anderson, and Erving Goffman, realizes. If Jameson were to contemplate these changing manifestations of lesbian life, he would regard them as abstractions and fantasies about purity and danger that promote themselves rather unattractively, but inevitably, via envy and loathing of the Other and abusive generalizing.[52] While I'd prefer to avoid such behavior in carrying out this project, I recognize with regret that it could be construed as coming with the territory and acknowledge my own responsibility in perpetuating categorical and other theoretical violences.

Lesbians themselves not only disagree about the senses in which it could be considered that "we" have a "culture," high or popular, but some ignore what we do have and thus help to maintain the historical relationship of invisibility, struggle, and ambivalence. Whether or not for reasons as malign as those Jameson gives, lesbians frequently fail to cite each other's work and otherwise treat it fairly casually. That we no longer have to like everything about it is one of the strongest pieces of evidence that we do indeed have a culture. The chief attitudes expressed by lesbian cultural critics are these: that there is at present nothing worthy of the name; that lesbian cultural productions tend to be non-canonical, under-read, and unknown; and that a culture popular among (some) lesbians currently exists and deserves study.[53]

Current resistances to formulating the links between lesbians and culture persist, however, even among lesbians who are open to the possibility that queering gayness will produce a more inclusive cultural and political practice. For example, *Village Voice* journalist Alisa Solomon found more to critique than to celebrate in the Cultural Festival of Gay Games IV during New York City's recognition of the twenty-fifth anniversary of the Stonewall riot. Solomon criticizes the absorption and cooptation of gay and largely male culture via commodification, but is much more concerned, in a way recalling

Jameson's argument, with the political dangers of adopting a multiculturalist model, which she sees as intrinsically essentialist and most likely racist:

> for it buys into the reductio ad absurdum of all identity movements: that one *inherits* a culture by being born into it. In this model, gays and lesbians are pushed into an essentialist corner, in which we end up asserting, "Yes. We're a culture, just like the others." Inevitably, this leads to the impossible assertion of gayness as an ethnicity. And that, in turn, leads to an assumption of whiteness, as queer culture positions itself *against* African, Latino, and Asian cultures. The distinction is ludicrous. (The Harlem Renaissance, Henry Louis Gates has suggested, could be described as *either* a black movement or a gay one.)[54]

Like Jameson, Solomon refuses to maintain the separation between culture and politics, and like him too, she sees cultural politics as inevitably nasty and othering, but of course, her fears about adopting a multicultural—actually a monocultural model—originate in the contemporary gay and lesbian concern about repudiating and avoiding essentialism. Meritorious as this attempt might be, I have no interest in taking it up yet again because I regard it as something of a red herring, a pseudoproblem of the 1980s which distracted and enervated oppressed groups while dominants either passed over it in silence or used the old nature/culture controversy to maintain their own hegemony. Clearly, Solomon's formulation about inheriting a culture by being "born into it" is absurdly inapplicable to gays and lesbians, who, like everyone else, are raised within heterosexist social and cultural relations. Furthermore, if one simply assumes lesbianism, as I do and as the writers, artists, and activists who are the subject of this book do, rather than arguing, explaining or defending its marginalized status, one effectively shortcircuits the whole tired debate between essentialism and constructionism.

Though Williams is probably right in claiming that the extension of notions of culture via ethnographic analysis to include the productions of subcultures has lessened some of the hostility directed at the supposed refinement of (high) culture, most notions of popular culture are still caught up with cultural discourse's other ugly twin, anxiety.[55] Is a group or subculture attractive enough, affluent enough, recognizable enough, or even oppositional enough, to find its niche in popular culture? Whether popular culture is regarded neutrally (or not so neutrally) as what is left over and out from high culture, most definitions seem to exclude lesbians. By that I mean that lesbians, outside of the discourses of pornography, are not popular, if by that one means "liked by the public or by people in general."

Lesbians are still usually regarded, when they are regarded at all, as invisible women, or as the ladies' auxiliary of the gay movement, not as consumers or creators of culture. For example, here's a passage from a fairly progressive Canadian political satire magazine deploring the presence of fat and ugly lesbians on public television:

> Of course, these women are all very well in their place—the pretty ones in pornographic films, the ugly types in the armed forces, lacrosse teams and so on—but surely not on a television screen at 6:00 in the evening, disturbing the family dinner and terrifying the cat.[56]

At the same time that "lipstick lesbians" and "lesbian chic" were discovered and promoted by the popular press, there were rumors about attempts at appropriation and reverse passing by "male lesbians" and "queer straights," but these phenomena were so rare that they failed to elicit much comment among lesbians.[57] By comparison, Camille Roy's contemporaneous judgment about the contradictory implications of lesbian invisibility in popular culture seems to still hold: Lesbians have difficulty being taken up by popular culture because "a community of female sexual perverts resemble nobody, and nobody desires to resemble us."[58]

Though we claim that "we are everywhere," we are not generally thought of as being popular in another sense, of being "of the people." Since lesbians haven't been accorded the privilege of being thought of as having an "everyday," lesbians don't seem capable of having a popular culture in the ordinary meaning of the term. Lesbians among ourselves may worry or joke about what it means to go off to Yale to play at being a lesbian, but the rest of the world thinks of us exclusively in sexual terms. A *Guardian* book review offers an example of how lesbians are excluded from the everyday:

> Helen Dunmore's new novel is about a relationship between a 16-year-old prostitute and a cabinet minister with a fetish for bondage and urination. Let's face it. If you were picking a team of sleazy novel plots for the nineties, this one would be first-choice captain. And that's before you even mention the lesbian subplot (yes there really is one).[59]

Because the triplet "lesbian/popular/culture" names a space where several lacks overlap, it's difficult to locate contemporary lesbian cultural productions securely either in high or in popular culture. As a sexual culture, it is too low to be genuinely high, but as a culture created by women it is too genteel or too marginal to be genuinely popular. While the arguments of feminist literary historians against the exclusion of "women," that is, apparently heterosexual women, from both canonical modernism and postmodernism have attained some critical credibility, their work largely ignores or subsumes lesbians.[60] Moreover, most of the common claims about postmodernism's tendency to efface the differences between high and popular culture or to promote itself as a new avant-garde which can successfully appeal both to the left and the right, neither fit nor offer much illumination of lesbian culture. Even an emerging lesbian postmodernism seems not to fit the description of male or mainstream postmodernism, perhaps because its peculiar overlap of high theory and low culture is neither formally experimental enough to attract theoretical interest nor popular enough to attract mass attention. To my knowledge, Charles Russell's recognition of the avant-garde potential of radical feminism, which frequently subsumes or overlaps with lesbian-feminism, is unique because of the tendency to define the avant-garde as a falsely autonomous and virtually content-free expression of shock and outrage, and so to exclude any kind of work tainted by feminism. According to Russell,

> the radical feminist investigations of literary form and social discourse have the potential to be the most significant expression of a revitalized avant-garde sensibility in the postmodern era, precisely because they bring together an aggressive aesthetic activism and a social collectivity that sees itself acting in society and its history.[61]

"WITHOUT YOU (LESBIAN/FEMINISM), I'M (LESBIAN POSTMODERNISM) NOTHING"

Postmodern lesbianism is at once a marketing strategy, a legitimizing tool, and a necessary fiction emerging from the current crisis in representation, in particular the identity crises and border disputes within 1980s feminism and lesbianism. It both creates and assuages anxieties about lesbian identities, sexual practices, and cultural productions.[62] It is perhaps most useful and illuminating to consider postmodern lesbianism as a complicitous critique of lesbian-feminism. As the comedian Sandra Bernhard, herself an extremely complicitous and not so critical postmodern lesbian, remarked in another context, "without you, I'm nothing."[63]

Just as postmodernism divided feminist intellectuals in the late 1980s, so too the more recent conjuncture of lesbianism and postmodernism has begun to inspire another and, one hopes, a more useful or interesting round of debates, grounds for which can be found in the collection, *The Lesbian Postmodern*, edited by Laura Doan in 1994.[64] Given that the critical establishment's interest in the first round of debates has long peaked, with the celebrators of postmodernism or those wearily resigned to it having "won," and given that the feminism/postmodernism rematch essentially had the same outcome (as illustrated, for example, in the collection entitled *Feminism/Postmodernism*, edited by Linda J. Nicholson in 1990)[65] there will probably be few surprises this time around. Nonetheless, it must be said that, while the theorists, writers, and artists I study are delighted that perhaps with postmodernism's help, older notions of the lesbian as victim, respectable deviant, and invisible woman are finally being parodied or rejected utterly by lesbians themselves, they are ambivalent about the tendency of some lesbian postmodernists, more accurately post-feminist lesbian postmodernists, to sever lesbianism completely from feminism and so to disconnect sexuality and aesthetics utterly from politics. (Even if, as in the dethronement of lesbian-feminism from its position as feminism's magical sign, sexuality is understood as not necessarily linked to any particular political stance, fundamental questions about the relationship between sex and politics remain to be asked.)

In spite of the claim that postmodernism is supposed to display incredulity toward metanarratives, it's tempting to tell the tale of the development of lesbian postmodernism as the narrative of the evolution of a subculture in which lesbian-feminism, a political perspective, is not only decentered but frequently demonized. The political and cultural accomplishments of lesbian-feminism in the 1980s, including the creation of alternative institutions ranging from battered women's shelters to women's centers and bookstores, and their promotion of more inclusive women's studies programs, "women's" music festivals, and publishing houses, tend to drop out of the picture. Instead, there's a fascination with the lesbian and gay cultures of the pre-feminist 1950s or the campier aspects of the gay liberationist 1970s. The hyphen connecting lesbianism and feminism then comes undone. Lesbianism next reemerges not merely as a resexualized identity, but as a set of increasingly perverse and avant-garde sexual practices, which in turn are promoted, theorized, and linked to the hypersignifying aestheticizing category of postmodernism which can mean all things to all people. Consider the marketing possibilities!

Though lesbian theorists who've taken the postmodern turn agree that it is crucial for feminists to deconstruct binary models of female sexuality, they differ in the ways they relate lesbianism and other sexual minorities to feminism, in the degrees to which their work is enabled by feminist thought, and on whether their emphasis falls more on the intellectual or political effects on feminists and lesbians of binary thinking. For example, though they generally agree that binary thinking fueled the sex wars and kept feminists at an impasse, some believe that out of the impasse over these debates came a more complex way of imagining sexual differences, such as the proliferation of sexualities beyond the simple "gay/straight" split.[66] In "Producing Sex, Theory, and Culture: Gay/Straight Remappings in Contemporary Feminism," Katie King suggests that

> Situationally other differences that cannot be imagined as opposites may be as salient or more salient: race, class, nationality, language, religion, ability. All suggest that sexualities are too plural, too politically granulated to be named in a gay/straight division, as women have too many genders, sexes to be seen simply across such a "gay/straight" divide; indeed, any such centering of a gay/straight divide is in itself deeply divisive: mystifying the power dynamics feminists play with each other, and our accountabilities to each other.[67]

King's suggestion provides a point of entry for understanding postmodern lesbian theory, especially with respect to how lesbianism and sexuality in general have been theorized in the emerging disciplines of lesbian (and gay) studies and in "queer theory." Though what to call this theoretical enterprise is itself controversial, there is no doubt that lesbian theorists such as Teresa de Lauretis and Judith Butler are among its originators, along with the non-lesbian, Eve Kosofsky Sedgwick. Though their work uses feminist, poststructuralist and psychoanalytic analyses, they differ on whether theorizing lesbianism is central to their project and in how relevant feminism is to it.

To recap what I take to be their most important insights, here are capsule summaries as they relate to what follows in this book. Eve Kosofsky Sedgwick is the most celebrated of queer theorists, perhaps because she argues in her book, *Epistemology of the Closet*, that the binary opposition "homosexual/heterosexual" is central to every other important binary relation of knowledge and ignorance in western twentieth-century culture.[68] Because her analysis is more focused on sexuality than on gender, Sedgwick calls it "antihomophobic" and indicates that it shouldn't be taken as coextensive with feminism.[69] Sedgwick calls attention to what is enabled and made more difficult in minoritizing views of homosexuality (that lesbian and gay issues are of interest only to a minority) as well as universalizing views (that the production of the category of the homosexual minority is interesting to everybody because it constructs and normalizes the heterosexual majority, which wouldn't make sense without it). Sedgwick prefers to identify herself as a queer or a pervert.[70] By making queerness a theoretical perspective that is open to anyone regardless of their sexual experience or identity, she seems to have found a way of transcending the gay/straight splits within feminism. Sedgwick's writing has received a lot of critical attention and has for many readers a great appeal because she rejects the boundary-keeping preoccupations and "normalizing/deviantizing" discourses that have driven feminist as well as most earlier lesbian and gay theory.

ða ða ða

Judith Butler's book, *Gender Trouble: Feminism and the Subversion of Identity*, has played a similar role in "queering" and que(e)rying the identity of lesbian and gay studies. Butler argues that constructing the lesbian as the vanguard position of feminism is a mistake which actually reinforces compulsory heterosexuality. Lesbian theorizing based on essentialist notions of identity is nothing more than a theoretically naive and politically disastrous reverse discourse. Butler solves the problems created for lesbian theorists by the binary oppositions of sex and gender by "denaturalizing" gendered and sexed identities and encouraging them to be seen as performances.[71] Queer theorists can further subvert identities, under some but not all conditions, through the exploration of practices such as drag, butch-femme, cross-dressing, transsexuality, and the proliferation of erotic minorities, performed as self-conscious and voluntary parodies.[72]

ða ða ða

By comparison with Butler and Sedgwick, Teresa de Lauretis's writing offers a more materialist as well as lesbian approach to what has variously been called lesbian and gay studies or queer theory. Like them, de Lauretis deconstructs the binary "heterosexual/homosexual," but unlike them she worries that lesbians will be the silent partner in the new enterprise of (lesbian and) gay studies. In essays about lesbian and feminist subjectivity and representation, such as "Sexual Indifference and Lesbian Representation," de Lauretis has done more than other lesbian theorists to break out of the theoretical immobilization induced and marked by either/or thinking—study sexuality or study gender, do antihomophobic analysis or do feminist analysis.

Unlike Butler and Sedgwick, de Lauretis is concerned about what is missing, undone, or displaced from lesbian and gay studies, especially from "Queer Theory," a term she herself coined in 1991 but now rejects as politically problematic.[73] Attentive to the politics of naming, de Lauretis chose "queer" because she thought it would be more inclusive than "the by now established and often convenient, formula" "lesbian and gay."[74] In discussing why she re-appropriated the previously hateful epithet, "queer," de Lauretis concisely mapped the development of lesbian and gay studies to date. Explaining the significance of shifts in the nomenclature of deviance, from the medicinally flavored "homosexual/ity" in the titles of books written in the 1970s, to the more positively affirming "gay," to the more inclusive "gay and lesbian," and then to the pro-feminist sequencing, "lesbian and gay," de Lauretis observes that the whole sequence conceals the differences in power between the much more visible, moneyed, and older (white) gay male culture and its "others."[75]

De Lauretis addressed the definitional tasks confronting the emergent field of lesbian and gay studies without denying their political urgency. She hoped that queer theory would produce a paradigm shift in the study of the intersection of the construction of gender and sexuality, "another way of thinking the sexual."[76] She defines lesbian and gay sexualities as "an agency of social process whose mode of functioning is both interactive and yet resistant, both participatory and yet distinct, claiming at once equality and difference, demanding political representation while insisting on its material and cultural specificity."[77] Unlike the other major queer theorists, de Lauretis refuses to ignore or displace feminist and lesbian perspectives on sexual representation. More than the others, de Lauretis made it explicit that queer theory needs to be written both with and against the institutionalization, the accomplishments, and the failures of other minority discourses, most obviously women's studies, but also African-American and other ethnic studies. De Lauretis urges that queer theorists not only interpret lesbian and gay cultures, but talk back about the constructed silences in them.[78]

FROM VANGUARD TO AVANT-GARDE

In the intellectually formidable texts of Butler and de Lauretis, among others, lesbian-feminism, a political vanguard which was unpopular not because it wanted to be but because it had apparently failed, transformed itself into lesbian postmodernism, a sex-cultural avant-garde, which was unpopular because it wanted and needed to be, because that was a hallmark of success. Around 1990, critics began calling the new cultural formation "lesbian postmodernism."[79] By the time more cautious critics caught up with the phenomenon, the name had stuck and it was too late for reasoned arguments about its appropriateness or accuracy.[80] Reworking the defiant yet ambiguous claim Jill Johnston had made in 1973 that lesbians were going to legitimize themselves as criminals, lesbian postmodernism appears determined to acquire the status and visibility of an un/popular culture.

Trading in their Birkenstocks for Doc Martens or stilettos, postmodern lesbians have created a microculture that is re-imagining lesbianism by making it once again, as it was during modernism, edgy, difficult, and stylish, without apology. This microculture, or subculture of a counterculture, has already achieved some measure of visibility and notoriety in academic circles as well as in the mass media through its preoccupation with written, visual, and film and performance erotica and pornography.[81] In the "critic-as-fan" spirit of cultural studies, lesbian-generated trends in fashion and pornography—from lesbian chic haircuts and high end clothing to state of the art dildos, harnesses and body piercings—have been analyzed as serious fun on the queer conference circuit. As such technologies of the self lose shock value, they have become more available for reading as outrageous parodies,[82] or have been replaced by potentially more disturbing phenomena, such as the growth in popularity of female-to-male transsexualism and a lesbian postmodernist take on it as cosmetic surgery rather than as an ethico-political crisis of and for lesbian survival.[83]

Intellectually influential out of proportion with its size and its possession of cultural capital, these forms of postmodern lesbian culture have attracted attention as a provocative mix of high theory and low culture. So far what has received little attention are the written texts of lesbian postmodernism: (both elite and low) lesbian theory, fiction, and autobiography, particularly those that self-consciously treat the development of this new cultural formation and critically engage with and against it. Those texts and their reception are the subject of this book.

COMING ATTRACTIONS, DISTRACTIONS AND REFRACTIONS

Because it is futile to work backward to one originary moment of twentieth-century lesbian thought, I attempt more modestly only to provide a history of the present, and a partial present at that. I have tried to cut through some of the glibness that goes along with the postmodern fondness for replacing genuinely historical accounts of social and cultural change with decade-by-decade or even year-by-year calendars, by displaying some caution about relying too much on claims about the repressive lesbian-feminist 1970s or the gay 1990s, or calling 1984 the "year of the lusty lesbian."[84] Disturbing somewhat the implied narrative by which lesbian-feminism becomes lesbian postmodernism simply by deep-sixing feminism—a narrative as smooth and uncomplicated, and as satisfyingly reductive as terminating all discussion by remarking that "that was then, this is now"—I show how the most significant lesbian theorizing and some of the most provocative work in autobiography, fiction, and graphic art of the last "generation" or so (in lesbian as well as gay terms, about five years) struggles with rather than simply casts off feminist analyses about subject positions, representation and the politics of desire.

Since lesbian writing often and characteristically mingles the theoretical and the literary,[85] along with theoretical essays, I analyze the theoretical implications of "creative" texts, such as graphic art and cultural commentary by Alison Bechdel, experiments in autobiography by Joan Nestle, and deconstructed lesbian genre fiction by Sarah Schulman, to determine how these texts elaborate contemporary theoretical issues. I have chosen these particular texts, rather than those that are either more formally experimental or more on the fringe, both because they are widely available and because they could be considered as postmodernist rewritings and revisions of the most characteristic and preferred lesbian-feminist modes of cultural expression. Since teachers are beginning to introduce such texts in university courses on lesbian and gay studies where they frequently face enormous resistances to reading, I end with a chapter offering a symptomatic reading of my own and other teachers' failures to enact a pedagogy that queers feminist and other assumptions about who and what is implicated by texts such as these.

With the exception of a handful of articles on contemporary lesbian literary-theoretical texts by Biddy Martin, Diana Fuss, and Judith Butler, and on avant-garde lesbian representation in film, video, and performance by Teresa de Lauretis and Sue-Ellen Case, most of the written texts that could be considered under the heading of postmodern lesbianism have so far been treated casually. I see a need to study them as literary and cultural texts as well as social and psychoanalytic documents.

That this area in lesbian and gay studies is as yet under-theorized is itself noteworthy. Lesbian critics have not seriously studied the development of lesbian theorizing in English since its rise in the late 1970s. A whole generation of exciting theoretical work has been largely ignored in important books such as Diana Fuss's *Essentially Speaking: Feminism Nature and Difference;* Judith Butler's *Gender Trouble: Feminism and the Subversion of Identity;* Fuss's second collection, *inside/out: Lesbian Theories, Gay Theories;* and Judith Roof's *A Lure of Knowledge: Lesbian Sexuality and Theory.*[86] Theoretical writing not discussed in these books includes work by academics such as Catharine Stimpson, Elaine Marks, Biddy Martin, and Teresa de Lauretis, as well as writer-theorists such as Gloria Anzaldúa, Judy Grahn, Audre Lorde, and Joan Nestle. I have therefore attended in this book to what has been left out by both cultural studies and women's studies, namely, lesbian representation, subjectivities, and reading practices.

My method of approaching the texts I discuss varies from chapter to chapter, depending on the degree to which I contextualize and analyze them in terms of what was happening in developments and debates in feminism, lesbian and gay studies, and literary theory. The more I behave like a literary historian, the less deconstructive and the more essentialist I become. Moreover, I am painfully aware that, to many lesbian readers, my choice of texts is charged with significance. Simply put, presence can be taken for approval and absence to disapprobation, even dismissal. A chapter on Joan Nestle as autobiographer/lesbian theorist? Where's Audre Lorde, or Minnie Bruce Pratt? What do those absences reveal about my theoretico-political allegiances and blindspots?

One answer is that Katie King, Biddy Martin, and Chandra Mohanty have already done superlative and readily available readings of their work. Another is that in the cultural politics of feminist/lesbian difference in the U.S., "racial" difference has often been reduced to the binary white, middle-class/Black (African-American) working-class. I hope to have upset that binary a bit by concentrating on the work of hyphenated Euramerican lesbians who are not only highly aware that "whiteness" is a color but that their own "whiteness" is frequently complicated by the fault lines of ethnicity, class, political affiliation, and nearness to the bi-coastal metropolitan epicenters of postmodern lesbian culture, New York and San Francisco. I approach these texts as an insider/outsider, as a white working-class convert to Judaism, and ex–New Yorker who emigrated to Canada for political reasons in the early 1970s but has lived for most of the time since in Toronto, one of the most multicultural, politically fractionated and lively gay cities in the world. Living as I do an hour's drive away from the border between the most powerful imperial state in the world today and its unknown, underappreciated, culturally and politically insecure, effectively colonized good neighbor to the north, might be an advantage, providing as it does some analogical commentary on the relationship between lesbians and the rest of the world.

In some cases, I have attended to creative or fictional texts primarily as they illustrate developing theoretical or political discourses or shifts. For example, in the chapters on Alison Bechdel, Diane DiMassa, Joan Nestle, and Sarah Schulman, their texts are studied for what they suggest about shifts in thinking among various American lesbian communities. In the part of this chapter where I summarized some of the most important developments in lesbian theorizing, I attempted to map a field, in trepidation both of oversimplifying and of foreclosing rather than of opening questions, but at the same time recognizing that theorizing lesbian anything is for most readers like embarking on *terra incognita* and so, perforce, I am willing to play the fool and offer myself as a guide.

In response to an earlier version of a part of what became this chapter, a piece intended as a chapter in a book about feminist theory, readers who identified themselves in their reports as women's studies academics indicated that, while they thought the argument important, the overview useful and original, and the writing clear, they were not familiar with most of the material and could not understand it. Admitting that they had to re-read sections several times before they could understand the issues being discussed by lesbian theorists post-Adrienne Rich, they argued that their having difficulties proved that their women's studies students could never hope to follow my argument. One might compare this response to feminist philosopher Susan Bordo's similar remarks in a book review about why she cannot imagine teaching Butler's *Gender Trouble*.[87]

Could I rewrite the article, my reviewers asked, leaving out or at least shortening the discussions of poststructuralist, psychoanalytic, and queer theories? Chagrined, even angry, I realized how these academics were defining "lesbian" writing in their classrooms: important, but too difficult—for themselves as well as their students—and therefore untaught and unteachable. If in previous generations lesbianism was considered too disturbing to be suitable for public discussion, now, apparently by becoming postmodern, lesbianism has become "too difficult."

It is urgent, when queer theory and the institutionalization of (lesbian and) gay studies at elite American universities threaten to marginalize contemporary lesbian culture, that this writing, as well as that of post-gay theorists such as Eve Kosofsky Sedgwick and Judith Butler, be studied as a theoretically sophisticated discourse in women's studies, English, and cultural studies courses, among others. Postmodern lesbianism needs to be acknowledged as the next stage in a far more inclusive history of lesbian culture than the one we already know, the one which skips from Sappho to Gertrude Stein and then concludes at gay liberation and the women's movement.

When I was first researching the connection between lesbian feminism and popular culture, I accidentally came upon a cartoon by a well-known male political cartoonist that had appeared in a Toronto newspaper in 1983. The cartoon addressed the relationship between self-conscious lesbian identities and reading practices. While I knew of two provocative essays which theorized how active and creative one has to be to become a reader of texts not apparently intended for lesbians,[88] these critics did not imagine that the reading of lesbian texts might pose difficulties for lesbian readers or might be resisted by them in any way. Studies of lesbians as readers are not theories of lesbian reading, however, and lesbian reading practices still remain undertheorized. In a sardonic way, the cartoon I found engaged that issue, and because I couldn't forget it, it became the provocation for this chapter.

In a single panel, two hip-looking women in a café are shown discussing lesbian sex and reading. The caption reads: "But, Marla," I said, "Where have you been? Why, I was a radical feminist lesbian 8 years ago. And the sex was allright but I just couldn't deal with all that literature."[89] The cartoon piqued my curiosity for a number of reasons: What role did reading play in the induction of lesbian identities and communities? Did you have to read certain texts, and read them with pleasure, in order to be or to remain what the cartoonist calls a "radical feminist lesbian"? Did a grass-roots, urban version, revolt against lesbian-feminism start earlier than one might think, circa 1975, and was it textual rather than sexual? As "all that literature" grew even more abundant and more theoretically sophisticated in the 1980s and 1990s, how had the demands that difficult reading made on readers helped to transform lesbian identities and communities?

I wrote the second chapter, "Paper Lesbians and Theory Queens," to explore what the cartoon could only assert—that lesbian identities could be considered effects of reading. "Paper Lesbians" is not an empirical investigation of lesbians' taste in reading, but a study of the reception of several recent lesbian theoretical or critical texts. These texts, as different as they are from one another in terms of disciplinary and ideological formation, all take up the role reading plays in the induction or transformation of lesbian identities and communities, particularly butch-femme and lesbian-feminist identities. I read these texts like a critical ethnographer to explore how reading and resistance to reading has helped to create and transform identities such as the lesbian-feminist, the butch-femme couple, the sex radical, and the queer. Paper lesbians who read and write theoretical texts offer an intriguing site for observing the resistances to as well as the seductions of theory. As a leading indicator of the possibilities for resistance to and seduction by theory, I conclude by reading how the queer fanzine *Judy!* reads theory-star Judith Butler.

Before there were theory stars and queer zines, the coming out story and other forms of life-writing dominated the lesbian-feminist literary landscape. These very popular autobiographical forms, from brief fragments collected in anthologies to memoirs and autobiographical fictions, told a modernist tale about how to claim an authentic lesbian identity. In the 1980s, genre-blurring theoretical autobiographies by Audre Lorde, Cherríe Moraga, Gloria Anzaldúa, and Joan Nestle deconstructed the coming out story and decentered notions of lesbian identity. The fourth chapter reads Nestle's controversial collection of autobiographical essays and erotic fiction, *A Restricted Country*, published in 1987, as a dense or thick description of a lesbian subjectivity treated not in terms of fragmentation but as a multiplicity.

While Nestle's accomplishments as political activist and social historian, particularly the part she's played in rethinking butch-femme lesbian cultures and sensibilities as editor of *The Persistent Desire*, have commanded considerable attention, not enough critical attention has been given to the way her writing theorizes what it means to restore the queerness to lesbianism. Because of the prominent part she played as a pro-sex femme lesbian in the sex wars, Nestle's writing has most often been considered within the framework of feminist debates about butch-femme, pornography, and sado-masochism. Indeed, when I delivered the earliest version of this chapter at a small but international gathering of lesbian theorists in Florence in 1989, the very fact that I had chosen to write about Joan Nestle was met with threats, name-calling and other forms of verbal abuse. In the heat of lesbian controversies about the reception of her work perhaps what tended to go unnoticed is how her writing of a singular history furthers understanding about the process of subject-formation and political resistance. But the reception of un/popular culture is never smooth. When I gave a more theoretically elaborated version of the paper in a session entitled "Theorizing Subject Positions" at a 1991 conference in Glasgow called "Questions of Feminist Theory: An International Debate," a number of participants walked out in the first five minutes as soon as they realized that the subject of my talk was lesbian.

One of the many things Nestle disturbs is the notion that subject positions must be negotiated. Rather than "negotiating" abstractly and disembodiedly between and among her subject positions as working-class woman, Jew, lesbian, intellectual, and sex worker, Nestle offers and exchanges herself with her readers as an erotic and political gift. Like other lesbian theorists, she keeps returning questions about the lesbian or feminist subject to the logically prior question of lesbian sexuality and desire, but perhaps more than other theorists, she insists that such questions be historicized. Unlike most other theorists until the recent dildo debates, Nestle concentrates on questions of explicit sexual practices and produces a political and erotic economy of the lesbian body.[90] Arguing that as a flamboyantly sexual femme lesbian she is permitted to be visible only when she can't be seen, Nestle's situation seems to parallel the problematic reception to date of most lesbian un/popular culture.

Visibility and un/popularity hardly seem to be issues for one of the two chief subjects of the next chapter, Alison Bechdel, the creator of the award-winning series of cartoons, *Dykes To Watch Out For*. Although when I was invited to give an early version of what became this chapter at the first sessions on lesbian representation at Harvard's English Institute in 1990, only the three other out lesbian speakers in this group of three hundred or so leading literary and cultural critics had heard of Bechdel's cartoons. At the time when Queer Nation and queer theory were coming into being—and the most famous queer theorists were in attendance—the audience laughed nervously about their inability to "recognize a lesbian" and wanted me to tell them how. Now that many lesbian zines exist, such as the more avant-garde *Hothead Paisan* by Diane DiMassa, perhaps high theory will catch up with low practice.

In the 1970s and early 1980s, lesbian-feminist cartoons and comic strips functioned like graphic versions of the coming out story. They were extremely didactic, rather heavy-handed and amateurish in their draftsmanship, and much more involved with describing the process of leaving the heteropatriarchy than they were with exploring what happened once a lesbian came out the other side. If Nestle's autobiographical essays deconstruct the written coming out story, then Bechdel's comics do so for the graphic version. Bechdel's lesbians are so out they're dykes. They have virtually universalized themselves as a minority and so have become more preoccupied by their own internal differences of race, sexual practices, and style. Bechdel's art, which more and more is coming to resemble a graphic serial novel, deserves consideration both as a manifestation of lesbian pop culture and as a form of low theory. I argue that Bechdel and DiMassa, though in different cultural and political terms, comically critique two major developments in lesbian un/popular culture: the resexualization of lesbian identity, and the assumption that there is a syllogistic relationship among lesbian sex radicals, radical politics, and radical culture.

The last chapter is an attempt to read what very often happens when texts like the ones discussed in this book are brought into university courses in women's studies or lesbian and gay studies. It's an exploration of what happens when lesbian and gay theoretical and other texts come into the classroom—one of the many places they belong—without a pedagogical practice queer enough to accommodate them. I've been there and done that myself. What tends to result is the course from hell.

Most of the earlier literature about teaching women's studies and gay and lesbian studies courses suggests that with the right curriculum and the right teacher and student identities present in the classroom, unpopular ideas and cultures will teach themselves, and the classroom will become a safe space for minorities to learn self-esteem and self-affirmation and for majorities to replace ignorance with tolerance. There are fewer happy stories being told now, both because of widespread shifts rightward in the political climate and because theories which refuse innocent readings, such as poststructuralism and postcolonialism, have begun to be incorporated into minority studies courses.

It's relatively easy to see and theorize about the effects on teaching consequent to the political changes that have made universities more hostile to radical teachers and classrooms, even those in minority studies, and more polarized between radicals who are usually in the minority and conservatives and the apathetic who are in the majority. It is harder to work out how those shifts, together with the introduction of theories which are not only cognitively difficult but emotionally unsettling for all the identities in the classroom, undermine the most popular assumptions about how to make pedagogy antihomophobic.[91]

While Sedgwick's arguments about why pedagogy needs to become antihomophobic have been influential, there has been little follow-up on her honest expression of uncertainty about what that might entail, apart from the expression of deep concern by feminist and lesbian theorists, many of them in women's studies, that queer theory or the most likely models of institutionalizing lesbian and gay studies further marginalize women and lesbians.[92] Instead of asking what it means to queer pedagogy, most of the recent literature in lesbian and gay studies is concerned with how the new field should be disciplined and institutionalized. Questions have yet to be asked about what could be taught or learned differently and better if homophobia isn't allowed to frame the limits of our classroom reading practices.

The final chapter asks questions about theory and practice in the women's studies or lesbian and gay studies classroom. It's a series of symptomatic readings of scenes of pedagogical failure, my own included, taken from accounts of teaching lesbian and gay material. It is my contention that courses become hellish not merely because teachers and students are sometimes resistant and unprepared for what happens when unpopular things in a racist, sexist, and homophobic culture are put on the syllabus, but because the pedagogical implications of theoretical shifts away from minoritizing discourses, shifts which have the potential to unsettle all certainties, identities, and knowledges, have yet to be traced out in the literature and are generally traumatic in the practice.

That the reception of lesbian and gay cultural texts in the classroom predictably results in trauma illustrates another facet of what I have termed un/popular culture. Though in everyday speech we tend to use the word trauma to mean simply painful and unpleasant situations, I am reminded that Laplanche and Pontalis's technical definition in *The Language of Psychoanalysis* suggests its other potentially educational and even beneficial implications, implications which fit very well the possibilities that I believe are invoked by engagement with lesbianism in its manifestations as an un/popular culture: "An event in the subject's life defined by its intensity, by the subject's incapacity to respond adequately to it, and by the upheaval and long-lasting effects that it brings about in the psychical organization."[93] The texts I discuss in this book, like those of the historical avant-garde, are not for everyone—they're not about accessibility but excessibility, in the sense of a desire to exceed what lesbians are or have been, and what one knows or thinks one knows about them and about the world.

CHAPTER 2

PAPER LESBIANS AND THEORY QUEENS

> *Resistance is...the current state of interpretation of the subject. It is the manner in which, at this moment, the subject interprets the point he is at. This resistance is an abstract, ideal point. It is you who call that resistance. It only means that the subject cannot advance more quickly.*
> —Shoshana Felman, *Jacques Lacan and the Adventure of Insight*

> *Nothing can overcome the resistance to theory since theory* is *itself this resistance.*
> —Paul de Man, *The Resistance to Theory*

At the current canonical and institutionalizing moment of lesbian and gay studies, queer theory puts a new spin on the old academic determination that some emerging area is theoretically sexy. In a paper entitled "Queer Readings" given at a recent conference where a "learned society" devoted to lesbian and gay studies was formed, one young scholar shared her fantasy about how to deconstruct the emerging canon:

> the Radical Think Tank of the Pacific Northwest...would bring together my favorite scholars, my best students and all of my academic comrades who need jobs...We'd all get along as we labor side by side for social justice, and we'd have a hot nightlife. Our work would be intellectually and politically

responsible. Interdisciplinary feminism, cultural studies and queer work would not be program options, but a way of life. Canons wouldn't matter because everybody would have read everything.[1]

That little problem resolved, days of deep discussion would inspire nights of partying. In fantasy, at least, nothing succeeds like excess.

There is neither resistance to reading nor to theory in this scholar's fantasy. Her fantasy treats queer reading as an exquisite form of eroticism. Things apparently have changed; in 1994, lesbians who read too much are no longer a problem, no longer a (sexual) turnoff. Unlike the cartoon from 1983 I mentioned in the first chapter, this fantasy involves no guilty scene of reading and the refusal to read. In that cartoon, the main character more or less reluctantly has to eschew lesbianism, not because of the sex, but because of the reading.[2] By contrast, this newer fantasy implies that, at least for lesbians who identify as queers, readerly and sexual bliss are deeply interconnected if not inextricable. Where have you been, if you don't already know that paper lesbians and theory queens are hot?

If membership in club lesbian has its privileges—good if not great sex—it also has its entry fees—hitting the books. This chapter uses the reception of several lesbian theoretical texts to explore what the joke and the fantasy in different ways can only assert: that there is a relationship between reading, especially the reading of difficult texts, and the opening up (or closing down) of different possibilities for the enjoyment of lesbian subjectivities and sexual expression. As a "leading indicator" of lesbian reception of lesbian theory, I conclude by reading how the queer fanzine *Judy!* reads theorist Judith Butler[3]

In spite of what the cartoon implies, the relationship between *lesbians and reading,* as a process which questions, complicates, and even transforms identities rather than merely affirming them, still remains under-theorized. On the contrary, mid-1980s lesbian-feminist reader response criticism,[4] current journalistic analyses of lesbian and gay reading preferences,[5] and best seller lists based on sales published in lesbian and gay bookstores and published in *Lambda Book Report* all portray the *lesbian as reader* who sifts through the available literature, chiefly canonical and non-canonical fiction, courageously and creatively seeking out her lesbian identity, that is, looking for what she already knows.

These studies and lists of what readers read or should read assume that the lesbian reader wants to know, needs to know, about lesbians and lesbianism as a matter of survival, literacy, and self-esteem. As one thoughtful analyst of the meaning of literacy for lesbians and gays argues: "lesbian and gay cultures have a unique dependency on literacy, and lesbians and gay men must be able to read and write their own stories if the culture and the people are to survive."[6] The lesbian reader, this model of reading assumes, seeks to replace ignorance with knowledge; resistance to reading exists "outside" in the hostile heterosexist world. Accordingly, the emphasis in this critical model falls on the construction and maintenance of marginalized and oppositional identities rather than on the processes by which identifications are constructed, changed, or exceeded.

From the lesbian reader response literature, which advises how to find and increase lesbian reading pleasure within what the lesbian theorist Terry Castle has recently called a "scarcity model" of mainiy heterosexist texts,[7] to empirical reports on what lesbian readers consume when the existence of lesbian and gay bookstores and the explosion in queer publishing offers them a seeming abundance, critics appear not to be interested in what occurs when increasing numbers of lesbian literary and critical texts, the latter offering methodologies for reading for the absence or against the grain, become more widely available. What is missing from these reports on lesbians as readers, then, is the question of *lesbian reading practices,* even and especially under ideal conditions, such as the fantasy of the radical think tank presented earlier in the chapter. Contrary to that fantasy, and based on the lists which appear in each issue of the *Lambda Book Report* lesbians are still resisting theory pretty unambiguously. The consistent best sellers are, as one might expect, romances, detective stories, and other works of genre fiction or subliterature, such as works on addiction, recovery, and "women's spirituality." Of all the lesbian critical and theoretical works published in the recent boom, only Lillian Faderman's study of American lesbian culture, *Odd Girls and Twilight Lovers,* has been popular enough to make it on these lists.[8]

The assumption of most lesbian critics, that reading will be easy when lesbian readers at last gain access to readerly plenitude and have an abundance and variety of lesbian-authored texts about lesbian subjects, seems unfounded. It fails to address the complex relationship between reading, knowledge, and desire.

My notions of what it means to read are themselves, as Michel de Certeau candidly observed about other readers, "poached" across and from fields in which I do not write.[9] In an age in which the binary production/consumption has been remade into writing/reading, de

Certeau wanted to claim reading as poaching as one of the practices of everyday life in which readers are not necessarily passive but have the opportunity to "turn to their ends forces alien to them."[10] Reading is a tactic of "making do," particularly for a reader such as myself, a lesbian critic who is a renter rather than an owner of cultural and other forms of capital.[11] The lesbian as critic is of necessity a plunderer, especially when she inserts herself into the "semeiocracy," making herself into what de Certeau, citing Witold Combrowicz, citing Musil, citing Freud, calls an "anti-hero" of knowledge who haunts what de Certeau tellingly calls "our research."[12]

I've plundered notions of reading from reception theory, which has more to say about aesthetic response and reader psychology than about the process of reading as meaning making. By cutting off in mid-sentence Jonathan Culler's definition, "an attempt to understand writing...," a useful emphasis is thrown on the process's inevitable incompletion and failure of mastery.[13] Unlike Iser, who in *The Act of Reading: A Theory of Aesthetic Response* disavows interest in reception in terms of the responses of existing readers, I want to explore modes of resistance to reading which operate intertextually between readers and writers of theory.[14] I've poached most obviously from feminist and deconstructionist as well as Lacanian approaches to reading, such as those by Gallop, de Man, and Felman, which, like all stories of reading, depict the subject-object relationship between text and reader as a drama, with potentially bad as well as good outcomes. I find the latter forms of analysis more useful than lesbian-feminist reader response criticism for attending to the problematic of lesbian reading because, unlike earlier humanist approaches, many of these stress and stage the difficulty, even the impossibility, of reading from *within* the reader and the project of reading. This insight is crucial in taking up the question of lesbian resistance to reading/theory, in particular how reading and resistance to reading produces anxiety and hostility as well as pleasure.[15]

This chapter began as a paper delivered at a 1993 conference at the University of Toronto entitled "Queer Sites." The conference organizers placed the paper in a session ambiguously entitled "Paper Lesbians." Given the context, I was both drawn to the phrase and disturbed by its implications. On the one hand, the title seemed particularly apt for the project I am engaged in, the exploration of the construction and reception of current lesbian theorizing in two modes, one of which takes the postmodern or textual turn, the other of which declines to do so or to do so fully. On the other hand, the title trivialized the very project of theorizing, and if applied unironically, gestures to the deep currents of anti-intellectualism that have marked much of contemporary American lesbian culture. Paper lesbians who write and read theory offer a site for naming the resistances to as well as the seductions of theory.

READING AT THE MOMENT OF THE LESBIAN THEORY BOOM

"Paper lesbians" are sometimes uneasy participants in a two-step; we read and write during a disciplinary shift in the writing of criticism and theory away from feminist historiography and women's studies and toward the writing of theory as disciplined by literature, philosophy, and film studies and the movement to institutionalize lesbian and gay studies in some American universities. If, as Paul de Man argues in "The Resistance to Theory," theory can be seen as an event, a moment of reflexive examination which is aware in a heightened way of its own self-resistance,[16] then the current explosion in the publishing of serious lesbian fictional and theoretical texts marks the 1990s as a moment in which lesbian theorizing offers its readers a chance to engage with the possibilities and problems of being self-subversively self-reflexive.[17] But will lesbian readers allow certainties of identity and identification to be problematized with all the resultant unleashing of unpopular things, the anxieties as well as the pleasures of exploring newness? And in this time, when brilliant theoretical texts are popping up like mushrooms in a rainy spring, are lesbian theoretical divas being read in, read off, or read out? This chapter explores rather than attempts to offer definitive answers to these questions, recognizing moreover that theoretical questions about reading practices are never entirely free from the cultural politics of publishing, reviewing, and teaching. Empirical data as compiled by the novelist Sarah Schulman suggests that what has been widely promoted as a flood in lesbian and gay publishing is more of a trickle where lesbians are concerned.[18]

Though many things are entangled in the decision to take or not to take the textual turn, what particularly fascinates me in my engagements with these "paper lesbians" is the likelihood that the theorists' decisions, like those of their potential and actual readers, are tied up with their investments in and fears of theory. Though the two are inextricable, I'd prefer to concentrate here on the resistances to theory in the writing and the reading of lesbian theory. By suggesting that the two chief forms of resistance to theory are resistances to the use of language about language and hence resistances to reading, de Man provocatively and surprisingly locates resistance to theory within rather than outside the project of theory. De Man's insight can therefore be used to shed light on the current moment of transition between two modes of theorizing by lesbian academics rather than to set up invidious comparisons between more or less theoretically advanced positions.

In any case, the jury is still out on whether lesbian theorists are part of "an army of theorists [that] cannot fail,"[19] or are merely "paper lesbians." De Man helpfully points out however that it is

> a recurrent strategy of any anxiety to defuse what it considers threatening by magnification or minimization, by attributing to it claims to power of which it is bound to fall short. If a cat is called a tiger it can easily be dismissed as a paper tiger; the question remains however why one was scared of the cat in the first place. The same tactic works in reverse: calling the cat a mouse and then deriding it for its pretense to be mighty. Rather than being drawn into this polemical whirlpool, it might be better to try to call the cat a cat…[20]

With de Man's advice in mind, I'll try to avoid both polemic and boosterism in announcing my own investments in and fears of and for lesbian theory.

My own interest in this subject is manifold: I read, write, and teach lesbian literary and cultural theory. My pleasure in these theoretical texts is or can be intellectual, political, and aesthetic. As a writer and a reader, I projectively identify with the who as well as the what of lesbian theorizing. I am frequently narcissistically delighted to find myself in the unusual position of being simultaneously the subject and the object of seduction by the theoretical, by theories, and by theorists. At other times, however, I find myself resistant, usually because I either leave myself out or have been left out by other theorists from the romance of lesbian intellectuals. Finally, more in my capacity as a teacher of lesbian and feminist theory to undergraduates than to graduate students, who tend to be "keeners," my pleasure recedes almost entirely in the face of their all too frequent indifference and hostility. Even and especially lesbian students are suspicious of most lesbian theory, particularly that which is poststructuralist: Do they really need it? Why does it have to be so hard?

Troubled by their routine resistance, I was nonetheless more startled than reassured when I tried to understand it in light of a key claim made by Bonnie Zimmerman in her study of lesbian fiction, *The Safe Sea of Women: Lesbian Fiction 1969-1989*. Zimmerman states that "the books a woman reads are what make her a lesbian feminist, or a member of 'the lesbian community'."[21] Her claim reminds me, yet again, of that cartoon. In similar ways, the cartoonist and Zimmerman valorize the role reading plays in the construction and transformation of lesbian identity and community. I want to interrogate their claim in an attempt not to decide the question whether texts make the lesbian, because to seek closure on this subject is impossible both theoretically and politically speaking. Rather, I want to open the claim up to scrutiny by speculating about the investments which support claims both pro and contra about the role reading by lesbians about lesbians and lesbianism plays in the construction and transformation of identity and community. How has the reception of theoretical texts induced changes in lesbian identities and communities? Who reads the two modes of lesbian theory and what needs do they fill? What counts as lesbian theory?

LESBIAN MODERNIST READING PRACTICES: ZIMMERMAN AND KENNEDY AND DAVIS

Let me suggest how difficult these questions are to answer by showing how they are implicitly addressed in two lesbian critical, if not exactly theoretical, texts by Bonnie Zimmerman and Elizabeth Kennedy and Madeline Davis which are informed by modernist or anti-poststructuralist reading practices. While Zimmerman's claim about the importance of reading is addressed to fiction rather than to theory, the way she reads fiction as a social document and instrument of historical change blurs generic distinctions at the same time as it begs the question about the role of texts in inducing social change. Fictional texts are theoretical and they produce change because that's what lesbian fiction does.

Zimmerman, a lesbian-feminist and a women's studies academic, is writing a book about fiction produced by people like her, about people like her, for people like her. This fiction, she argues, should be read as a myth of origins, but she does not appear to notice the degree to which she too is a mythmaker who is producing an interested story about them. In her article, "The Situation of Lesbianism as Feminism's Magical Sign," Katie King has suggested that feminist and lesbian theoretical texts can be read as ethnographic objects in order to illustrate that "identity is ephemeral, shifting, and inevitably contested."[22] Doing ethnography poststructurally makes it impossible to claim that ethnographies tell real stories, maintaining that they are instead "only different stories, all concretely situated, all interested."[23] Though King treats the two texts she studies as objects, reproducing their covers and paying careful attention to their graphics, in the body of her own theoretical text she does not deconstruct the claim that texts induce individual and communal change. Moreover, she relegates those claims to her notes, a practice I'll bring to the foreground later in my own ethnographic discussion of how recent lesbian theoretical texts address the role that reading plays in transforming lesbian identity.

King's discussion of the ways texts have shifted identities reminds us why reading and writing are highly contested sites. For example, in a footnote to her article, King says that a theoretical text by Adrienne Rich written in 1976 "totally eclipses Abbott and Love in subsequent feminist constructions of lesbian experience."[24] In a later footnote, a theoretical text by Rich is termed a "polemic," which constructs a new "lesbianism" elaborated upon the operation of "lesbianism as magical sign."[25]

Implicitly, lesbian-feminism functions as magical sign in Zimmerman's study of lesbian fiction. Moreover, there is an utterly silent slippage throughout the book between lesbianism and lesbian-feminism, and, for all save one chapter on difference, between "the lesbian community" and a white and middle-class American lesbian cultural mainstream. Because Zimmerman's literary critical model operates with a realist and mimetic view of the relationship between language and experience, the work by which readers fit themselves into texts is largely effaced. In Zimmerman's story of reading, there is neither complicity nor resistance. According to Zimmerman, one discourse fits all. To make lesbian culture, you follow the recipe, as follows:

> We mix together Sappho, amazons, Gertrude Stein, and Natalie Barney…; add bar culture from the fifties; season liberally with new left politics and new age consciousness; strain through traditional literary metaphors; and cover over completely with feminism to produce a lesbian culture. Today when a woman comes out as a lesbian, she has an identity and belief system waiting for her…[26]

Zimmerman's account of the role of reading in lesbian-feminist culture makes reading a non-event. To begin, it effaces the possibility that all readings are re-readings or misreadings. Though Zimmerman's book concentrates on the ways writing and reading change identities and communities, it mystifies the activities by which readings are produced. It fails to account for a re-reading and re-writing process like the one King carefully documents in her article. King shows that what many of us have heard and then further reproduced as a rallying cry for lesbianism, feminism is the theory and lesbianism is the practice, is actually a re-writing of an earlier and very different formulation, "Feminism is a theory; Lesbianism is a practice."[27]

For these reasons, even if it's true, as Zimmerman claims, that lesbian-feminism is primarily a reading practice, it becomes important to ask questions about the roles reading can play in the production of lesbian cultures. It becomes more urgent to explore how sexuality and textuality produce and are produced by each other. How have the reading of texts, particularly theoretical texts, helped to create and transform individual and collective identities such as the lesbian, the lesbian-feminist, the butch-femme couple, the sex radical, the queer, and my favorite, the theoryhead? What is productive, seductive, or destructive about theorizing identities in and through texts? What might it mean when a political movement appears to see its greatest effectiveness and lasting power in terms of the creation of texts? And most of all, where do lesbians who don't read or write theory (or anything else) fit into this grand scheme?

Those very lesbians have been given pride of place in Elizabeth L. Kennedy and Madeline D. Davis's very important book, *Boots of Leather, Slippers of Gold: The History of a Lesbian Community*.[28] Both more self-reflexive than Zimmerman and more desirous of decentering rather than recentering a lesbian-feminist mainstream of culture, Kennedy and Davis still nonetheless largely reject poststructuralist critiques of historiography and ethnographic authority, and appeal to the truth of a prediscursive "reality." At the same time as they reject most aspects of poststructuralism, their oral histories of forty-five lesbian "narrators" during their fourteen-year-long research into the largely working-class lesbian subcommunities in Buffalo, N.Y. from the 1930s to the 1950s were intended from the outset to be a suspicious reading.

Kennedy and Davis's initial suspicions of lesbian-feminism's critique and marginalization of butch-femme lesbians (whom they generally elide with working-class lesbians) were not only confirmed, but, they claim, their narrators' stories made them see how these Black and white working-class lesbians were simultaneously oppressed people and historical actors who self-consciously created a twentieth-century gay and lesbian consciousness. Kennedy and Davis conclude that that consciousness, formed in the public space they fought for in the bars, rather than that of the more closeted middle-class lesbians who restricted their socializing to safer but more isolating domesticated spaces, made possible the development of the homophile, gay liberation, and lesbian feminist movements of the late 1960s and 1970s.

(RELATIVELY) INNOCENT READINGS

My reservations about Kennedy and Davis's project come from their failure to critique their desire to tell the true story of butch-femme life from the insiders' point of view. Their initial suspicion of lesbian-feminist readings of butch-femme lesbians does not extend to their own revisionist reading. Because they announce their bias, they think they have rendered their reading innocent.[29] If lesbian-feminist readings such as Zimmerman's, which they do not mention, or Adrienne Rich's and Lillian Faderman's, which they do discuss, are false, then theirs is true, or at least truer.

Unfortunately, there's no such thing as a seemingly innocent reading and one of their harshest critics, the lesbian historian Sheila Jeffreys, catches them up on this point in a chapter of *Not a Passing Phase: Reclaiming Lesbians in History 1840–1985* entitled "Butch and Femme: Then and Now."[30] Although I agree with Kennedy and Davis's contention, stated in an endnote, that Jeffreys "seriously misreads" their work,[31] Jeffreys, who herself is a sworn enemy of poststructuralist feminist theory, ironically critiques the innocence of their reading practices, the absent/presences in their citational practices, and their valorization of "authenticity" in lesbian culture, just as a feminist poststructuralist might.[32]

In a preface where the co-authors speak in their own voices, Kennedy indicates that she set out to write a revisionist ethno-history which would not only add new ingredients to Bonnie Zimmerman's standard lesbian-feminist recipe for lesbian culture, but would at the least create a brand new dish and perhaps even reject the notion of a single recipe altogether. Kennedy's goal was "to correct the assumption of my students that lesbian history consists of Sappho, Gertrude Stein, and gay liberation."[33]

That assumption derives from the hegemony of desexualizing lesbian-feminist theories, such as Rich's notion of a transhistorical and transcultural "lesbian continuum" and Faderman's privileging of a bourgeois lesbian tradition of romantic friendship. Kennedy and Davis discuss these approaches in their introduction before explaining why they reject both as class-biased and reductive. While both Faderman's previous book, *Surpassing the Love of Men*,[34] and her more recent update on the fate of romantic friendship, *Odd Girls and Twilight Lovers*, are critiqued for their insistent and repetitive claim that sexological texts induced the formation of late nineteenth and early twentieth-century working-class lesbian subcultures that were unequivocally oppressive to lesbians, Kennedy and Davis do not clearly indicate at this point in their book how resistant they are to the idea that texts of any kind have induced lesbian or gay communities.[35]

Kennedy and Davis's resistances to reading are thus twofold: they resist a self-consciousness towards their own process of reading and they resist the idea that reading theoretical or even literary and medical texts played any significant role in inducing (at the very least) working-class lesbian communities during the time period they have studied. In this, they are following the example of George Chauncey's argument in "Christian Brotherhood or Sexual Perversion? Homosexual Identities and the Construction of Sexual Boundaries in the World War I Era." Chauncey argues that

> medical discourse still played little or no role in the shaping of working-class homosexual identities and categories by World War I, more than thirty years after the discourse had begun. There would be no logical reason to expect that discussions carried on in elite journals whose distribution was limited to members of the medical and legal professions would have any immediate effect on the larger culture, particularly the working-class. The culture of the sexual underground, always in a complex relationship with the dominant culture, played a more important role in the shaping and sustaining of sexual identities.[36]

Like Chauncey, Kennedy and Davis take a materialist stance about the relationship between the social and the symbolic. They argue that an outlaw community culture rather than the dissemination of ideas through reading or speech created working-class lesbian and gay consciousness. The struggle, then, as Kennedy and Davis present it in the first phase of their study, is for the right to be visible, to take up public space, rather than to speak or to read about same-sex desires in private spaces. For this reason, they term the culture of resistance of working-class lesbians "pre-political."[37] But even if we agree that community forms consciousness rather than the other way around, what then enables the formation of community and how are the cultures formed by community passed along?

These questions are provoked for me in Kennedy and Davis's discussion of the absence of language about sexuality in their narrators' accounts of most of the period under study, as well as the general reluctance of lesbians of the 1940s to help bring women out into bar life.[38] That the relationship between (linguistic) community and speech about sexuality is still one primarily of lack is attested to by Marilyn Frye in her article "Lesbian 'Sex,'" which Kennedy and Davis cite, although it disconfirms their claim that matters changed for the better in the 1950s.[39]

There are as well other contradictions produced by Kennedy and Davis's decision to reject the role played by texts in inducing identities and communities. For example, after discussing why they reject the lesbian-feminist theoretical claims about working-class and butch-femme lesbians offered by Rich and Faderman, they indicate that they hope their work will help create a counter-discourse in its place. This move is not so much a rejection of the notion that texts induce communities, but a decision to venerate an alternative textual tradition.

Kennedy and Davis see their work as building on and using an alternative tradition begun by the writer-theorists Joan Nestle, Audre Lorde, and Judy Grahn, all of whom were themselves involved in working-class lesbian communities in the 1950s. With very few exceptions (among them, most interestingly, is Monique Wittig), Nestle, Lorde, and Grahn are the only lesbian writer-theorists whom Kennedy and Davis frequently and consistently cite in the body of their text. Other lesbian and feminist theorists are consigned, without comment, to the extensive endnotes. Furthermore, discussion of their quarrels with Faderman are dropped from the index, as are their citations of the theoretical formulations of Teresa de Lauretis, Biddy Martin, Marilyn Frye, and Sue-Ellen Case. If a reader didn't read the endnotes, she would be unaware that Kennedy and Davis knew the work of these lesbian theorists and thought that it sheds enough light on their research to be worth mentioning at least in notes.

In a similar way, Kennedy and Davis indicate that they are aware of but knowingly reject the theoretical, methodological, and historical operations and implications of a poststructuralist ethnography which would render "the authority of the ethnography, the ethnographer, and the reader...always already suspect."[40] Instead they want to to take up a middle of the road position between discourse theory and objective historiography in an attempt to achieve "the best approximation of 'reality'" in order to get an insider's view of working-class lesbians into the historical record.[41] Unfortunately, as with their desire to produce a relatively innocent reading, their nostalgia for an ethnographic and historiographic "real" on which to anchor the authority of their text only defers but cannot totally avoid coming to terms with the crisis in representation.

DE LAURETIS'S READING OF THE CRISIS IN LESBIAN REPRESENTATION

The crisis in lesbian representation not only has dared lesbian theorizing to become more self-conscious about its theoretical investments and its positionality, but to take greater risks in problematizing its own certainties. Two articles by Teresa de Lauretis, "Sexual Indifference and Lesbian Representation," and "Film and the Visible," illustrate the risks and the possibilities of a lesbian theorizing in what I earlier called another mode that engages more fully with poststructuralism.

It seems appropriate to study these articles alongside Zimmerman and Kennedy and Davis not only because de Lauretis's texts resonate intertextually with the problematic of butch-femme representation, but because one of the de Lauretis articles, "Film and the Visible," is a re-reading of her earlier text, "Sexual Indifference and Lesbian Representation."[42] Moreover, the later text was given as a conference paper where de Lauretis's readings were largely ignored and displaced first by respondents at the conference and then again in print by queer journalists.[43] In a sense, both her re-reading of a lesbian film and her audience's refusal to read her reading offer possibilities of studying resistances to theory within and without the bounds of her text. As theory is rendered invisible in the citational practices of Zimmerman and then Kennedy and Davis, so de Lauretis's theoretical work is displaced into the commentary of others: What is remembered about what de Lauretis said is what *she* didn't say.

In both articles, de Lauretis explains why she believes that even lesbian theorists and practitioners are still caught in the unresolvable paradox of socio-sexual (in)difference which renders the literary, critical, and filmic representation of butch-femme sexuality difficult if not impossible to make legible or visible. Her position highlights the fact that lesbian visibility still has to be fought for within the new disciplinary regime of "queer theory" or lesbian and gay studies (upscale turf) as it was in the days of the bar culture celebrated by Kennedy and Davis.

In both pieces, de Lauretis makes a theoretically and politically remarkable decision to read Sheila McLaughlin's "She Must Be Seeing Things," a non-commercial lesbian-made film about lesbian representation that addresses itself to lesbian spectators. While one might think that such a film must make lesbians perfectly queer, both the film and de Lauretis's reading of it explore the difficulties of representing lesbian desire, rather than celebrate a triumph for lesbian visibility.[44] Thus many lesbians (in my teaching experience) are resistant to the pessimistic thesis of de Lauretis's articles: "the discourses, demands, and counter-demands that inform lesbian representation are still unwittingly caught in the paradox of socio-sexual (in)difference, often unable to think homosexuality and hommosexuality at once separately *and* together."[45] For the same reason, they have been known to be viscerally resistant to McLaughlin's film, which suggests that "heterosexuality inevitably informs" even lesbian "conceptions of sexuality," to the extent that on at least one occasion women stormed the screen or attempted to destroy the film.[46]

In the later article, "Film and the Visible," de Lauretis tries to attend to the problems posed by the film's failures in representing lesbian sexuality. While she explicitly admits that this failure is just one of the absences in the film, and names another as the ethnic or cultural displacement of racial differences between the lovers, she chose not to take up this displacement as central to her argument. In a note, which may or may not have been added to the written text after the heated discussion during the conference of her failure to attend sufficiently to the racial displacement, de Lauretis insists that "[a]lthough the reasons for this displacement would be an interesting and important point of speculation in an interpretive account of the film, they are not directly relevant to the present argument."[47]

It thus seems that de Lauretis is herself resistant to theory in that her desire to make one item on her theoretical agenda present (the role of fantasy in butch-femme lesbian sexuality) unintentionally renders absent another key marker of socio-sexual indifference (racial difference) from her analysis. What de Lauretis didn't say, rather than what the film and the other texts she analyzed didn't make visible, then became the focus of attention during the ensuing discussion.[48] In the course of the discussion, things are attributed to de Lauretis that she did not say, and indeed the failure of the conference as a whole to handle race equitably is laid at her feet. Still later, in brief printed summaries of de Lauretis's contributions to feminist, lesbian, and queer theory, this particular attempt to theorize lesbian representation is always mentioned as significant, but it is in actuality effaced, and her paper is displaced by the discussion.[49] Could this be the fate of lesbian theorizing at the present moment?

READING AND THE DISPLACEMENT OF THE LESBIAN SUBJECT

The study of the displacement of the lesbian subject has in recent years shifted its focus, becoming in the process increasingly full of nuance, from relatively safe but apparently foreign sites, such as in Freud and in mass culture, to more dangerously familiar turf closer to home, such as in feminist literary and film criticism. Judith Roof's *A Lure of Knowledge: Lesbian Sexuality and Theory* cites all of the above to make an elegant Lacanian psychoanalytic argument about how lesbian sexuality is used as a figure of immaturity, incompleteness, inauthenticity, or erotic excess.[50] These traits signify something else, such as anxieties about knowledge and identity. More recently, in *The Apparitional Lesbian,* Terry Castle, underlining that she writes against the theoretical tide of psychoanalytic and poststructuralist anti-humanism, connects the displacement of the lesbian in queer theory with older ways of "ghosting" her. Castle argues that the lesbian figures paradoxically in modern western culture, present everywhere, but "many people have trouble seeing what's in front of them."[51] While the goal of Castle's book is to bring her back into focus, like de Lauretis in the discussion above, even in the act of doing so, the lesbian subject is displaced.

Castle indicates that when she was delivering her chapter on the apparitional lesbian as a lecture, the first question she was usually asked was, "but what about gay men?"[52] Although her argument about the centrality of the lesbian to the dominant culture is obviously informed by Eve Kosofsky Sedgwick's universalizing model of (male) homosexuality, and could even be seen as a bold and inspired attempt to construct a similar paradigm for lesbians, Castle doesn't stop there but criticizes Sedgwick for ghosting lesbians and lesbianism in her work. Citing the same offending passage in *Between Men*[53] that other lesbian critics, even those who are usually considered theoretically correct, such as de Lauretis in *The Practice of Love*,[54] use as evidence in arguing that Sedgwick finds lesbian sexuality unimaginable, Castle shows how in *Between Men*, Sedgwick's "blockage" of interest in lesbian desire or representation effectively "dismisses lesbianism as a useful category of analysis."[55]

In Castle's study, lesbian characters in fiction from Defoe to Henry James are waved away with a blocking gesture of the hand. It's my contention that a similar blockage is in effect in contemporary lesbian and gay theory. In the work of some prominent queer theorists, lesbian theory is waved away with a blocking gesture of the pen-wielding hand. Queer theory all too often refuses to cite (in the sense of mention as well as use) lesbian theory or assimilates it as a less developed suburb of gay male theory. I will call attention to two popular forms that the blockage takes by using different typographies. When the theory in question brackets lesbianism and thus amounts to gay male separatism, as in Sedgwick or Edelman[56] I indicate it by writing it thus, (lesbian and) gay theory. When the theory in question assimilates lesbianism to male homosexuality, as in Halberstam,[57] I indicate it by writing it as if it were one word, lesbianandgay theory.[58]

Quite possibly, an analogy holds between the earlier reception of lesbian fiction and the current reception of lesbian theory. If the telltale signs that fiction is lesbian, according to Castle, are that they are under-read, largely unknown and therefore unappreciated texts standing in a parodic relationship to canonical writings which they strive to displace,[59] then lesbian theory demonstrates its lesbian-ness by getting much the same treatment.

Admittedly, even lesbian theorists who want to despectralize the lesbian sometimes ignore each other's work and the intertextuality of their theoretical elaborations. Though Castle's argument is framed very differently than Roof's, both books make large claims for the centrality of apparently absent or under-represented lesbian cultural productions and try to explain this paradox. These two texts, currently among the most accomplished full-length studies in lesbian cultural and literary theory, construct a kind of counterpoint with each other on the grand theme of lesbians as a present absence. Castle, however, does not sufficiently credit what Roof's articulation seems to have enabled. Roof, for example, in *A Lure of Knowledge,* calls Adrienne Rich's concept of the lesbian continuum in "Compulsory Heterosexuality and Lesbian Existence" a "spectral definition of lesbianism," an attempt to allay anxiety about sexuality,[60] but Castle, apart from two endnotes, does not cite Roof's contribution to her working out of the ghostly metaphor.[61] Neither does Castle cite Sue-Ellen Case's imaging of her critique of heterosexual feminism as the "ghosting of the lesbian subject" when she admiringly cites Case's essay on the lesbian vampire, a figure she describes as a "kissing cousin…of my own figure of the apparitional lesbian."[62]

Admittedly, the senses in which citation refers to mere "mention" or "putting to use" blur, but citation of lesbian sources leans in the direction of conferring "realness" because there is so much anxiety and contentiousness about the (un)representability of the lesbian subject. And, given that she has been and continues to be signified as a series of lacks—of desire, language, history, culture, and style—a generous citational practice can lend dignity and value to lesbian writing. However much one might want to break from the onto-theological project of fixing and stabilizing lesbian identity and therefore depicting it as exclusionary and monolithic, lesbian, gay, and queer theorists' seeming reluctance or downright refusal to cite the work of lesbian writers, particularly theorists, is not in itself a solution to this ethico-political as well as theoretical dilemma.

As I have been arguing and will continue to argue throughout this book, because there is no necessary connection between lesbianism and particular sets of political, aesthetic, or sexual preferences, no single theoretical discourse fits all lesbians. Indeed, many lesbians do not see a need for discourses which could be considered theoretical, even in the simplest sense that they attempt to explain lesbians to themselves or to others. Therefore, while it's important to acknowledge that all ways of theorizing lesbianism are flawed, partial, or exclusionary, it's equally important to acknowledge that all of them are relatively obscure, if we take the example of Foucault as the standard of a theoretical model that everyone must know and acknowledge.

Lesbian theoretical multiplicity *already* exists. It's not just a threat. Consider King, Meese, Martin, Pérez, Stimpson, Lorde, Marks, Fuss, Moraga, Rubin, Brossard, de Lauretis, Wittig, Roof, Anzaldúa, and Castle, for starters. Welcome aboard, brilliant Barbara Johnson. (I will not mention all the still closeted "feminists" and the semi-closeted psychoanalytic and deconstructionists.) There are more differences here than there are similarities and they confound reductive "generational" models. Though many are not now nor perhaps ever were "lesbian-feminists," most are filed under that currently dismissive category and given short shrift (from the Old English *scrifan,* impose as penance, and the Latin *scribere,* to write). Advancing the project of lesbian theorizing means genuinely recognizing lesbian theoretical multiplicity. That means acknowledging that the range hasn't been exhausted when a critic lambastes the naiveté of lesbian-feminist manifestos of the 1970s in order to praise the perspicacity of Judith Butler. If this means citing people for whom one feels disdain or with whom one disagrees strongly, and the practice merely seems futile, then lesbian critics and theorists might consider the creatively sadistic possibilities of refining and advancing their project by doing to other lesbians what Derrida did with "John R. Searle" in "Limited Inc."[63]

A greater dilemma involving the citational politics of lesbian theoretical texts concerns those that don't seem to bear citation in the perhaps more significant sense that they do not appear useful in advancing current understandings. For example, some texts such as Adrienne Rich's "Compulsory Heterosexuality and Lesbian Existence," Audre Lorde's "The Uses of the Erotic," Monique Wittig's "One Is Not Born a Woman," and Gayle Rubin's "The Traffic in Women," while considered foundational or at least formational both in the fields of women's studies and lesbian and gay studies, seem to have less relevance or to be even antithetical to the affiliational project of lesbian and gay studies, both because of the ways they configure lesbian identity and ignore or criticize male homosexuality. All were, however, included in *The Lesbian and Gay Studies Reader*.[64] Solving this problem by invoking an ostensible generation gap, whether the gap is of chronological or disciplinary age, seems problematic.

Doing so is like combining the worst sins of our founding "mothers and fathers"—the generational and even familial language used by those who have begun to critique this phenomenon is a dead giveaway.[65] Setting up a binary between the critics who are creatures of the old theories and the critics of the newest order seems at once like the creation of an explicitly lesbian and gay version of the anxiety of influence, to which a nasty queer spin of attention deficit disorder and chickenhawkism has been added, as well as a specifically lesbian rerun of the "repressive feminist mother/subversive sexy daughter" scenario that Julia Creet, in her 1991 article, "Daughter of the Movement: The Psychodynamics of Lesbian S/M Fantasy," suggested fueled the sex wars for so long.[66]

As it affects citational practices with respect to theoretical texts, reliance on the old/new binary seems obviously ageist, but it is more subtly discriminatory against "older" forms that lesbian writing in particular tended, and in some cases, still tends to take. Though there is more than equal lesbian representation in *The Lesbian and Gay Studies Reader*, the editors' decision to exclude certain forms of writing in which lesbian-feminist representation has been strongest and perhaps most creative relegates it to the pre-theoretical past. Though they praise works of personal testimony, poetry, fiction, art, cartoons, and photographic essays as the "kinds of cultural activism and analysis that have contributed so crucially to the growth and sophistication of lesbian and gay consciousness,"[67] their decision mitigates against the possibility that readers will think of lesbian theoretical discourse as having been around for a few decades by merely displacing one version of the "old."

As well as displacing lesbian theory by defining "theory" so that it excludes what lesbians tend to write, there are at least four popular ways of ignoring or failing to cite, in the sense of using, lesbian theorizing: define it as empiricist;[68] define it as a reactive polemic;[69] define it as essentialist and homophobic;[70] and most creatively, define it as "formally innovative writing" rather than theory proper.[71]

READING *JUDY!*: THE EX-CITING CASE OF JUDITH BUTLER

In another and weirdly paradoxical gesture of blockage, lesbian theory is cited parodically, almost excessively, evidenced most dramatically in the iconization of Judith Butler. Butler is one of the very few lesbian theorists who are cited in the arts and humanities rather than the social science index. After Butler published her instant classic, *Gender Trouble,* in 1990, citing her became *de rigueur* in lesbian and gay academic circles.[72] By the time of the 1991 Rutgers conference on lesbian and gay studies, Butler was running neck and neck with Eve Sedgwick, if not surging ahead of her in the citational sweepstakes.

Given the density of Butler's argument and style, it is not so surprising that her whole involuted argument has been reduced to the mantra "gender is performativity." Nonetheless, her construction into an instant star is somewhat curious. It's as if the academic establishment, gay as well as straight, in a virtual replaying of the 1980s fetishizing of each year's singular African-American female writer, can only bear one or at most two of this year's marginalized theoretical divas. The choice can appear arbitrary. The intuition that these trends might be as ephemeral or as volatile as other subcultural fashions is borne out if one consults lists of theorists canonized in recent books such as Donald G. Marshall's *Contemporary Critical Theory: A Selected Bibliography,* in which the only female is the non-feminist, non-lesbian, Julia Kristeva.[73]

Merely getting cited is not the solution to the ghosting of the theoretical lesbian. As every academic who writes and reads knows, the politics of citation are complex and frequently nasty. Information scientists working in the area of bibliometrics often study noted scholars' citational patterns; observing, among other things, the frequency and distribution (very often narrow in the humanities) of scholars' citations of each other's work. From the slavish citational practices of the graduate student who must display that she or he has covered the field, to the citational practices of the rich and famous who must not cite just anybody, citation is a minefield. If I cite you, will you cite me? Like real estate, citation comes down to location, location, location.

Citation, then, as a form of adoring fanship might be readable as a more subtle form of resistance; another way, ironically, of de-realizing or ghosting the lesbian subject. As de Certeau suggests, citation might be "the ultimate weapon for making people believe. Because it plays on what the other is assumed to believe, it is the means by which the real is instituted."[74] In a populist culture like the American one, where hatred and fear of intellectuals has typically taken the form of ignoring them or turning their work into jokes, the construction of the "theory queen for a day" through excessive citational practices of her and her sexy topics seems far from a new development or a solution to the problem of ghosting.

Resistance to reading takes a spec(tac)ular form, as in the fanzine *Judy!*[75] Taking this marginal production as an instance of reading the theory of Judith Butler in itself demands explanation. I became aware of *Judy!'s* existence when I was researching queer zines. A zine or fanzine is an obsessional work of bricolage, a cheaply produced tabloid or photocopied item disseminated via word of mouth to other fans. Zines juxtapose a variety of different texts and images, including letters, photographs, drawings, and fantasies, many of which are meant to be shocking or pornographic. They originally concerned celebrities or their personae who were significant in teen and youth culture, such as the characters in "Star Trek." Now, many zines are of the personal sort, focusing on the lives of the obscure and the uncelebrated. Few of the zines are named after celebrities known for their writing; the *Dead Jacqueline Susann Quarterly* is exceptional in this regard. Apart from *Judy!*, only one other queer zine included fantasies about literary or other theorists.[76]

From the moment I sent away my two dollars for a copy of *Judy!*, I could be considered complicitous in the zine's project of creating a cult of personality around Judith Butler in a way I would not have been, perhaps, when I purchased *Bodies That Matter*,[77] a book which when it first appeared was so popular that it sold out in two cities with many fine bookstores and largish claques of queer theorists, Toronto and Ann Arbor. My initial response to the zine was mixed. On the one hand, I was delighted. Its existence marked the arrival of lesbian theory on the (sub)cultural scene, much as Sedgwick's appearance as a performance artist in a crowded smoky club in Toronto's bohemian area in 1993 announced that queers could be contenders as the new Beats. The zine's author, Miss Spentyouth, was at the time an undergraduate at the University of Iowa, and, unlike most of my students, loved theory (or theorists). Clearly, she keeps up with her reading when she is not stalking academics. On the other hand, Spentyouth's reading of Butler reduces her and by extension her work and that of other theorists, not all of them lesbian, to sexual fantasies and malicious gossip. Have lesbians finally evolved into campers?

As crude transference onto Judith Butler, *Judy!* displays the author-reader's resistance to theory and to reading. Substituting acting-out repetition for verbalized or written recollection, *Judy!* exemplifies the downside of the American cultural studies model of the intellectual or proto-intellectual as fan or groupie who is him or herself turned into a celebrity.[78] That chain reaction was then amplified in the fall of 1993 when Larissa MacFarquahar, in *Lingua Franca,* the journal which calls itself "The Review of Academic Life," reported on *Judy!* as a "sex-positive love letter" to Judith Butler, in the process interviewing Miss Spentyouth and Butler herself.[79]

That the "love" which apparently inspired this "impertinent reading"[80] is more than lightly sprinkled with a regressive narcissism and overt hostility is explicit from beginning to end of the seventeen-page zine. Miss Spentyouth's *Judy!*, including her "responsibility for my actions statement," is a manifesto of reading as really aggressive poaching (in the *Concise Oxford* dictionary sense of "to trample, cut up [turf etc.] with hoofs; trespass on [land etc.] capture [game, fish] by illicit or unsportsmanlike methods…from F. *pocher* put in pocket"): "I swear to god I heard every bit of dish from someone I know or read it someplace so you know it's true. If your name is in here and you're pissed, you might as well know I'm too poor to bother suing and also if you did you'd look dumb…Also you should be nice while reviewing this. It took me twelve years to write."[81]

Reading *Judy!* suggests how essential the writing and reading of queer theory has been in the production and promotion of the pomo queer. Without the queer theorist and his/her readers, there would, I suspect, be very few neo-queers. Compare the placard held erect over the title of Linda Garber's collection of essays, *Tilting the Tower: Lesbians Teaching Queer Subjects:* "Another Queer Theorist for Lesbian & Gay Studies." Being queer might be the larval (from the Latin for ghost) and pupal (from the Latin for girl) state of the tenure-track professor of cultural studies.[82] The not so hidden trope of the generation gap between queer theory producers and consumers is everywhere in this monument to the new pederastic pedagogy, which gleefully records happenin' theory's inevitable transience. Is the moment of the triumph of queer theory also the moment of its fall? *(The Lesbian and Gay Studies Reader,* the *Lesbian and Gay Studies Newsletter* published by the MLA and the new Canadian parallel association have all decided after much debate not to name themselves "queer.") In the very moment of inscribing Judith Butler into the academic firmament as a superstar, Spentyouth implies that Butler is tired, passé: "Judy's a hot ticket but those naughty fickle grad students have probably picked another famous theoryhead to lionize by now (so be sure to read our predictions for the next wave of homo-icons in forthcoming issues. Who will it be [sic(k)]. Honey, I'm not sure I can wait."[83]

Does "hypertrophic reading," "a cancerous growth of vision, measuring everything by its ability to show or be shown and transmuting communication into a visual journey…a sort of epic of the eye and of the impulse to read," of this sort help to bring the lesbian back into focus, as Castle desires, and establish a lesbian writing and reading economy of plenitude?[84] In her own chapter on the nineteenth and early twentieth-century collective lesbian fixation on Marie Antoinette and on coming out as a diva worshipper of the mezzo-soprano Brigitte Fassbaender, Castle argues that it can. Resisting her own embarrassment, a feeling Miss Spentyouth apparently never experiences, Castle remarks on how "scandalously" energizing such reading can be, and for this reader, so it was, because I wanted to hear a witty and erudite lesbian intellectual give in to the desire to admire another woman's accomplishments.[85] "Give in"? Yes, the sense of eroticized surrender is intended in my formulation. If in her book Castle comes out as an opera queen, in my perhaps equally "crude transference" to Castle, I have outed myself as a lesbian theory queen. This is where I am in my story of reading, this is my point of resistance, and I acknowledge that mine is no innocent reading either. I prefer to find lesbian theorizing smart and sexy rather than naive and puritanical, etc., etc.

Though the impulse to replace the scarcity model of lesbian culture with one of plenitude seems to me theoretically problematic, the desire for it, a kind of strong reading, is psychologically understandable: The object of lesbian divahood, such as Marie Antoinette then or Judith Butler now, "gave those who idolized her a way of thinking about themselves."[86] Far more persuasive and erotic is Castle's argument based on fanship's potential for producing more and more sensitive readings:

> If I have, however crudely, inspired a desire to hear, or hear again, the singing of Brigitte Fassbaender, I am glad: in the presence of such brave and tender artistry, there is nothing in the end to fear, and much—oh, so very much—to love."[87]

CHAPTER 3

BACK TO THE FUTURE WITH DYKES TO WATCH OUT FOR AND HOTHEAD PAISAN

WHEN RETURNING TO THE PAST LOOKS LIKE PROGRESS...

So I'm walking out of the gym where I use the stairmaster to keep me from obsessing about whether two of my favorite lesbian cartoons are aesthetically innovative enough to be considered avant-garde (and that's if it's possible to have a movement or even for individual artists to do avant-garde work anymore) or whether they're just old-fashioned tendentiously realistic lesbian-feminist agitprop. Only a hard workout on the stairmaster makes me stop ruminating. While I'd rather imagine I was an infallible (if psychotic) critic like Hothead Paisan, I know I'm only neurotically ambivalent, like Mo in *Dykes To Watch Out For*.

Hothead Paisan, the self-described "Lesbian Homicidal Terrorist," is incendiary enough to have made it into Re/Search's *Angry Women*, but she was in advance of the editors.[1] Perhaps they had less trouble imagining an academic like bell hooks as a performance artist than contemplating that a cartoonist like DiMassa might share their vision of "a new consciousness which for the first time would integrate political action, cutting-edge theory, linguistic reconstruction, adventurous sexuality, humor, spirituality and art toward the dream of a *society of justice*".[2] Since 1991, Hothead, the creation of cartoonist and tattoo artist Diane DiMassa, has appeared four times a year in a small black and white zine.[3] Hothead is a young urban proletarian Italian-American lesbian with Medusa-like hair, Doc Martens, and a tattoo. A "paisan" is the Italian-American equivalent of a "homegirl." She looks like a queer trendoid, but she's more extreme and nihilistic than bohemian in her cutoff pajama bottoms. She converses with her talking familiar, a cat named Chicken, and the cat talks back, as well as the moon goddess and a lamp that represents "The All That Is." Hothead is armed and deadly, partially because she "really checked out for lunch" after watching too much TV.[4]

By comparison, Mo and her friends in Alison Bechdel's long-running graphic novel, *Dykes To Watch Out For,* are a lesbiantic Brady Bunch.[5] The strip, which began to appear in book length volumes in 1986, takes the form of an extended and unresolvable debate about sexual-political practices in a self-consciously lesbian-feminist subculture. By *Spawn of Dykes To Watch Out For,* Bechdel's fifth volume, they've evolved into "cultural workers, young professionals, and hot-blooded housemates."[6] If the unidentified back cover blurbwriter for this most recent collection calls Bechdel the "well-loved chronicler of contemporary lesbian life and times," then how does that compare to Sarah Schulman's endorsement on the first page of Diane DiMassa's *Hothead Paisan: Homicidal Lesbian Terrorist,* as the book that American lesbians (at least those who come to her readings) most love to read, even if they feel that they have to deplore the violence in it and keep on reminding those not so enchanted with it that it's only fantasy?[7]

Is this another good girl/bad girl thing? "The lesbian community's premier visual archivist/gossip columnist" versus "the bible of man-hating ball busters driven over the edge of insanity into our own state where anarchy reigns and no man is safe to walk the streets"? Perhaps *Dykes To Watch Out For* is a femmes' comic and *Hothead Paisan* is the zine for butches. (Are femmes to agitprop as butches are to the avant-garde? Yikes, as Hothead would say.) Nonetheless, it must be acknowledged that the look and the preoccupations of *Dykes To Watch Out For* seem to reflect expert claims about gendered taste in comics, particularly with respect to the gendering of visual languages and to the insistence that the "outsider" vision of the great American cartoons is ultimately gentle and conventionally affirmative.[8] Everybody knows that it's girly to prefer more sentimental, talky, and domesticated comics and macho to dig action comics with superheroes and aliens. In terms of visual language, boys' comics privilege movement and girls' concentrate on feelings, especially of faces in close-up, "subtle expressions and body movements" which "supplement the dialogue."[9] Neither *Dykes To Watch Out For* nor *Hothead Paisan* smoothly fit into this predictable binary. Both, albeit in very different ways, focus on the everyday, that is, the sometimes extraordinary reality of everyday lesbian micro-political life, and emphasize the feeling activities, including erotic activities, of undomesticated women. Unlike the superheroes in Thomas Inge's *Comics as Culture,* dykes and hotheads offer different kinds of threats to the representational status quo. While these two cartoons show one site of feminist popular culture in the process of transforming itself from lesbian-feminist vanguard to lesbian neo-avant-garde, determining which is most in advance of culture and society is not as easy as it might appear.

As I return to my ruminations, a bullet-shaped man, who physically resembles the men Hothead frequently terminates, makes appreciative sucking noises at the young blonde "spritzhead" (this is hotheadian for what a lesbian-feminist like Mary Daly would call a "male-identified fem-bot") in front of me. Still lost in thought, I reluctantly leave my dreams of the avant-garde and return to the world I share with both my comic book anti-heroes because the man has turned his attention to me, growling, "Get out of my way, dyke." I don't, but with respect to lesbian cultural and political analysis, this incident reminds that when anarchic avant-garde desire meets reactionary social and political conditions it unfortunately looks like déjà vu all over again. Getting revenge, widely thought to be a victim's desire and tactic, one especially favored by lesbians and feminists in the 1970s, is once again fashionable in the gay '90s.[10]

ANGER AND SEXUALITY IN "WOMEN'S" COMICS AND QUEER ZINES

As violently surreal as *Hothead Paisan* appears to be compared to the gentle "realism" of *Dykes To Watch Out For,* DiMassa's work, like Bechdel's, takes up the same major themes of anger and sexuality that have preoccupied women's alternative comics in general and lesbian comics in particular since the second wave of feminism began in the late 1960s.[11] What makes *Hothead* seem more queerly postmodern is that her anarchic spiritual and poetic vision makes her a credible candidate for a place in the tradition of the aesthetic avant-garde, which could be making a comeback. The less formally innovative but more lesbocentric *Dykes To Watch Out For* seems stuck in the collectivist lesbian-feminist political vanguard which currently seems out for the count.

If a generation in lesbian and gay cultural terms is about five years, then Alison Bechdel, who published her first book length collection of *Dykes To Watch Out For* cartoons in 1986, is a generation behind Diane DiMassa, who began to publish *Hothead Paisan* as a slim quarterly zine in 1991. In terms of crude chronology, though, they are contemporaries. DiMassa is actually the older of the two, having been born in 1959, a year earlier than Bechdel. While both cartoonists have devoted followings among different segments of the American lesbian subculture, signs of which include *Dykes To Watch Out For* calendars and *Hothead* T-shirts, neither has attracted "serious" study yet by the cultural studies crowd even when they discuss queer zines.[12] Even Lynda Hart's ferociously theoretical *Fatal Women: Lesbian Sexuality and the Mark of Aggression,* which is dedicated to so-called lesbian serial killer "Aileen Wuornos and for all the women who have been vilified, pathologized, and murdered for defending themselves by whatever means necessary,"[13] fails to mention Hothead Paisan, the "Lesbian Homicidal Terrorist." Is it because Hothead always gets away with it or because she's just a cartoon?

Moreover, in feminist as well as mainstream analyses of comics, even Bechdel's ingratiating treatment of everyday lesbians hasn't received any attention. Though Bechdel has now published five collections of Lambda award-winning cartoons, including *Dykes To Watch Out For; More Dykes To Watch Out For ; New, Improved! Dykes To Watch Out For ; Dykes To Watch Out For: The Sequel* and most recently, *Spawn of Dykes To Watch Out For,* which appear in more than forty lesbian and gay publications in North America, and she routinely makes the bestseller lists in gay bookstores, there's no mention of her work in *Comics as Culture* and she was left out of all the books and articles about women's and feminist humor. Not popular enough to be mainstream, not straight enough to be feminist, and not queer enough to be avant-garde—who's watching out for these dykes?

Perhaps Bechdel's titles have something to do with those omissions—"dykes" are not women and they aren't considered part of popular culture or history. Perhaps Bechdel's in-your-face title, with its various connotations of looking, being vigilant, keeping a person in sight so as to be aware of any movement or change, and of being on one's guard, sounded too militant for the reactionary 1980s. What readers/spectators are requested or commanded to "watch out for" are, after all, not "woman-identified women," not "feminists," not even "lesbians," but "dykes." When most feminist cultural workers were still in the closet in their work, and mainstream presses hadn't yet realized that lesbian and gay studies titles could be a gold mine, it's important to remember how blatant and unapologetic Bechdel was about her subject matter. Bechdel's small press publisher, Nancy Bereano of Firebrand, said the cartoonist was worried about details of the first cover's design rather than the presence of that word, "dykes," in the title.[14]

By contrast, in a much shorter time, *Hothead Paisan* has been noticed enough to inspire debate among readers, who, in typical zine interactive fashion, respond in print to the writer as well as her characters (including Chicken the cat) in the back pages of each issue. When I bought the collection as well as the most recent issues that I have been able to sneak across the Canadian border, I had the longest and most appreciative conversation about books and ideas I've had in some time in a bookstore, or anywhere else for that matter. The queer clerk, who shares each issue with lots of his friends, said he had spent the evening before defending Hothead's "violence" against men as fully justified and as a fantasy in any case. These loyal friends of Hothead, I suspect, wouldn't be swayed by Laplanche and Pontalis's correction of their commonsensical assumption that "fantasy" should be understood as an opposition between "illusion" and "reality."[15]

That there's more than one way to "read" Hothead hasn't even occurred to Canada Customs, which has banned the zine as hate literature. Like earlier avant-garde work, the success of *Hothead Paisan* can be judged by the degree to which it has inspired outraged reactions from members of previous waves of the avant-garde as well as by members of the establishment. Even friendly readers want to hear the cartoonist talk about bricks being thrown through her windows by "feminists chanting anti-violence slogans."[16] Canada Customs has confiscated shipments in raids on women's and gay bookstores because the strip combines "'sex with violence,' despite the absence of sex scenes in the offending issue."[17] Hothead herself might not be surprised: the cover of Issue three warned that this publication is "a dangerous little zine" that is "not for the weak" well before the cover of Issue nine proudly announced "Banned in Canada! (cause we're ascared of it, that's why!)."[18]

On two occasions, DiMassa interrupted her narrative with surrealistic segments addressing patriarchal censors and outraged pacifist lesbian-feminists who would suppress her work. In the second issue, a giant censor in the form of a panopticonic eyeball invaded Hothead's apartment, objecting that the comic was too violent. To which our acute cultural critic had a ready reply: "What about Bat-fuck and Nintendo and the Road Runner?" The censor wasn't swayed by logic: "That's different! Boys will be boys."[19] The incident ended when Chicken, Hothead's mild-mannered feline sidekick, scratched the eyeball out. In Issue five, righteous lesbian-feminist Fran calls DiMassa to complain that she's undoing the last twenty years of feminism by behaving just like men. DiMassa enters the frame, explains that the whole thing's a satire on the media, and a revenge fantasy. When those "reading lessons" aren't convincing, DiMassa shrewdly asks Fran whether there's any man in the family she'd like to have Hothead blow away, and before you know it, DiMassa's made a convert.[20]

But before drawing the conclusion that this is the first time that government or feminist p.c. police have tried to censor lesbian comics, it's useful to remember that this too is something of a rerun. Comic books have always had a dubious relationship with "realism" as well as with good taste; that has always been a major part of their appeal to readers as well as why they have threatened the tender and mature sensibilities of parents and members of the bourgeoisie. Mainstream comic books engendered major moral panics in the 1950s. Sexually explicit adult and underground comics created more scandals in the 1960s, and when the first "women's" comics—I use scare quotes because the word is very often a euphemism for lesbian—appeared in the late 1960s and early 1970s, some feminists were not amused. One of the reasons lesbian erotic artist Tee Corinne researched and wrote an 1977 overview of "Comics By Women" for a feminist alternative magazine was that even then many women's bookstores refused to carry them, utterly missing their cultural importance in disseminating new ideas in the feminist and lesbian communities.

> [M]ost women's bookstores do not carry them because: "They are too dirty," "They are too violent," "They do not further the revolution," "They don't uplift women's ideals," etc. Or, as one East Coast Women's Bookstore owner put it: "Women have better things to spend their money on than that trash…" Many of the comics done by women do deal with sexuality and anger as major themes. They also deal with coming out, future visions, communal living, transsexualism, foremothers, abortion, herstory, loving men, loving women, self loving and the use of vibrators. Their themes have roughly paralleled those of

the alternative women's press magazines and sometimes predate the popularization of those issues by a year or more. They also function as a place for women artists to develop their skills and share who they are and who they are becoming.[21]

After the sex wars, the same thing happened again, as many women's bookstores in the mid to late 1980s took a stand against pornography and sado-masachism by refusing to sell lesbian sex magazines such as *On Our Backs* and *Bad Attitude*. Though these magazines rejected and sometimes parodied the moral outrage and sexual puritanism of the lesbian-feminist alternative press, in inventing a pornography for women, they also necessarily rejected the older publications' drab layouts and amateurish graphics. Though sexual pleasure was their goal, and they were fairly successful at producing it, their relative slickness and commercial appearance distinguishes them from the punk and post-punk queer zines which succeeded them. Their goal was not so much pleasure as outrage. In traditional avant-garde fashion, they aimed their target not at straight society, but at the older and assimilationist lesbian-and-gay establishment.

Works of youthful bricolage, handwritten or using a mish-mash of computer typefaces like ransom notes and held together with staples, zines look anything but slick. Their contents might include a wide range of writings and graphics, from personal narratives illustrated with cartoons and doctored photographs, to poems, manifestos and analytical essays, but their intent is always to reinvent what it might mean to be lesbian and gay outsiders by venting spleen in extreme, obscene, and imaginative ways. Because their editors reject the profit-driven economy that drives conventional magazines, even pornographic ones, zines are intended to be labors of love that lose rather than make money. Intended for a small and select audience—*Bimbox* says it's "free to those who deserve it"—they're usually distributed at the price of postage and handling alone. Like earlier avant-garde work, the zines are supposed to be incomprehensible and repellent both to the brain-dead bourgeoisie and to the lesbian and gay avant-garde that *they* hope to supersede. Though their operating definition of avant-garde work resembles Peter Bürger's thesis about the characteristic positioning of the historical European avant-garde outside and in opposition to the art institution, unlike him, zine editors and readers are entirely optimistic about the possibility of doing neo-avant-garde work now.[22] Propaganda from the 1992 Decentralized World-Wide Networker Congress Subspace International Zine Show emphasized that zine editors both resembled members of earlier avant-garde movements and expressed a totally new artistry:

> As foreseen by the DADAists, Futurists, Situationists, Fluxus and others, a new kind of artist has developed—the networker. In total autonomy and independent from the art and culture institutions, the networker is manifested through the international networks of mail art, tourism, copy-art, computer bulletin boards, fax art, cassette labels, and the underground press, etc.[23]

COMIZINE DIVERSITY AND PERVERSITY AFTER THE SEX WARS

In a landscape whose major landmarks are *Holy Titclamps, Taste of Latex,* and *Brat Attack,* Bechdel looks pretty tame compared to DiMassa. The work of both, however, like that of the lesbian sex magazines and the newer queer zines, is similar in that it has been enabled as well as fueled by the fracturing of the feminist cultural consensus after the sex debates. The work of both is informed by twenty or so years of American feminist theoretical practice, especially the bitter and failed attempts to "include" women of color, working-class women, and lesbians in (white, middle-class, heterosexual) feminism. The hidden injuries of racism, classism, and heterosexism can be traced through these cartoonists' responses to what journalists and scholars refer to as the sex debates and the "crisis of representation" within feminism.

Bechdel, the liberal pluralist humanist, has tried to heal the wounds by representing all the factions as a multicultural multiplicity of lesbian diversity. When she speaks to primarily lesbian audiences about her work, fans often ask her why she hasn't drawn (enough or any) bar dykes, lesbian mothers, older lesbians and so forth and pointedly urge her to do so soon.[24] Bechdel, a white, recovering Catholic lesbian, has apparently not been criticized for being a racist through under-representing lesbians of color or through arrogantly appropriating their cultures. She herself is not sure why this hasn't happened, because she acknowledges how her own struggle against racism plays itself out in her difficulties in drawing lesbians who are different from herself.

Bechdel thereby suggests how the struggle to know and love the apparently self-same is fundamentally entangled with the struggle to delineate social differences. When she began to draw her lesbians of color, she says that she depicted them more like the central white character's "ethnic sidekicks" than as fully fleshed lesbians in their own right.[25] Nonetheless, even after five volumes, the center still belongs to the dominants within "the" lesbian community, rather than to leather dykes, butch daddies, or femme tops. While Bechdel's strip has interracial luppie moms, twelve-stepping Asian-American new agers, a cute young queer girl, and a disabled dyke, they're all second bananas. The lead is still Mo, a white, downwardly mobile but middle-class lesbian-feminist, who distracts herself from her sexual miseries by endless whining and ranting about what is to be done about every political issue in and out of this particular midwestern lesbian subculture. (Bechdel based the strip loosely on lesbian life in Minneapolis, where she lived when the books began to be published.)

Her spectators' apparent craving to be included representationally, of course, can never entirely be fulfilled, no matter how broad the representational sample that Bechdel depicts. They will never entirely find themselves there in that simple way, no more than the urge to de-essentialize lesbianism or lesbian representation will be satisfied by producing a multiplicity of lesbians as an answer to a craving for identity that is still perceived as a unity.[26] In fact, lesbians watching *Dykes* and waiting for themselves to slip into the representational frame "just as they are" in a documentary sense might still be frustrated when a somewhat plump and somewhat older lesbian appears because she works as a human rights investigator, let's say, and not as a bookkeeper or a waitress.

If Bechdel's chief subject is diversity between and among lesbians after the sex wars, then lesbian perversity, in both the specifically sexual sense and in the sense of the mechanisms of splitting, disavowal, and defensiveness that tend to operate in the perversions, is DiMassa's. Hothead's diversity lies within her—in the splitting between her evil personality #2, who emerges all too easily "with all the answers,"[27] to incite her to violence, and her guardian angel, who surfaces only with great difficulty[28] to urge her to hope and love, and whom she tunes out. Hothead's psyche is the battlefield of lesbian diversity rather than the kitchen table, as in the wrangling that goes on between old friends and lovers in *Dykes To Watch Out For*. Though her circle of friends, like the ones depicted in *Dykes*, is multiracial, Hothead frequently and explicitly points to her own positioning as raced, as living a particularly white ethnicity, which she shares with the white men and women who oppress world majority people.[29] Her personal psychodrama is the central focus, as befits the intensely personal ethos of avant-garde writing, rather than the more extroverted and leftist discursive debate about political praxis that characterizes *Dykes To Watch Out For* as a lesbian-feminist sermon of the week.

While Hothead has a few friends, unlike Bechdel's tight little "Herland," she goes into her existential nightmares and visions as well as out on her homocidal adventures alone and without the support of a lesbian community. Like other junkie outsiders—rage and coffee are her drugs of choice—it's hard to imagine Hothead settling down into coupled domestic bliss. Because she's fond of drag queens and transgendered people and her vision of utopia is hermaphroditic, she gets "as much shit from the politically correct police as from anybody else."[30] When she does have sex, it's rough, with an s/m air about it, something that has attracted the positive attention and curiosity of the leatherdyke zinescene.[31]

AVANT-GARDE EXTENDA MIX: SPIRITUALITY AND POLITICS

The epiphenomena of new-age spirituality, so popular among lesbian feminists, from twelve-step programs to rituals for healing one's inner child, are generally treated as insider jokes and met with the same initial "political" outbursts of scorn by both Mo and Hothead. But once again, as with the treatment of sexual diversity, the treatment of spirituality is more complex and contradictory in *Hothead Paisan*, allowing for difference within, than in the consistently secular and rationalist *Dykes To Watch Out For*. In *Dykes*, new-ager Sparrow's crystal-wearing, sage-burning, affirmation-spouting is never taken very seriously and only played for laughs. Since most lesbians are aware of the acute analyses launched by First Nations People and others concerning the culturally appropriative practices of Euramerican shamanistic wannabes, it's a bit of a copout that Bechdel has laid the new-age trip on an Asian-American dyke. Because spiritual practices are simply and not very effectively proselytized for, and then defended or rejected, they function only as a site of polarization in lesbian cultures.

In *Hothead Paisan*, the main character also rejects religious practices, whether her family's Catholicism or Roz's new-age rituals; but unlike the characters in *Dykes*, who live in an everyday if lesbian reality, Hothead is willy-nilly a mystic, a seer, and a madwoman, who is transported on a regular basis between heaven and hell through her utopian and dystopian visions, dreams, and nightmares. Those momentary illuminations suggest that there is more, much more, to perceive, feel, and do than her ordinary reality presents her with.

Though the scenes in which Hothead scorns the new-agey advice of Chicken, who urges her to replace caffeine with yoga and Roz, the blind visionary lesbian-feminist, and who recommends that she sublimate her rage into other forms of creativity by entering therapy, are played for the same kinds of laughs as in *Dykes,* the visionary episodes make "spirituality" far more than a trope for cultural diversity. It's presented as bittersweet and even tragic but alas all too human that the moon goddess and the droopy lamp that represents "The All That Is" get her attention only fitfully. DiMassa doesn't simply present goddess and lamp as revelations of a transcendental reality that stands in opposition to Hothead's paranoid fantasies, but as other manifestations of her longing. Accordingly, the seriousness with which spiritual and even metaphysical issues are treated in this zine links it to the essentially religious and idealist basis of the aesthetic vision of the historical avant-garde.[32]

In *Hothead,* as in other avant-garde work with anarchist leanings such as postmodernist fiction by William Burroughs, Thomas Pynchon, and Kathy Acker, paranoid violence and visions of alternative realities are closely connected: sex n' violence. The narrative core of each issue is the same—Hothead gets high on caffeine and television, and then goes out into the hostile heterosexist world to seek equal space. Like clockwork, she is assaulted by misogynist street toughs, doctors, homophobes, rapists, and neo-Nazis, and then she blows them away with a variety of deadly weapons, from hugely phallic guns to hand-grenades, in a variety of blood-curdling ways. Though each issue has the same pattern of movement out of apathy or despair into murderous rage, the catharsis never seems identical because each one is such an inspired vision of radical destruction. Unlike a socialist transformation, which as Oscar Wilde complained, would be very nice but it requires too many nights of tedious meetings, Hothead's revolution takes but a moment, and doesn't involve endless discussion. Hothead is a revolutionary only in the sense that she's a terrorist.

Like earlier avant-garde writers, her goal and her highest value is personal freedom. As DiMassa states in the introduction of her book, she's a "battler for the right to take up a little space."[33] Her murderous rampages are presented as a poetic quest in which she is taken over by personality #2 in a simultaneous act of negation and creation. Unemployed because her rage puts her on permanent disability, Hothead is free of the workaday world that frames life in *Dykes To Watch Out For.* She only leaves her apartment to commit mayhem and then to be saved from her dissipation by Chicken and Roz. In the first issue, which predated the Lorena Bobbitt case by two or more years, she chopped off a penis and imagined six different fantastic uses for the severed member.³⁴ Sometimes, she bursts into rhyme and grows additional arms like Kali, the Hindu goddess of destruction:

> *Oh, I'm just a thick-headed Italian, Can't tell me shit!!!*
> *It's my God-given birthright to yell and have a fit!!!*
> *Yessss, I'm the homicidal Lesbo Guinea Goddess!!*
> *And I don't like to be calm!*
> *An' I get pissed when I look around an' see what's going on…so…*
> *This is the legend of Hothead Paisan,*
> *No time for guilt, and packin' a gun*
> *Some say I'm insane but it's simply this:*
> *Stand tall when you walk and don't take any shit!*³⁵

COMICS AS A SIGHT OF LESBIAN REPRESENTATION

By comparison with DiMassa, Bechdel is much more concerned with the older lesbian theoretical and creative project of getting lesbian diversity into the frame of representation. Making lesbians visible, making their differences from each other as well as from straight women clear, has generated as well as been the goal of her work from the beginning. Bechdel tells a story in her slide show text about her inability, before she came out as a lesbian, to draw women "from her head," as she could easily do with men. This inability bothered her, she says, "ideologically." She didn't want to draw men and she couldn't draw women, whom she saw as, like Minnie Mouse, merely Mickey in drag. The inability made her almost stop drawing. Then she asked herself, "Why not draw a lesbian?" and she found she could do it. She could draw a woman if she thought of her as a lesbian. Bechdel attributes the breakthrough to being with "all these wonderful, gorgeous lesbians, all these women who were really at ease with themselves and their bodies and their self-image," and she "found that it was possible to draw real women who weren't in drag."³⁶ This story can be interpreted, of course, in a variety of ways and various conclusions can be drawn about the artist's conception of her work's relationship to realism and the project of inserting lesbians as the "explosion in the seme (seem)"³⁷ that rips the joint apart. Bechdel can suddenly draw "women" when she can draw "lesbians," once she knows she is one and she sees, for the first time in a sense, others like herself. But the question remains, as in the impasse over lesbian essentialism, which came first epistemologically and which recognition enables the other?

When mainstream comics are discussed, it's generally taken for granted that the appeal of the strip is mainly visual. With respect to a strip about lesbians, responses to what is being represented might be more complicated. When I gave the first version of what became this chapter at Harvard's English Institute in 1990, in their first lesbian session ever, I distributed copies of a few frames from *Dykes To Watch Out For* in which the chief characters are formally introduced as if they were protagonists in a Russian novel with a great number of characters, all of whom are related in complex and convoluted ways. I asked my audience of approximately three hundred or so of America's most insightful literary critics and cultural analysts, including those who would become the most celebrated of queer theorists, whether they recognized these "types" of lesbians—types I saw, actually, as stereotypes. My audience indicated that they had not; apparently, they wouldn't have known, in 1990, which dykes, if any, were the ones to watch out for.

Bechdel, in any case, thinks of her intended audience as primarily self-conscious lesbians and gays. She claims that "the humor in my work is the shock we get from seeing ourselves. We're not used to seeing ourselves represented as lesbians and gay men, and things become funny simply by virtue of their familiarity."[38] That is, even for the intended audience, the funniness lies in the shock of what is simultaneously familiar but has until very recently been almost completely unrepresented. The humor might resemble the erotic shock of unexpectedly seeing same-sex lovers kiss in a mainstream commercial film. Though the watching conditions might be very different in the two situations, both experiences are cognitively incongruent, however much seeing them represented might be desired by a spectator. The paradox of the representations being simultaneously in some sense familiar and everyday but difficult to see or get enough of is reminiscent of the way pornography frustrates and satisfies desire. According to pornographic film maker Bette Gordon: "pornography guarantees that representation will never fulfill desire while maintaining the desire for that representation."[39]

In a tightly argued and funny essay entitled "Between Women: A Cross-Class Analysis of Status and Anarchic Humor," Regenia Gagnier suggests that Victorian women in their autobiographies, that is, when "they were alone" without men to overhear them, used what current theorists of humor call the humor of incongruity, rather than of temporary release, to mount a "prolonged anarchic assault upon the codes constricting them." Their particular use of incongruity has implications, Gagnier argues, "for exploring difference rather than merely disparaging it and for prolonged critical action rather than momentary release."[40] Though Gagnier's focus in the essay shifts between "difference," meaning gender differences between women and men, and class differences between women, her finding of an unexpectedly radical edge to these women's humor and its location in a prolonged if anarchic assault on social difference not only suggests how Bechdel's humor of "women alone together" works (like that of Gagnier's Victorian heterosexual women, it has nothing to do with hating men), it also suggests that its goal involves more than the temporary release of inhibitions, the purchase of a moment's pleasure.

Bechdel's dykes can be watched in the light of Gagnier's suggestions for a number of reasons; for example, to celebrate their prolonged and radical assault on the code of heterosexuality; to suggest that the endlessness of that struggle is well-suited to the usually reassuring but potentially destabilizing conventions of the soap opera or serialized novel that she has adapted for her strip; and to argue why lesbian sexuality is never a completely stable or satisfying refuge against sexual indifference. The dykes one really must watch out for are always in transit, especially, but not only, when they are about to come.

If one looks at the strips in *Dykes To Watch Out For* in which lesbian representation or exclusion from it is the subject of the strip, one can see how "visibility" becomes more and more fraught with contradictions as the representations become more and more "lesbian." Moreover, older critical-theoretical questions about whether these cultural productions merely offer more opportunities for repressive desublimation or whether they can produce a genuinely liberatory discourse might not only miss the point with is sort of marginal "aesthetic activism," as Charles Russell memorably defines the core of avant-garde writing,[41] but fail to acknowledge the scarcity model of lesbian representation that strongly operated when Bechdel began to publish.

It's important to remember that Bechdel's chief competition for the hearts and minds of self-conscious American lesbians in the mid-1980s was the pulp fictions and romances of Naiad Press. Bechdel's texts exist in an aesthetic, sexual, and ideological realm far beyond that of the sentimentalized coming out stories that had been the mainstay of the popular lesbian press, which Bechdel in a detail of one cartoon panel depicts as a Naiad Press "generic romance #423."[42] Lesbian textuality in strips like these bears an ironic and distanced relationship on the one hand, to a despised subculture whose existence has been either ignored, seen from the outside, or pathologized, fetishized or trivialized, and on the other, to the cozy, naturalized world of the lesbian in neo-pulp who is like everyone else, only more so. While Bechdel's work and that of DiMassa too necessarily remain a long way from

Stimpson's call for a lesbian "writing degree zero,"[43] it cannot be contained within the older frame of radical/cultural feminist texts of the 1970s, which seek to provide "positive images" of lesbians and lesbianism as a not too demanding form of propaganda and protest.

In the first volume of *Dykes To Watch Out For*, which appeared almost ten years ago, when the central characters had not yet stabilized, figures who resemble the later Mo and Ginger appear in a strip entitled "The Rule." The two want to see a movie, but the Black lesbian explains her "rule." She only goes to movies that have at least two women in it, who talk to each other about something other than a man. The white lesbian acknowledges this is a strict but good idea. The only problem is that it eliminates all the available films. They give up the search for representations that will satisfy themselves and go home—together.[44]

In the second volume, *More Dykes To Watch Out For*, which appeared in 1988, Lois and Mo argue about "The VCR." Lois is excited because she's just bought one, but Mo is anxious and critical. The VCR is an immoral, self-indulgent, consumerist disease, part of the "heteropatriarchal plot." First, according to Mo, "you buy their VCR, and then you start watching their movies."[45] Only a few films are inoffensive. Lois's response is to offer two that apparently pass the test, *Desert Hearts* or an unnamed Whoopi Goldberg film, which we can take to be *The Color Purple*. While both films have repeatedly been criticized for the ways they grossly or more subtly reinscribe lesbians within sexual indifference, our cartoon figures are literally stuck with them. Mo sees the path to doom before them: "You can only watch Desert Hearts so many times! Next thing you know you'll be bringing home Clint Eastwood flicks!"[46] Queer Lois, who, like Hothead seems younger than some of the other characters in *Dykes* and much more comfortable and accepting of popular culture, takes her pleasures where she finds them, however tainted they may be. She replies with, "Desert Hearts it is!" Mo is finally seduced and demands even more repetition: "When we get to the part where they kiss in the rain, can we play it back?" Lois encourages her, "As many times as you want."[47] Is this an example of using the technology and even the recuperated form of the so-called lesbian romance against its reproduction or is it a creative subversion?

READING COMIZINES INTO AND OUT OF THE AVANT-GARDE

In some gay and women's bookstores and catalogues, *Dykes To Watch Out For* books have moved from the humor section into the fiction section. Bechdel's most autobiographical strip, "Serial Monogamy," the only one narrated in the first person, and the coda to volume four, *Dykes To Watch Out For: The Sequel,* has been chosen for inclusion in the critically acclaimed anthology, *The Penguin Book of Lesbian Short Stories.*[48] As the series has progressed, each volume has become more serial in form, adopting some of the conventions of soap opera, including a central character, the ever-anxious Mo, and her friends and lovers. The main plot, the invention of ways of being lesbian in a non-lesbian world, offers the dramatic structure of subtle and not-so-subtle threats of recuperation by and struggles against heterosexuality, which is encoded in a variety of ways by this particular lesbian-feminist subculture.

Though heterosexuals and heterosexuality are virtually absent from the world depicted in Bechdel's strip, they loom menacingly in DiMassa. Nonetheless, the implications of this present/absence are not necessarily obvious for determining which comic or zine represents a lesbian representational practice that is more "in advance" aesthetically, politically or sexually. In DiMassa's *Hothead Paisan,* harassing heterosexuals are present even in queer Provincetown.[49] In spite of Hothead's and avant-garde culture's desires to escape ordinary reality, they and she are able neither to leave it completely nor to change it utterly. In fact, their and her desire to transform it only serves to increase the time, energy, and attention they give to it.

DiMassa's, far more than Bechdel's, is a counter-discourse that gets recuperated by what it says it wants to eliminate. Male readers, straight and gay, were the first to write fan letters to *Hothead Paisan,* and continue to express fascination and support for her murderously misanthropic vision. Ironically, DiMassa, the cartoonist probably preferred by younger and queerer readers, employs a "feminist" analysis heavily dependent on concepts like "the patriarchy" and misogyny in the mass media, as well as language like "male-identified fem-bot"[50] that were old in the 1970s and are usually thought of as heavy artillery in the ancient and outmoded idiolect known as lesbian-feminism.

If DiMassa seems to have the avant-garde edge over Bechdel, it's only because she advances by looking back to an earlier and apparently discarded feminist theoretical tradition. The theoretical underpinnings of DiMassa's vision aren't, however, what one might think—that is, the post-identitarian queer theory of Judith Butler or the anti-essentialism of Diana Fuss—but the "lesbian chauvinism" of Mary Daly and Valerie Solanis, particularly her 1967 *SCUM (Society for Cutting Up Men) Manifesto.* The extremist, outrageous language and vision of Solanis, whom most people remember as Andy Warhol's would-be assassin, is apparent in this, the opening shot of her manifesto:

Life in this society being, at least, an utter bore and no aspect of society being at all relevant to women, there remains to civic-minded, responsible, thrill-seeking females only to overthrow the government, eliminate the money system, institute complete automation, and destroy the male sex.[51]

Solanis's vision is what underwrites DiMassa's. In fact, in one frame, Hothead is shown reading Solanis's manifesto with great excitement. When her friend Roz suggests that she read to her instead from the new "Queer Brains" magazine modeled on the now defunct *Outlook*, Hothead is outraged by all the boy butt.[52] By comparison, one would guess that the far more lesbocentric but never "man-hating" discourse created by Bechdel out of more recent issues in feminist theory and praxis is probably a lot less interesting to male readers.

In Bechdel, the discourses of heterosexuality have figured most recently and, for some readers, in whom I must include myself, most disappointingly, in the relentless fascination throughout the eponymous volume five, *Spawn of Dykes To Watch Out For*, with Toni's alternative insemination, pregnancy, and childbirth. Doing one's reproductive duty, with the typical ambivalence Bechdel employs, could be considered a form of selling out. This possibility is suggested in Bechdel's comic by the desire for upward mobility, yay, even unto yuppie- and buppiedom, the attempt to seek relief for politically induced pain through psychotherapy, and the lure of sexual practices, including principled monogamy as well as non-monogamy (as these practices are sometimes most curiously and revealingly referred to by lesbians), as threats to retrap lesbians within sexual (in)difference. Be vigilant! Watch out, Dykes!

Both the fear of reinscription and humorous, inventive and erotic resistances to it have become more intense as the strip evolves. In the third volume, *New, Improved! Dykes To Watch Out For*, the central characters are introduced for the first time, formally, accompanied by a brief, novel-like narrative, at the beginning of the volume. Each character is presented, whether in profile or frontally, in physical isolation or connected by touch to the others, bristling with lesbian iconographic indicators and accompanied by a brief character sketch that indicates what she represents in the dialectic between complicity and resistance.

And it is a dialectic and not a case of simple oppositions. Lois, for example, is more of what Maria Maggenti, Eva Yaa Asantewa, and others call a "modern lesbian," because she performs lesbianism through a butchy kind of seduction.[53] Lois is more "modern," what would now be called "postmodern," that is, less politically correct, than Mo. However, unlike Mo, who believes in lesbian monogamy and constantly obsesses over macro-political issues, Lois is even more politically correct in a seventies-style lesbian-feminist way because she lives collectively with lesbians of color and eats weird macrobiotic vegetarian food. Though it could be argued that the introductory still-life portraits, coupled with the almost didactic yet deadpan narratives of character, deprive the figures of their dynamism, the way they have been constructed as a group denies there is one way to be a lesbian, that is, of refusing reinscription in sexual indifference, resisting its compulsions and experiencing its pleasures.

Reading these cartoons is not necessarily all that easy, even for insiders, because part of the labor as well as the pleasure of consumption derives from the spectator's investment in decoding the issues and the players and attempting to decide, after all, what to make of these things.[54] Consequently, knowing how to read Bechdel requires, as a necessary but not sufficient condition for readability (no text is completely readable), some information about a particular and probably small part of the lesbian subculture. This subculture self-consciously obsesses over micro-political or personalized political issues as they work themselves out through: multicultural erotic relationships; gay and lesbian studies committees; women's bookstores; downward mobility for middle-class whites; attempts at upward mobility for lesbians of color; food fascism; communal living; controversies over the place of therapy in a reactionary political climate; and the appropriateness of monogamy and commitment ceremonies in an erotophobic climate.

Bechdel's "realist" subject matter, her serial structure derived from realist fiction, and her traditionally representational visual style make her work seem readable as a lesbian-feminist realism, rather than as a formally and aesthetically innovative and anti-realist contender for avant-garde status. Her reception, or rather lack of it, by the lesbian critics who have done the most to advance the theorizing of lesbian cultural productions in the last decade derives from their desire to put the lesbian-feminist and cultural-feminist legacy of expressive realism behind them.

It's helpful in determining whether Bechdel's and DiMassa's work are credible as neo-avant-gardist to contextualize their accomplishments in light of the recent history of lesbian literary and cultural theorizing. When lesbian literary theory in English began to take off into the nuanced theoretical stratosphere in the late 1980s, the critics who were making those advances rejected lesbian realist texts in favor of emerging avant-garde performance art, theater, video, and film. In order to promote what was newly new, they had to put distance between the work they were championing and that which had seemed new enough just a decade before.

These critics, including Teresa de Lauretis, Sue-Ellen Case, Kate Davy, and Jill Dolan, found lesbian avant-garde texts, by which I primarily mean texts that were too raunchy or challenging to be high art and too tendentious to be called camp, the most exciting sites of application of postmodernist and poststructuralist theory to feminist cultural production.[55] While the work of Case and the other performance theorists chiefly addresses questions of lesbian representations and aesthetics as produced by the construction of lesbian spectatorial communities in performance and theater, de Lauretis, in her essay, "Sexual Indifference and Lesbian Representation," cautions that such attempts to define lesbian desire are somewhat premature and insufficiently deconstructive. That is, those who would attempt to describe that desire are still grounded in sexual indifference, or a hom(m)osexuality which amounts to heterosexuality because within its terms of reference, desire for the self-same cannot be recognized. Keeping the double senses of homosexuality or lesbian sexuality separate yet in tension demands a double response from theorists who must live within a contradictory regime of "constant affirmation and painful renegotiation."[56] In this essay, which originally appeared in 1988, de Lauretis traced different lesbian strategies of representation of gender, but kept returning to the logically prior question of theorizing lesbian sexuality and desire, which she insisted must be regarded as open to question (See her most recent work on this subject, *The Practice of Love: Lesbian Sexuality and Perverse Desire.)*[57] In the work of all the performance and film critics mentioned above, as well as of lesbian literary critic Elizabeth Meese, however, no matter whether the focus is on articulating lesbian sexuality, its representation, or its reception within various lesbian communities, some attempt is made to suggest how the three are connected. Tracing those connections is an important part of the notion of political accountability of lesbian avant-garde writing, which, however tendentious it might appear to be, grounds their work in earlier feminist theory and practice.

Case's polemics against realism, which she averred was unhealthy and even lethal for women, reiterate what was obvious to the traditional avant-garde but what was at that time blasphemy to most North American lesbians.[58] As powerful and compelling and necessary as it was to have her polemic appear at that moment in American lesbian culture, Case's case against realism is somewhat misleading in that she treats it as a monolithic mode, which is odd given her critical background as a Brecht scholar, and in that she rejects out of hand the radical potential for materialist lesbians of a progressive realism such as Brecht's.

Like the historical avant-garde and its preferred critics, these poststructuralist lesbians valued texts which suggested how aesthetic, political, and sexual practices ought to be merged so that formal ruptures could help to produce revolutionary behavioral and political transformations. In Jill Dolan's earlier writing in particular, she implies that for lesbian performance artists, being ideologically aware as a materialist feminist equals being aesthetically hip equals being a lesbian sex radical. From her viewpoint, cultural feminist artists were ideologically simplistic (humanist) and therefore aesthetically backward (realist), and sexually vanilla (boring).[59] This syllogism may have been new to lesbians in the late 1980s, but it was old hat to the historical avant-garde.[60]

These critics, perhaps in part because the new possibilities for creating sophisticated lesbian spectatorial communities through the avant-garde work of groups such as Split Britches and other performers loosely coalesced around New York City's WOW Cafe seemed so fresh and so promising, appeared to have high hopes for the radical aesthetic and political potential of the reading practices they would help to produce and disseminate. If these critics believed that the new work of avant-gardist lesbians, as if in paraphrase of Nicole Brossard, could reinvent the wor(l)d and thus produce lesbian plenitude[61] then this work would unite spectators and readers with performers and writers in an erotic and political frenzy which could slash the representational practices of heterosexism and usher in new social practices. These hopes were consistent with typical avant-garde notions that changes in writing practices would change consciousness, erotic, and even political behavior, and that change in one sphere of life would necessarily affect change in the others. While the utopian appeal of such anti-realist hopes for aesthetic activism is compelling in these depressing times, even the critics most responsible for producing these determinist readings concerning the new lesbian spectatorial communities came to acknowledge that they hadn't paid enough attention to the contradictions within discourses and within spectators or readers.[62] These sorts of internal contradictions are used, metaphorically, in the last issue of *Hothead Paisan* included in the book length collection, to suggest the limitations and strategic errors of Hothead's impatient, anarchic, and avant-gardist approach to change. Roz's lover, an older Black lesbian educator named Alice, forcefully rebuts Hothead's insistence that education and all "slow" change is useless. According to Hothead, "The way I operate...it's eat my dust!!! The problem is gone!" Alice responds, as agents of the political avant-garde tend to do, "Don't you sit there and sass me about what works and doesn't! Your arrogant little butt can't see the forest for the trees!...That's not the way to blow off steam! It's just a quick fix! Slow change is lasting change!" And Hothead retorts, as perennially adolescent-spirited avant-gardists tend to do, "Well, I just think we're short on time! An' some people just ain't teachable!"[63]

The difference between the aesthetic and especially anarchist avant-garde preference for sudden and dramatic rupture and the political avant-garde's insistence on working perhaps more slowly but strategically is illustrated in the different narrative structures of Bechdel's and DiMassa's work. Whereas DiMassa's issues characteristically end with a bang, Bechdel's strips end with a whimper. The typical structure of a Bechdel strip offers the spectator a problem, an open-ended discussion or argument about the problem, and then an anxious irresolution, coupled frequently with a request to stay tuned for more developments. This is a cliché of cartoons generally, of course, but here it means, stay tuned for more questions without clear answers. Pomo, huh? Even the sometimes lengthy erotic scenarios have an open-ended, anxious aspect to them. What will happen? What will we be allowed to see? Will a couple be formed, continue as lovers or break up and regroup? (See Harriet and Mo making love the first time, in "Down to the Skin: A Mildly Erotic Epilogue," in *More Dykes*; this is one of only two silent frames in her oeuvre.)[64]

To a lesbian spectator, watching *Dykes To Watch Out For* offers more than the pleasurable recognition of the old game of "spot the dyke," even if it's the cartoonist's chief intention to promote lesbian visibility. Because, as Derrida remarks in a very different appropriation of a possibly lesbian photographic text, "one sees the characters speaking,"[65] endlessly to each other, the spectator is brought into an open dialogue with the artist about the speaking and desiring subjects of lesbianism. As Bechdel uses it, the comic book form achieves what Lucy Lippard says it can, the closest possible imitation of speaking in writing.[66]

...MAYBE IT'S TIME TO GO BACK TO THE FUTURE

The notion of an avant-garde, as Charles Russell reminds us, has typically been so loosely defined that since it began to be used in the eighteenth century there's never been complete agreement on who or what counts.⁶⁷ Even so, most male theorists of the avant-garde sympathetic to the left, such as Huyssen, Bürger, or Russell, have all been skeptical about the possibilities of reviving an avant-garde movement even under the capacious umbrella of postmodernism.⁶⁸ It's difficult to conclude that surrealistic work like *Hothead Paisan,* let alone the much more traditionally representational *Dykes To Watch Out For,* deserves inclusion in what I've been hedging my bets by calling a neo-avant-garde. Neither seems innovative enough in linguistic and formal ways. Much as I hate to admit it, that notorious theoretical lesbophobe, Julia Kristeva, may have been right when she asserted in her 1980 article, "Postmodernism?," before *Hothead Paisan* or *Dykes To Watch Out For* were even a gleam in their creators' eyes, that postmodernist women writers haven't yet merited a place in the avant-garde because they "have no stylistic and hence no literary novelty." She's right. Both *Dykes To Watch Out For* and *Hothead Paisan* suffer from the "defect" of having too much "interest in significance."⁶⁹

Both these cartoonists are only marginal contenders for avant-garde status because they are too serious. Neither is un/popular enough, playful enough, politically incorrect enough. Neither really measures up completely in terms of offering a self-conscious lesbian cultural critique designed to transform representational practices while being cognizant of the fictiveness of truth and realism. Both, in their very different ways, are aware that it's not possible to create new work, as the historical avant-garde thought it could, entirely *ex nihilo.* They also, in different but significant degrees, acknowledge two awkward things about the relationship between cultural and political change: that one cannot create advanced work without reliance on one's theoretical and cultural predecessors, in this case, those much derided lesbian-feminists of the 1970s, and that without the material and political conditions that make revolutionary cultural and political praxis possible, avant-garde writing may have to go back to the future.

CHAPTER 4

TOWARD A BUTCH-FEMME READING PRACTICE:

READING JOAN NESTLE

GETTING "MORE PERSONAL"
JOAN NESTLE, *A RESTRICTED COUNTRY*

In the particular lesbian subculture I move in, butch-femme is a non-issue and has been for some time. It's become part of the cultural and sexual surround. It's no big deal and no longer a very interesting or urgent political question. I'm still a bit confused as to what I am, of course, but I no longer dwell much on it, because the positions keep proliferating. On the continuum from butch daddies to femme tops, where does Alison Bechdel's "lentil-lapping leftist" belong?[1] Reading one's own butch-femme barometer also grows more complicated as one ages. I think I'm a femmey butch—on a good day—but my friends laugh at that self-assessment. You wish, they say. Butchy femme—on a good day. Maybe I should attend a JoAnn Loulan lecture and volunteer to be rated by the audience, since she claims, in *The Erotic Dance*, that lesbians observing other lesbians virtually always agree on who's who.[2] Funny, since we don't agree on anything else. My lover—she should know, shouldn't she?—says I'm butch, but she means in the head, where she thinks it counts.

If butch-femme matters, does it affect how one reads texts other than living, breathing ones—written ones, that is? And if so, how? This chapter on the life/work of butch-femme theorist and practitioner Joan Nestle is framed by my own curious, hypocritical, and sometimes mildly traumatic inability to "read" butch-femme lesbian subjectivities and representational practices adequately. I want to write a chapter on what makes it difficult to develop a butch-femme reading practice that brings to the foreground my own tentativeness about these categories as well as the ways it has inflected my reading of the work of Joan Nestle. If it's theoretically misconceived in 1994 to talk about reading "as a lesbian," it might still be possible to imagine a reading position which slides along a continuum from butch to femme with as much fluidity as necessary to engage the text and the reader pleasurably and enthusiastically, as one engages a lover.

What Katie King, following Chicana theorist Chela Sandoval, calls "conversations" about sexuality and politics in self-conscious lesbian and feminist subcultures are always ongoing and impossible to date with the precision that is possible in dating many other cultural events.[3] In Toronto, where I was active in the lesbian-feminist community in the first half of the 1980s, the impact of the imported American sex debates was intense. My friends, most of them lesbian activists and intellectuals, all of them feminists, were violently polarized over butch-femme, pornography, sex toys, and s/m. Most were opposed to all of the above for what they said were political reasons, and they were forthright in their opinions. My lover at the time and I were privately dabbling in all of the above, and, while we were theoretically sympathetic to the sex-radical writing that was beginning to be published and discussed, we rarely identified ourselves as sex radicals or mentioned what we were doing in and out of bed.

It was a difficult situation in which to learn more about sexuality, even and perhaps most especially one's own. In some ways the hypocrisy, self-protectiveness, and defensiveness which characterized our reading practices around these sexual issues resembled what Samuel Delany courageously critiqued some ten years later with respect to the very serious, even lethal consequences of failing to take responsibility for the silences in both street talk/straight talk around safer sex practices.[4] In the early 1980s, however, most lesbians I knew were discussing sexual practices and how to read them in an abstract and impersonal way, applying pre-fabricated cultural feminist distinctions like those between "vanilla" and "s/m" sex; between "erotica" and "pornography;" between "egalitarian" and "abusive" relationships—without ever questioning what these distinctions concretely and personally distinguished. We judged others without ever mentioning what we liked to do sexually. It was another case of having all the answers and none or not enough of the questions.

During this time, if there was one text, one passage, that made me change my mind, made me rethink what I thought I thought, what I knew I knew, about butch-femme—a subject and a practice I thought I knew and cared little about personally but that my lesbian-feminist analysis said was wrong—it was the often cited one from Joan Nestle's essay, "Butch-Femme Relationships: Sexual Courage in the 1950s," where she discusses in explicit erotic detail how the semiotic code of butch-femme worked.[5] The part that thrilled me, that made me think that I didn't know what I was talking about when I dissed butch-femme, but that I did know something, on another level perhaps, that I felt less comfortable in talking about was this: "I loved my lover for how she stood as well as for what she did. Dress was a part of it: the erotic signal of her hair at the nape of her neck, touching the shirt collar; how she held a cigarette; the symbolic pinky ring flashing as she waved her hands."[6]

I didn't know any women, even any lesbians, who looked like that one precisely, and I've always hated smoking, but something in the passage made me understand that this, some version of this woman, was what I desired. Given the usual waywardness of desire, I learned that mine is a deviant deviance: I identify as a soft, very soft butch, but I desire women who are butcher than I am. In the preceding part of the passage, which is quoted frequently, but perhaps not as frequently as the one that entranced me (and perhaps that says something about the positioning of the lesbians who have written theoretically about butch-femme), Nestle names what she enjoys hearing and doing sexually as a femme. That was interesting. But even though it was also a revelation to hear something that resembled my own sexual behavior at the time, it wasn't as exciting in teaching me to read my own desire.

Several years later, when some of the heat had gone out of the sex debates, or so I thought, and in point of fact my own sexual practices had become more like what was called "vanilla," I started to write versions of this chapter about Joan Nestle's book of theoretical erotica, *A Restricted Country*.[7] The first presentation I gave of it, in a small gathering of lesbian theorists and critics in Florence in 1989, was received by one or two of those present with great hostility and even verbal abuse. The lesbian historian who objected most vociferously threatened to leave when she met me and asked what I was writing about. To write about Joan Nestle meant that I was sold out to discourse theory, as well as bad sexual practices. In hindsight, I hope that she was correct.

Oddly enough, plumbing precisely that connection between theoretical developments in feminist and lesbian writing about subjectivity that had preoccupied many writers throughout the 1980s and Joan Nestle's autobiographical, theoretical, and fictional writings had been what I thought of as the chief focus in the first spoken and written version of what has become this chapter. The problem that most consciously beset me was that it wasn't clear to me how much Nestle's writings about her own far from unified subjectivity made use of, required, or helped to produce the writings of the lesbians I thought of as "high" theorists. In what ways were these different discourses in dialogue with each other? How did one illuminate the other? Was one the unthought of the other? Was lesbian "low culture/high theory" a butch-femme relationship in the way Nestle said the term "lesbian-feminism" was? That is, was the high theory the respectable lesbian who could pass in the academy and the low practice the hypervisible butch whom nobody wanted in their canon?

The problem I was less aware of was that I hadn't considered what my own personal investments were in thinking through these issues, that is, why reading Joan Nestle respectfully was privately important to me and why it gave me pleasure to extend her the courtesy of trying to read with her even in hostile public situations. When in December of 1993 I had a chance to talk with her and told her about what had happened when I discussed her writing at academic conferences first in Florence and then in Glasgow, she thanked me for taking her work into places where it was dangerous to do so. In effect, I was and have been reading Joan Nestle, the femme, from a butch or at least a butch-wannabe position.

DEEP BACKGROUND: CONNECTING THE THEORIZING OF LESBIAN SEXUALITY AND FEMINIST SUBJECTIVITY

In the last decade or so, lesbian as well as feminist theorizing about subjectivity has shifted from analyses preoccupied by what or who belongs inside/outside feminism and lesbianism and analyses more fascinated by surfaces than depths. The trajectory has been from the politics of identity to subject-positioning to performativity: the subject of pomo in fast mo. Those analyses were launched as feminist and lesbian applications or revisions of neo-Marxian, psychoanalytic, and poststructuralist theories of subjectivity. As the theoretical focus shifted, some of the most prominent lesbian thinkers as well as lesbians in the sheets or on the street changed their primary concern from "who am I" to "what do I represent" and then to "what do I do." But because answers seemed both easier to arrive at and more available than questions, some of the old questions keep returning. For instance, when controversies over butch-femme arose as a question for lesbian-feminists in the early 1980s, the debate within lesbian-feminism was structured over whether "it" (was butch-femme something you were or you did or you appeared to be?) was or was not authentically lesbian or feminist; was or was not good for lesbians and feminists; and was or was not old and outmoded or new and improved. Was neo-butch-femme a continuation or a revival or a parody of a working-class embarrassment gussied up as an avant-garde cultural treasure?

Subjectively speaking, in theory if not in practice, the focus shifted during the 1980s from prescribing or proscribing one or more lesbian identities to inscribing and then describing lesbian sexual practices, practices which might well be loosely if at all tied to identities. If Foucault was right that "homosexuality" began to be perceived by growing numbers of people in the nineteenth century as something a person was rather than an action he (or maybe even she) could engage in, then many lesbian theorists seemed to be going backward, theoretically speaking. Lesbianism, according to most of our most prominent thinkers, was more properly and usefully thought of as an activity or a desire than as an identity.[8] After struggling so hard to make lesbians a subject in and of feminism and to change the subject of lesbianism from deviant to political vanguard, butch-femme lesbians and others "in the advance" seemed to be giving up their positioning as transcendental subject to become performers of sexual practices which they were willing to share and share alike with a whole bunch of other folks, many of whom were not the sort you'd be likely to take home to mom. At a time when economic, social, and political progress for ordinary people seemed less and less possible, in theory, movement was all. Or was it?

Initially because of the controversies surrounding her and the other sex radicals at the 1982 Barnard conference where the sex debates ignited, and then because of the dissent ensuing from the publication of *A Restricted Country* in 1987, Joan Nestle's life/work became a limit text for these questions and answers. Joan Nestle, in many ways more egregiously than even Pat Califia, "stood for" the sex radical position. Her life/work meant "controversy." While many lesbians responded to the resexualization of lesbianism in theory and practice that she represented in moralistic terms of yea or nay, with just a few years' hindsight it seems somewhat easier to read what seemed so controversial at the time more as symptom and less as morality lesson.

In this chapter, I read Joan Nestle not as giving anything away—whether in terms of politics, sexuality, or aesthetics—but as giving them up as an eroticized and living gift of visibility and historical continuity from a femme lesbian. One doesn't have to be a butch to read her this way, but it probably makes accepting her gift easier. Her life/work confuses and refuses distinctions between political vanguards and intellectual avant-guards. She never uses the technical language of negotiating subject positions or decentering subjectivities. While she doesn't occupy a unified subjectivity, she does speak of being whole. The image of her sexual self as the hemp rope that binds all the parts of herself together sounds like a colligation or binding connectivity of subject positions. Her sense of her own subjectivity is definitely not fragmented or, it seems, even layered, to use the suggestive figuration of depth that Katie King has proposed in her analysis of Audre Lorde's inscription of her own subjectivity in *Zami*.[9]

The ambiguity and code-switching in Nestle's own choice of language as well as the fact that lesbian critics sympathetic to her life/work would like to legitimize her, theoretically makes Nestle very difficult to read. Though Clare Whatling, in "Reading Awry: Joan Nestle and the Recontextualization of Heterosexuality," realizes that questions of reading are what is most at stake in the reception of Nestle and she wants to open them up rather than shut them down, her article is almost entirely a defense of Nestle's sexual politics. In a most interesting one paragraph afterword, Whatling mentions Nestle's stress in the preface to *A Restricted Country* on her multiple identities, and thanks the lesbian-feminist critic Liana Borghi for pointing out to her what she refers to as her "failure to *name* Nestle's sense of her own Jewishness, a sense of Jewishness which I believe now is *central* [my emphasis] not only to her politics, but to the tone, the inflection, the voice that comes through so clearly and magnificently in her writings."[10] By making this correction, a brave and necessary one, in my opinion, Whatling recenters Nestle's subjectivity once again and undermines her own attempt to read Nestle deconstructively.

Nestle, furthermore, doesn't talk about herself as a "subject" but as a self. She has many selves—Jewish, lesbian, femme, working-class, among others. She doesn't speak of fragmentation but of multiplicity. Joan Nestle uses a language about her own subjectivity that is capable of being read in more than one way, and that switches codes between essentialist and anti-essentialist conceptual structures in mid-passage. For example, in "Butch-Femme Relationships: Sexual Courage in the 1950s," she says: "As a femme, I did what was natural for me, what I felt right. I did not learn a part; I perfected a way of loving."[11] In some pieces in *A Restricted Country*, such as in the short story "A Change of Life," a fictional exploration of the old adage that, after forty, femmes turn into butches, Nestle can be read as thinking of gender and sexuality, as well as other social differences, in terms of fluid rather than fixed subject positions. However, in her introduction to the anthology she edited five years later, *The Persistent Desire: A Femme-Butch Reader*, she can be read, as can many of the other contributors, as thinking of butch and femme as givens, how one is and has always been, rather than what one could become or cease to be. As the title proclaims, desire at least, if not subjectivity, is persistent and integral; while the subtitle, Nestle says, "herald[s] this new voice in identity politics."[12]

While Nestle doesn't use the technical terms employed by theorists of subjectivity, her writing in many ways takes up its theoretical and political problematic. In December of 1993 I attended a class in a course on the lesbian and gay literary tradition that Joan Nestle gave at the Center for Lesbian and Gay Studies in the City University of New York Graduate School. She remarked that the reading she had been doing more recently in lesbian theory helped clarify problems she had been working out in her own writing practice. It seems true enough to say that for her as for most of the Anglophone world of feminist and critical writing, the 1980s was the decade of the subject.[13] For my purposes here, I want to read the development of that theory as a trajectory, but not necessarily as teleology, from the female to the feminist and then to the lesbian subject; and I want to use Joan Nestle's fiction/theory to suggest how she *works* the contradictions between and among her subject positions rather than negotiates them, offering them instead as a gift.

This increasing specificity of theorization may indicate that feminists, especially as more and more came out of the academic closet in the late 1980s, attempted truly to carry through on the more general project of historicizing the subject. But at the same time, attempts to specify who could be such an agent tended not only to "risk essentialism," perhaps more cavalierly than they ought to, but also sometimes seemed to run the danger of producing another discourse by, for, and about a tiny elite audience. While having a small audience for theoretical writing and for avant-garde literary work might not necessarily make their theoretical and aesthetic project politically ineffectual, the question of who's listening continues to nag at those involved.

Though not all of the theorists who engaged in study of subjectivity could be called Althusserians, they did tend to argue, if only by analogy, that as "the" subject was caught in ideology, so was "the female" subject implicated in gender. While "the feminist" subject might be aware, as seen from her analytical position supposedly "outside" gender, of her contradictory location as "woman," she was also admittedly contained, as a historical and social subject, within its real ruling relations.

What traps the female subject is the heterosexual contract. The implication is that the feminist subject achieves whatever freedom she can by relocating herself outside the ideology of sexual difference. In the development of the notion of the feminist and then lesbian subject, there is a slippage in the arguments of essays written in the late 1980s by de Lauretis, such as "Sexual Indifference and Lesbian Representation," and Sue-Ellen Case's "Toward a Butch-Femme Aesthetic," not only between a feminist and a lesbian subject, but between a subjectivity simultaneously inside and outside of ideology, to one that is unbound by its constraints and endowed with agency. The desire to be fully outside, to revel in outlawry and outsiderness, marks the desire in these texts as typically avant-garde. If the very idea of a lesbian subject could be said to begin with Monique Wittig's claim that lesbians are not women, then in the development of the lesbian subject, there is also, most significantly, a movement away from the initial negativity of Wittig's claim, in "The Mark of Gender"[14] as well as in her other work such as *The Lesbian Body*, to a brash insistence on positivity, as in Case's claim that "the lesbian roles of butch and femme, as a dynamic duo, offer precisely the strong subject position the movement requires."[15]

Case and some of the other theorists of lesbian subjectivity within performance and drama, impatient about the impasse over essentialism, insisted that even attempts such as de Lauretis's to increase or enable critical movement left the reader "with the negative stasis of what cannot be seen."[16] Their cry for theorizing the lesbian subject was "freedom now." This goal is characteristic of other avant-gardes, but carries with its utopianism some dangerous disadvantages. It seems to me a mixed blessing if breaking up the lesbian logjam means settling on one lesbian subject, such as, for example, the butch-femme couple or whatever seems most transgressive at the moment, as "the" strong subject position.

While the work of Case and the other performance theorists chiefly addressed questions of lesbian representations and aesthetics as produced by the construction of lesbian spectatorial communities in performance, de Lauretis, in her essay on sexual indifference, cautioned that such attempts to define lesbian desire are premature and need deconstructing. Though de Lauretis's analysis of sexual indifference has become more carefully elaborated and self-critiqued over time,[17] her warnings that attempts to pin down lesbian desire are still grounded in sexual indifference, by which she means a hom(m)osexuality which amounts to heterosexuality, are still worthy of attention. De Lauretis argued that, within the terms of hom(m)osexuality's reference, desire for the self-same cannot be recognized. Keeping the double senses of homosexuality or lesbian sexuality separate yet in tension demands a double response from theorists who must live within a contradictory regime of "constant affirmation and painful renegotiation."[18] In tracing different lesbian strategies of representing gender, de Lauretis keeps suggesting that the theorizing of lesbian sexuality must not be shut down but opened up. In this regard, as I remarked in chapter three about the relationship between the theorizing of new lesbian avant-garde writing and the growth of lesbian comics and queer zines, it should be remembered that while de Lauretis's work in the late 1980s resembles that of other lesbian critics of performance, theater, and film in its broad theoretical and political allegiances, there is more tentativeness and less polemic in her discussions of the potential of lesbian avant-garde work for offering solutions to intractable questions of lesbian sexuality, aesthetics, and politics.[19]

The resexualization of lesbianism which occurred in the wake of a second and failed attempt to include lesbians in heterosexual feminism played a significant role in how lesbian subjectivity has been theorized by these and other lesbian thinkers and artists. If ambisexual bad girl feminists like Jane Gallop[20] first made the pleasure of the theoretical text undeniable in their written or spoken performances in the mid-1980s, then some lesbian theorists and critics soon did so as well. Joan Nestle gave readings of sexually explicit writing dressed in slip.[21] Lesbian performance artists such as Holly Hughes, and more recently her lover Phranc, who made hearts and other organs thump when she appeared in drag as Neil Diamond, heat up the stage as they make audiences rethink what they think they know about gender, sexuality and identity. In more subtle ways, a literary critic like Elizabeth Meese, whose earlier books contributed, in lively but measured prose, to the engagement between deconstruction and materialist feminisms, shifted to writing a more experimental style of theoretical erotica in *(Sem)erotics: Theorizing Lesbian: Writing*.[22] In my experience of hearing and seeing her read a chapter, Meese left audiences gasping.

Meese's essay, "Theorizing Lesbian: Writing—A Love Letter,"[23] is a formal experiment which builds on, even dances around, Elaine Marks's 1979 essay on "Lesbian Intertextuality." Meese uses Marks's texts of desire, in particular Violette Leduc's *La batarde* and Wittig's *The Lesbian Body*, to take her theoretically and erotically higher and higher, working through the letter of the law to get to the law of the letter "L," not stopping until she comes, perhaps even before her love letter arrives.[24] Meese's essay is remarkable not just for the elegant ways she poses the problems about the theorizing of lesbian textuality while daring lesbian essentialism but for the risks she takes by making her text an erotic performance.

RESEXUALIZING REQUIRES RETHINKING LESBIAN SEXUALITIES

Just as this writing and performance, particularly writing as performance, forced a reopening of the question of what lesbian sexuality had to do with vanguard politics and avant-garde aesthetics, it also implicitly raised the question of what counts as lesbian theorizing. Both questions created anxiety; they were difficult to answer and they made those who thought about them uncomfortable. The questions press themselves forward in the dilemma of how lesbians and other theorists of the subject ought to "read" creative texts which offered useful ways of inscribing fragmented and multiple subjectivities.

The 1980s was also the decade in which the split, fragmented, sometimes even torn apart subject "in and of" feminism was addressed in works, not of high but of low theory—theorizing in and as fiction, poetry, and autobiography. The classic texts here are the anthology, *This Bridge Called My Back: Writings by Radical Women of Color*, edited by Cherríe Moraga and Gloria Anzaldúa in 1981,[25] and Audre Lorde's biomythography, *Zami: A New Spelling of My Name,* originally published in 1983, and her collection of speeches and addresses, *Sister Outsider,* 1984.[26] As in earlier feminist foundational texts, the key form is the collection, the anthology, and the mixed genre. When such texts appear, it is suggested that new subjectivities are emerging and seeking representation. Those subjectivities are collective and communal, rather than individual or unique. Oddly enough, until the 1990s the collective subject of lesbianism does not seem to have been given to inscribing itself in lengthy tomes, but to brief lyrical fragments, topical addresses, polemics, manifestos, or personal narratives.

The most concrete evidence that the question of the subject may have been broached more or less simultaneously but was not being formulated, developed, or attended to by the same intellectual communities is apparent in the relative rareness of any references to the writings of the second set of theorists by writers in the first group, with the chief exception being Case and de Lauretis. Admittedly, it's difficult to build avant-garde theory on texts tainted by a realist aesthetic. De Lauretis's acknowledgment of these texts is far more varied and extensive than those by others, but in "Sexual Indifference and Lesbian Representation," in 1988, she acknowledges them in a way that presages the usual practice for high theorists who notice these works at all.

These high theorists do not work with the texts, but merely cite them, usually grouped together in endnotes, or quote brief passages, as in this: "Just a few lines from *Zami*,...will make the point, better than I can."[27] De Lauretis suggests that Lorde's phrase, "the very house of difference," "points to a conception of community not pluralistic but at once global and local." While de Lauretis grants Lorde's image complexity, it simply "points to a conception" rather than is a conception. It needs to be supplemented by or "read with" other texts by "others" like her, that is, who have the same "commitments," apparently without regard to differences of genre.[28] Admittedly, there are no citations to the first group of lesbian writers in the works of the second group. And, since there are none at all, I can only speculate why, offering the usual unsatisfactory explanation of "inaccessibility."

The point I want to make here is that the first set of texts is generally read, and taught, as "theory" and the second set as "women's studies." In such binaries, the second term is the devalued one. Perhaps, the relation between "women's studies" texts on subjectivity and "theoretical" treatments of "the female" or "feminist" or even, most recently, "the" postmodern lesbian subject, is another unequal partnership between a discreet and an indiscrete lesbian. I am using a play on the two related words, the homonyms, "indiscreet" meaning not circumspect in speech or action, not unobtrusive, neither prudent nor judicious, and "indiscrete" meaning not divided into distinct parts, to suggest how Joan Nestle, as a femme lesbian who is also a working-class woman, a Jew, a feminist and a socialist, refuses to make herself invisible or to cut herself off from a collective subject position.

What I would like to claim, further, is that this relationship between different sorts of texts of subjectivity can offer hints to what is missing from or is variously not developed or untheorized in both sorts. As the literature on the subject is traversed from the non-gendered subject of Lacan, Foucault, and Althusser to the female, then feminist, and then, in the late 1980s, the lesbian subject, many of those who read the theory became increasingly uncomfortable with its abstractness, determinism, intellectual vanguardism, and political quietism.

These discomforts are brought together in an accessible attempt to map the theoretical terrain as it appeared in 1988 in Paul Smith's *Discerning the Subject*. Smith favors that line of reasoning about the subject that hopes to restore a politically responsible focus on subjectivity by stressing the possibilities for resistance as locatable at the level of the "individual/subject," rather than at the level of discourse, in the theories of humanist feminism.

Because Smith emphasizes the role feminism has played in articulating the agentic possibilities of the subject and because his remarks on autobiography as a "singular history" seem to hold possibilities for further clarifying what is meant by a resisting female/feminist/lesbian subject who increases agency by negotiating her subject positions, it still remains useful. It puts those controversies into an historical context. Sadly, Smith's insistence on resistance now seems another dashed and unfashionable utopian hope. In the 1990s, critics and theorists speak a lot less frequently of resistance and more of transgression and subversion. This code-switching marks a discursive and political shift from socialist to anarchist language, frames of reference, and hoped-for outcomes of aesthetic activism. Nestle, a writer who straddles the divide, joyfully transgresses and subverts but always in the interests of producing resistance.

From the outset, Smith places the debate between determinism and agency into a political perspective that is extremely favorable, at a distance, to feminism. He claims that his two chief targets are the political consequences of theories of fixed or dispersed subjectivity, but he is much more concerned with the "indifference"[29] and "inability to theorize action"[30] following from theories of dispersion, which also trouble many feminist critics, especially those most suspicious of poststructuralism and deconstruction. (Compare Patricia Waugh, *Feminine Fictions: Revisiting the Postmodern.*)[31] Most of his book is devoted to critiques of Althusser, Lacan, and Derrida for failing to provide a theory of the subject that can account for and expand political agency.

By contrast, Smith praises certain kinds of feminist theorists for succeeding in theorizing subjectivity *responsibly,* that is, in a way that, while taking the decentering of the subject as a fact of critical life, enables and promotes a resistant agent.[32] Ironically, having praised feminism so highly, Smith, like many another sympathetic writer, fails to say much that is useful, in the sense of being detailed enough about feminism's actual practices. This is particularly tantalizing, given his attention to autobiography and critical pedagogy. Nonetheless, he advances understanding of possibilities for resistance by arguing that choice is made possible, if not easy, as a by-product of the agent's negotiations between subject positions[33] and by showing how moments of choice can be placed in relief in the writing of "singular histories."[34] Though he offers Barthes's last work as a demonstration of the "resistant force of jouissance," he also doubts the effectiveness of such "personal guerrilla warfare against the prevailing order."[35]

Smith's text is typical of a trend during the 1980s among the theorists of subjectivity who were more and more determined to find and even celebrate possibilities for agency within the female/feminist/lesbian subject. To do so credibly, they attempted to locate her more concretely and specifically within particular political conformations, aesthetic modes, and sexual practices. Because these theorists were almost as equally committed to a left cultural and institutional politics as they were to anti-essentialism in their feminisms and anti-realism in their aesthetics, they could be said to have a surplus of theory to operate on a deficit of texts/material. In some cases, this resulted in a cultural critique in which high theory fed off low culture, such as the Madonna semiotics industry. In other cases, it tended to produce a craving for more and more "exotic" texts on which to operate a theoretical apparatus.

Just what made these texts "exotic" was itself a fascinating phenomenon: Sometimes they were the colonized and appropriated texts of so-called Third World Women; sometimes they were, as in the case of lesbian writers such as Joan Nestle or Pat Califia, controversial because they were sexually explicit or sexually marginal; and sometimes, as in the case of feminist theorists who began to turn their critical attentions more and more on themselves and their complex and contradictory subject positions, they began to attempt to break down, and in some cases, to collapse the boundaries between theory, so-called creative writing and autobiography.[36]

This late 1980s feminist critical phenomenon of risky and increasingly risqué erotic writing of, around, and about the critic's subjectivity could be seen variously. Undoubtedly, for many of those following its development as a form of critical writing, such texts can offer a great deal of fun and pleasure. They can be read as marks of the so-called "turn to the personal" in feminist theory. Or they can be read as marking that turn at the expense of the perceived political need in other areas of cultural theory to "turn to history" and to address the ethico-political content and consequences of one's cultural identities and textual productions.[37] Better, they can be read as somehow, potentially or in practice, being co-implicated rather than as forks in the critical road.

Perhaps one turn was the unthought in the turn the other discourse took. Nestle's writing, in particular, raises for me the question of how to read women's, feminists', and lesbians' autobiographical writings in light of the development of theories of the subject. Biddy Martin's "Lesbian Identity and Autobiographical Difference[s]," opens this question up. This essay brilliantly problematizes essentializing tendencies in writing about lesbian identity, such as in the assumptions governing the way the word "lesbian" modifies "autobiography." The original placement of her essay in a collection otherwise framed as "women's" autobiography underscores her argument. Martin cites the work of de Lauretis, especially her introduction to *Technologies of Gender*, suggesting that de Lauretis's usage of autobiographical writing by American women of color illuminates the contradictoriness and multiple construction of subjectivity. That essay's argument also complicates de Lauretis's "own earlier formulation of the inevitable tensions between the negativity of theory and the positivity of politics by robbing theory of its exclusive claim to negativity and suggesting a new imbrication of theory and personal history."[38] Martin's attention, however, in the article is focused on analyzing how works of lesbian autobiography refuse essentialist readings and problematize the relationship between identity and politics, with an emphasis on how they consolidate lesbian and anti-racist writing and activism, rather than on the details of their negotiation between and among their subject positions.

In a later essay, "Sexual Practice and Changing Lesbian Identities," written in the wake of queer theory and its concomitant exploration of sexual practices, Martin uses King's metaphor of "lacquered layering" to suggest how Lorde's and Nestle's autobiographical writings provide thick descriptions of the dangers of centering lesbian sexuality, particularly the complex phenomenon that is butch-femme, as a distinct category of analysis.[39] Martin is particularly acute in her observations about the intellectual curiosity and generosity of writers like Susie Bright and Joan Nestle. Martin indicates that their work implicitly complicates the notion of negotiating subject positions by the way they resist the tendency to locate threats to destabilize beloved categories—whether current or out of favor—from an outside or an outsider.[40]

NEGOTIATING—SHOULD LESBIANS SAY "YES" TO THE TEXT, AND IF SO, HOW?

Apart from the essays by King and Martin, in most of the theoretical writing concerned with how lesbian writers negotiate their subject positions, there is an absence of detailed analysis. Notably, neither King nor Martin uses the term, which seems a strange one to use in any case. The phrase "to negotiate one's subject positions" came into the critical vocabulary some time in the mid-1980s and seems like appropriate baggage of the pro-business regimes of Reagan and Thatcher. I'm not even sure who originated the usage. Perhaps it was R. Radhakrishnan, a theorist who has written frequently about subject positions.[41]

The infinitive, "to negotiate," seems an odd choice to designate the conflictual and most probably risky process/business by which individual/subjects move or translate themselves over time between places or locations which have variously been assigned to them, rejected, chosen, or been struggled for. *The Oxford English Dictionary*, as well as *Fowler's Guide to Modern English Usage*, indicates that the word's origin is in sport, specifically hunting, and its original usages were "jocular":

> **negotiate** *v*. f. ppl. stem of L. *negotiare*, f. *negotium*, f. *neg* not + *otium* ease, quiet.
> 1. *intr. a.* To hold communication or conference (*with* another) for the purpose of arranging some matter by mutual agreement; to discuss a matter with a view to some settlement or compromise....*b*. To do business or trade; to traffic. *Obs*.
> 2. *trans. a.* To deal with, manage, or conduct (a matter, affair, etc., requiring some skill or consideration)....*b*. To arrange for, obtain, bring about (something) by means of negotiation.... *c*. To set right by negotiation. *rare*.
> 3. *a.* To transfer or assign (a bill, etc.) to another in return for some equivalent in value; to convert into cash or notes; to obtain or give value for (bills, cheques, etc.) in money....To deal with, carry out, as a business or monetary transaction.
> 4. (Orig. *Hunting*.) To clear (a hedge or fence); to succeed in crossing, getting over, round, or through (an obstacle, etc.) by skill or dexterity....*b*. To succeed in dealing with in the way desired; to get the better of. **1888** *Pall Mall G.* 14 Nov. 5/2 The difficulty of simultaneously negotiating creatures whose divergent natures demand...widely different tactics....Hence, *negotiated ppl. a.* (engaged, busy)...

As one reads through or negotiates among the various meanings the word evokes, the reader is shifted between a sense of a process which requires, stresses, and acknowledges the accomplishment and importance of producing a relationship of mutuality with another human being, to a different reading in which a Nietzchean power play is enacted. In the latter sense, the negotiator merely deploys a skill in order to get the better of another person, even if it means turning the other into an obstacle to be overcome, or a fence to be jumped. The pleasure and fascination of what's difficult resembles the thrill of the hunt and the clink of the cash register. Again, it strikes me that "negotiation" is an odd choice to name a process by which feminists and other cultural critics hope political resistance is to be produced.

Nonetheless, Gayatri Spivak reflects rather differently on the word in her essay, "Feminism and Deconstruction, Again: Negotiations," calling it in one instance a use rather than an ignoring of texts that influence us while not excusing them of their errors[42] and in another, "the giving of assent without excuse, so much that one inhabits its discourse—a short word for this might be 'love.'"[43] While the erotic possibilities for "critical intimacy"[44] produced by this form of saying "'yes' to the text"[45] sound appealing, in her framework, they are also implicitly and even explicitly hetero-relational. Compare Meese's question in "Theorizing Lesbian: Writing—A Love Letter": "What path can lead us to the 'yes' of the 'lesbian' beyond the male-female opposition of hetero-relational feminism,[46] 'the lesbian' beyond the Derridean refusal of lesbianism as homosexuality's opposition to heterosexuality (terms he also refuses)."[47]

Indeed, outside of literary theory, the major work on negotiation takes place at the intersection between business management, industrial psychology, and self-help manuals. As I studied this literature, I found some revealing absences. It is rare for the term to be defined, even cursorily. Although it is said to be an everyday activity, done by everyone, from child to adult, in order to get what they want, the language used to describe the process is inevitably of the "he/man" sort. While the examples given assume a genderless, classless, and raceless dyad of negotiator/negotiatee, the negotiators are nearly always male and fairly affluent. Of the very few instances in which women appear, almost all are designated as "spouses." In the literature of business negotiation, patriarchy as well as capitalism seems inevitable, and the heterosexual contract too.

In the most humane, thoughtful, and well-written of the books I looked at, Roger Fisher and William Ury's *Getting to Yes: Negotiating Agreement Without Giving In,* the authors offered an alternative way of thinking about negotiating which they describe as neither hard nor soft, but as both hard and soft. In their attempt to find a fair and mutually satisfying way of conducting negotiations, they reject the usual process of successively taking and then giving up a sequence of positions. They believe this locks both sides into their respective positions and that the positions, rather the interests of each party, control what happens. Not only is this process inefficient, it endangers a relationship which it is probably wise for those involved to maintain. Instead, the authors, who headed Harvard University's Negotiation Project, argue for "principled negotiation," a form in which the participants attempt to decide the issue on which they are conflicted by appealing to objective criteria, which they define as "market value, expert opinion, custom, or law."[48]

The "objectivity" of those criteria would be disputed by feminists generally, but Fisher and Ury's liberal humanism should make feminists and lesbians who wish to theorize about negotiating subject positions wince. Whereas socialist feminist historian and autobiographer Carolyn Steedman casually but tellingly remarks in her book, *Landscape for a Good Woman,* in light of her life and the life of her working-class mother, "we knew we couldn't always get what we want,"[49] the literature of business management, and perhaps even the literature of literary theory, seems to hold out that dream as an "option."

Theoretical writing on the subject tends to emphasize negotiation as an internal and largely psychological process in which the "differences within" destabilize the subject and bring it to crisis, more than do "movement" writers such as Anzaldúa, Moraga, Lorde, and Nestle, who seem to construct autobiographies not often considered as "postmodern," though they are written in deterritorialized languages, take place on "borderland" sites, and are usually acknowledged as worthy of some formal interest through their use of generic montage.[50] But even in the writings of overtly political theorists, there is a tendency to efface the differences or to overlook the differences in social significance between intra-psychic or cross-cultural negotiating and negotiating between and among subjects regarding relationships with each other, as well as ideological, conceptual, or even theoretical systems.[51] What I notice in this work, even the best of it, is a failure to realize the tension in theorizing the decentered subject that Couze Venn emphasizes in the following remarks:

> The constructive aspect of that recovery [of the domain of the unconscious] is the attempt to conceptualize the constitutive relationship between the so-called 'cognitive' and 'affective' dimensions of behaviour by decentering them from the subject and locating their construction in the domain of the social. Any discourse which aims to speak of the subject must at the same time speak of the social.[52]

Although gestures are made in the literature to distinguish between, if not to give equal time to, articulating the various aspects of subjectivity, the social or political subject has been the step-child of literary theorists' attention. As I have been implying, the phrase "to negotiate one's subject positions" seems suffused with idealist mystifications about agency and conflict and hetero-relational ones about love. What seems to be obscured in the transaction is a notion of the subject as agent of change, that is, as a materialist or a lesbian subject. Whether they are management professors or literary critics, they look to negotiation as a potential, or even likely, "win-win" situation. They express not only boundless optimism but also mystify the material and other differences between negotiants as they enter into the process of negotiation.

It may seem vulgar and self-interested to ask, as Cornel West does, but "who gains, who loses and who bears the cost?" as an outcome of negotiating,[53] but I'm curious nonetheless. Why has it taken so long even to raise the question of what exactly constitutes a subject position? Judith Butler, in *Gender Trouble*, argues that this has already been done and has not been useful, in her opinion.[54] Why haven't the theorists even noticed that the question was missing? Why has it taken recent questioning about the fundamental categories of feminist analysis, namely gender, sex and sexuality, to make it clear that the theorizing of the subject of feminism is beyond negotiation?

If gender is no longer acceptable for analysis by many feminists as the primary contradiction and if interlocking systems analysis is coming to be regarded as too difficult or as always already exclusionary, in which direction will theorizing of a feminist subject turn—toward the personal or toward history? These are the two most logical directions suggested by the 1980s theoretical agenda of "historicizing subject positions." Shouldn't the doubting be turned in the direction of asking not how trapped or limited we might *feel* in our identities, since each aspect of them represents some degree of struggle within subject positions that have only partially been assigned, but what are the ethical and "political consequences of this moral content and cultural identity"?[55]

JOAN NESTLE AND THE REFUSAL TO NEGOTIATE

In the indiscreet/indiscrete fiction/theory written by Joan Nestle, who insists on selecting all aspects of her subjectivity, the word "negotiation" never appears. In *A Restricted Country,* even the juxtapositioning of very different sorts of texts, indiscreetly published together, represented a political risk for the author and the publisher, Nancy Bereano of Firebrand Books, a small lesbian-feminist press. While the book is now generally shelved in the lesbian theory section of women's book stores, it was originally banned from some stores altogether because of the controversies about Nestle's reputation as a sex radical. Whether read as a work of sexual indiscretion or infamous for being unread, *A Restricted Country* was not usually read as Nestle wanted it to be read, that is, as a work of history.⁵⁶

Nestle introduces the binary with which the text plays, restriction/liberation, particularly as it operates in very different historical, political and sexual contexts, along with her refusal to negotiate with that binary, in the piece of autobiographical criticism which gives its name to the collection as a whole. "A Restricted Country," an essay not to my knowledge ever discussed in treatments of Nestle as a "controversial" sex writer, traces a failed exodus from the Nestle family's restriction in poverty in the Bronx, to a promised if temporary liberation at two guest ranches in Arizona. Not knowing the rules of the new land, they are met with anti-Semitism at the Shining Star Guest Ranch, their "best bargain."⁵⁷ On arrival, they are seated as far away as possible from the other guests, and a white card is placed by each plate at dinner, which reads, "Because this guest ranch is run like a family, we are restricted to members of the Gentile faith only."⁵⁸ After dinner the manager offers a negotiation. "Since it was off-season, he was willing to compromise. If we told no one that we were Jewish, if we left and entered through the back door, and if we ate our meals by ourselves, we could stay. We looked at each other. Here was an offer to the Nestles to pass as Gentiles. To eat and walk in shame."⁵⁹

Nestle and her family refused to pass, but this story sets in motion the trope of passing in the civil rights movement, in the women's movement, and in lesbian-feminism, as an almost inevitable condition of her specific history—a necessary if not always willed disguise from both enemies and friends. That night, however, they refused to negotiate, that is, to make themselves invisible by passing, and are graciously taken in by a Jewish guest ranch. There, however, though they are received sympathetically as fellow Jews, the Nestles don't belong either, particularly Joan's mother, because they are working-class and fatherless. "We were Jewish, but we were different,"⁶⁰ Nestle says, evoking Audre Lorde's observation in *Zami* that "we were different" and so were unable to find a home or liberation anywhere except in the "very house of difference" as "sistah outsiders."⁶¹

Just as Nestle does not find out the full meaning or terms of the restrictions imposed upon her until the end of the story—when it is explained to her that the real estate signs proudly designating the beautiful land she is riding through as "the most restricted," that is, free of Jews, in the state—she lives through many sites of struggle in which she can have no permanent home if she refuses to be invisible.⁶² If it is true that the opening of an autobiography tends to offer an account of origins and therefore foregrounds the autobiographical subject's position, then *A Restricted Country's* first essay, "I Am," suggests that Nestle's is a "destitute" subjectivity and a study in negativity.[63] In three poetic paragraphs, she reiterates what she does not have—mythologies, goddesses, secret languages, rituals, noble histories, or ancient memories. What she has, or is, is a shallow pool of time, her present as history, her collective subjectivity with the common working people who do not have those things.

Nestle's claims in this opening passage suggest that it would be useful to connect her juxtapositioning of genres, erotica, and history as autobiography or perhaps autobiography as history, with her provocation of curiosity if not transformation on the part of her readers as they struggle, along with the author, to find a way of interpreting Nestle's presentation of her subject positions. As she says in a later theoretical chapter in which she claims connections, another indiscretion, between the historical sisterhood of lesbians and prostitutes, "The reclamation of one's history is a direct political act that changes both the hearer and the speaker."[64] This reclamation is another gift Nestle offers readers.

In terms of generic and other transgressions enacted in this text, *A Restricted Country* can be read as re-memorializing and re-privileging moments of desire in the text of necessity. Two British feminist historians, one a theorist of Victorian working women's autobiographies, Julia Swindells, and the other a theorist and writer of a twentieth-century working-class women's autobiography, Carolyn Steedman, suggest what the difficulties are in producing and interpreting those moments, at least as they relate to working-class heterosexual women, if not lesbians, (the "not quite" women). Swindells relates the theoretical "progress" of autobiography as the "not quite" discourse, caught between the disciplinary and interpretive devices of history and literature.[65] From the perspective of history, the discipline she argues with more extensively in her article, autobiography is a text of low status. It provides inadequate evidence and has been dismissed, until very recently, as a text of those who are "not quite historians."[66]

As autobiography came up in the disciplinary world because of its importance to social historians, and the debate arose about the autobiographical subject and who can speak for history, social historians tended to conflate autobiography, and working-class autobiography and claimed the latter as a privileged historical text. So much so, that when Carolyn Steedman wrote *Landscape for a Good Woman* and refused to call it a history, it seemed that she had committed class treason. From the perspective of the other discipline that has begun to claim autobiography as its own, literature, the conflation has gone in the other direction, toward the personal, the merely fictional. Swindells states in her footnote that:

> it might be tempting to glance again at English studies, if it were not for the suspicion that "the personal and the social" is a dimension too much for the literary critic. He (occasionally she) is, rather, busy being a voyeur, getting too busy with the personal, getting personal. Why have recourse to "the social" when you can privatize your author—take your autobiographer to the confessional, or out for the talking cure? For the literary commentator, it is as if the autobiographical "I" reminds too much of the sexed (sexy?) deep psyche.[67]

Squeezed between disciplines, autobiography remains perhaps a marginalized, indiscrete discourse, with working-class women's life writings being difficult to see and to interpret because of the absence of interpretive frameworks to do so. Using irony, dislocation, disruption, and perhaps envy to tell her own as well as her mother's story, Steedman uses, while she deconstructs them, the frameworks of psychoanalysis and Marxism. She cautions that what she has to tell is not yet a story, but pointless narration until it is accepted by readers as a story.

> All the stories that follow, told as this story tells them, aren't stories in their own right: they exist in tension with other more central ones. Accounts of working-class life are told by tension and ambiguity, out on the borderlands. The story—my mother's story, a hundred thousand others—cannot be absorbed into the central one: it is both its disruption and its essential counterpoint: this is a drama of class.[68]

In making these claims, Steedman suggests that her text could function like Paul Smith's notion of a singular history which presents subjectivity as a series of moments produced in the course of social life. Doing that depends, however, on her success in making her readers, however they are located, connive in receiving the text as a story with a point which is the same for reader and writer. Like Nestle, her goal is to create a narrative exchange which will transform both speaker and hearer, but as in the case of Nestle, that seems next to impossible.

The two working-class female autobiographers are caught in a contradiction. The subject positions from which they speak are assumed by the interpretive and ideological frameworks on which they

..ty to be unintelligible and unworthy of notice. And yet they must use them to be intelligible, and, in Nestle's case, worthy, on their own terms. And so, Nestle, who is unintelligible not only as a working-class woman, but as a lesbian (among other things), decides to use a strategy of indiscretion, not negotiating her subject positions with her interlocutors within and without her text but offering her split subjectivity, and that of the gay and lesbian community as a sexual people, as a gift to the world.[69] Because although Nestle does not write in the language of subject positions, she seems to be aware that a split subject may be nothing more politically useful than the flip side of a unitary one. She writes to acknowledge that the point of remarking on the splitting is to bind together the differences in such a way as to mobilize resistance, to effect revolutionary change. She says about co-founding the Lesbian Herstory Archives:

> [M]y different identities led me there: my Jewish self that knew memory was a holy thing, never to be bartered or sold; my old femme self that knew the sacredness of a scorned courage; my new feminist self that wanted the delight of a women-only creation; my socialist self that believed all resources must be shared; my teacher self that had been taught by First World students the burden of colonization and the pain of exile; my psychological self that called on me to carry my mother and her loneliness into my own conflicts about security and freedom. And, like a hemp rope binding the parts together, ran my sexual self, taking on all these forms of being and rearranging them in stunning new ways.[70]

As this passage suggests, the treatment of her sexuality as that which binds all the aspects of her subjectivity together makes Nestle's autobiography as history different in some significant ways from other autobiographical texts such as those studied by Biddy Martin in her critique of identity politics and lesbian autobiography. As similar as Nestle is to Mab Segrest or Minnie Bruce Pratt, by virtue of being American lesbian writers who are dedicated as white women to antiracist struggles, in her treatment of the interrelationships between the restrictions of gender, race, class and sexual orientation in *A Restricted Country*, Nestle does not go as far as the other writers do, that is, to conflate her sexuality with a concern with "larger struggles."

Though the emphasis in the passage from Nestle above seems to be on the colligation of subject positions rather than on what unsettles them and brings them to crisis, any colligation is a temporary one. As her autobiographical trajectory and her advice to lesbians suggests, lesbians should be mistresses of discrepancies. Nestle cannot fully identify her own interests with any one discourse, and so is highly conscious of her need to slip in and out of subject positions.

> This is what my history has taught me: if we choose to involve ourselves in the antipornography movement, it would be helpful to keep in mind that many of us were the early victims of vice raids...If we sign the NOW resolution against, among other things, the public display of affection, we should remember that others, like myself, made love in public bathrooms because we had no other place to go.[71]

Nestle's notoriety among many lesbian feminists rests on her writings about butch-femme relationships and her attempt to write a lesbian history which includes rather than dismisses them. Nestle's revisionist history as autobiography which links lesbians and prostitutes, also disturbs lesbian historians who want to stress the centrality of middle and upper-class lesbians who achieved cultural respectability through their invisibility in the private sphere of romantic friends at home, and at exclusive resorts and salons.[72]

In writing a chapter on the joint history of lesbians and prostitutes, Nestle works the contradictions between oppression and resistance, rather than attempting to marginalize the indiscreet. In the process of constructing and then deconstructing the first concrete reference to a lesbian history from the garbled mutterings of a Victorian misogynist named William W. Sanger who, in order to speak about prostitution, "was forced to enlarge upon an even more repulsive theme," that is, lesbian sexuality, Nestle traces the path from Athenian flute-playing prostitutes who pleasured themselves and each other to the celebrations of lesbian separatists at the Michigan Women's Music Festival.[73]

In producing an analysis of the processes by which a lesbian subjectivity can be deciphered, Nestle also writes a history of her own formation and reformation as a lesbian subject. Not coincidentally, following that path helps her not only to reconnect dykes and whores but to find yet another way of linking herself with her mother and of honoring their disreputable and heroic ways of surviving as working-woman and lesbians. Whether the reader reads this writing as gift or excrement—lesbian-feminist philosopher Janice Raymond takes the latter view in "Putting the Politics Back into Lesbianism"[74]—Nestle demonstrates that it is historical. Her account of how she came to relate her mother's history as a prostitute both to her own changing relationships to whores and her later identification as a sex worker deserves to be called an analysis of a "lesbian subject-in-process."[75]

Paul Smith calls the process Nestle has just recounted a "dialectical thickening" and remarks that only if it "takes place is it possible to see the way in which the agential elements of subjectivity, formed in and by the contradiction of subject-positions and by conflicts of self-interest and ideology, are themselves historical and historicizable."[76] Smith does not, however, mention the pain that accompanies such a process or the courage it takes to see it through. Nestle's gift of this self-revelation qualifies as one small example of what Fredric Jameson meant when he defined history as "what hurts."[77]

Nonetheless, the most concrete aspect of Nestle's gift of herself is that her text lessens the shame and humiliation that she learned from both heterosexism and lesbian-feminism to attach to devalued aspects of lesbian subjectivity. She discusses, side by side, what she learned from both: "Because I quickly got the message in my first Lesbian-feminist cr group that such topics as butch-femme relationships and the use of dildoes were lower class, I was forced to understand that sexual style is a rich mixture of class, history and personal integrity."[78] "My butch-femme sensibility also incorporated the wisdom of freaks. One day many years ago, as I was walking through Central Park, a group of cheerful straight people walked past me and said, 'what shall we feed it?' The *it* has never left my consciousness."[79]

The pain of being treated as an other, whether by lesbian-feminists or straight people, forces her to understand how her subject position disturbs the effective functioning of a hierarchical system. Nestle unfortunately tends to emphasize the colligating and triumphal aspect of her multiple subject positions at the expense of their unbinding action. Though a snub, a rejection, an insult, or a threat jolts her into self-awareness, into history, once the rupture is over she seems to join her threatened and secure selves together again into a new formation which seems at least momentarily unified, as in the through-line of her butch-femme sexuality which has gifted her "with sensitivities she can never disown."[80] In the new colligation there is no room for negativity, for moments of subjectivity that are non-unified and inconsistent. To look for them, would that be like turning her gift into excrement? And yet without negativity, some possibilities for resistance lose their theoretical and political force.

Nestle's text attempts to induce the formation of a minority community and to offer a revisionist view, a performative view, of recent lesbian history: "Let this be the history we make ours."[81] Nonetheless, like the lesbian-feminist historiography she is re-writing, Nestle too has a need to persuade readers of her own whole(some)ness. She is thus sometimes tempted by the privileged site of lesbian contestation: the pure and the sure. Unlike them, she does admit to doubt about the truth of her writing.[82] But like those she opposes, Nestle is not always willing to own her readings as interpretations which she makes rather than finds, and which are, in any case, open to question.

Since I too run the risk of doing that, I acknowledge that interpretations, my own included, are sometimes gifts and sometimes just excrement. Sometimes readers simply accept them in the spirit in which they are offered, but I hope they still ask: what are the political consequences of Nestle's text, her gift? On a first reading of *A Restricted Country*, I assumed it was just another document in the sex wars, what some critics hostile to lesbians like Nestle call the "re-sexualization" of women.[83] On a second reading, I noticed that Nestle's first word was "History" and that she offers it to her readers with even more urgency and with mingled expectations of producing delight and rejection than when she gives her aging, fat, femme body to her butch lovers.

For this reason, I'm more taken with what Nestle implies are ways of theorizing action through becoming lesbian desiring subjects than with the accounts offered by other lesbian theorists. We still live in restricted countries, but Nestle, as would-be unrestricted feminist historian and autobiographer, urges us to imagine the enabling, agentic potential of nuns, queers, and whores. She does not, on the one hand, simply ignore or recuperate them too for some kind of respectability, as does Lillian Faderman or Janice Raymond, or, on the other, offer one and only one strong subject position, the butch-femme couple, who are always together and never split or fractured, as does Sue-Ellen Case. Nestle's indiscreet/indiscrete lesbian exhibits herself, insisting that what is culturally and politically acceptable only as long as the femme lesbian remains an invisible "I" must be looked at. She shifts and exchanges herself with us like a gift.

CHAPTER 5

SARAH SCHULMAN:
URBAN LESBIAN RADICALS IN A POSTMODERN MAINSTREAM

Novelist, playwright, essayist, and activist Sarah Schulman has large ambitions—to help forge a lesbian literary avant-garde that refuses to disconnect from progressive politics. As an example of how she plays this edge, she reinvents lesbian activism in a pomo mode by founding the Lesbian Avengers, whose handbook is excerpted in her collection of essays, *My American History: Lesbian and Gay Life During the Reagan/Bush Years*.[1] In this chapter I discuss how she uses the symbolic geography of the city-island in her five novels in light of three ways of imagining Euramerican lesbian literary history, through Sapphic, Amazonian, and Romantic friendship models. None of these models provides the perfect matrix for Schulman, but because she writes in response to developments in lesbian culture, these models, particularly the Sapphic one, function like a palimpsest, as an imperfect but almost necessary fiction for her fiction.

Why I would look to the lesbian past rather than to the present in order to place Schulman's accomplishments first needs explaining however, because of the reception her writing has thus far been given from reviewers and critics. Wanting to promote her ascendancy from small press writer of paraliterature to serious artist, they deck her with high cultural honorifics, deem her a lesbian postmodernist, and say that, as did Fay Weldon, with Schulman's latest novel, *Empathy*, "the lesbian novel comes of age."[2] Though her work merits all the critical attention it can get, this kind of reception is problematic because it legitimates Schulman by universalizing her writing, thereby ignoring its relation to the far less well-known, less prestigious, and "insular" history of American lesbian fiction. Because Schulman's work is a reaction and response to what she found wanting in the lesbian writing immediately available to her when she began to write, her accomplishments first need to be placed in the lesbian-feminist context from which she emerged in the mid-1980s.

Sarah Schulman began to publish fiction in 1984, in the immediate wake of the American feminist sex wars. She was one of the first lesbian novelists to write in detail about lesbian sex. She has been claimed as a sex radical who believes that the sex radicals won the war over sexual representation. Such criticism simply adds Schulman to the list of lesbian and feminist writers and thinkers whose work is explained in terms of the following syllogism: sex radical equals poststructuralist equals postmodernist. What does the sex-radical victory mean for contemporary American lesbian fiction and the reading public? Critics have begun to answer: out with dykey stylelessness, in with lesbian chic; out with expressive realism, in with meta-fiction; and, most of all, out with minoritizing discourses, such as feminist and lesbian separatisms, and in with universalizing discourses, such as queer theory.

Before the celebration begins, I would urge another look at Schulman's writing practices, especially her last two novels, and at the syllogism itself, which is reductionist as well as triumphalist. Though Schulman's first three novels seemed so different from prevailing patterns in the last two decades of American lesbian-feminist writing that critics were quick to claim her as a lesbian postmodernist, I believe that her break with lesbian-feminism is not clear-cut. Also, ascertaining her relationship to traditions of lesbian writing may be more illuminating than claiming her as a postmodernist as, for example, Sally Munt attempts to do in her essay, "'Somewhere over the rainbow…': Postmodernism and the Fiction of Sarah Schulman."[3]

Since, however, "lesbian" is a negative identity and an unimaginable ontological category, lesbian literary histories, like all other notions to which the modifier "lesbian" is attached, are at best epistemologically suspect. Though much has been written about these conundrums, the immediate consequence of these questions is that the very existence of a lesbian literary tradition, as well as its make-up, is a matter of controversy, even to lesbian writers and critics.

For them, even more than for the general reading public, Terry Castle's definition of the typical lesbian novel as something that is not only non-canonical, but under-read, unknown, and unappreciated suggests that these putative lesbian literary traditions might be difficult to access even for the writers and readers who need them most.[4] This, I argue, is the case with Schulman, one of whose protagonists often asked "why she tried to write lesbian fiction when she never read any."[5] Schulman's novels first need to be read with reference to how she imagines a lesbian literary tradition as well as to how she complicates our understandings of lesbian literary history before they are fitted into the legitimizing and slippery category of lesbian postmodernism, particularly if all that is meant by the buzz word is "serious fun."

This takes me to notions of lesbian culture and separatism. While notions of insularity, even separatism, are intrinsic to lesbian culture, their meanings are obviously contested, complex, and less obviously, perhaps, contradictory. My reading of Sarah Schulman's five novels queries assumptions about what happens when American lesbian-feminism, assumed to be insular and totalizing, meets postmodernist aesthetics, assumed to be suspicious of all meta-narratives, on the terrain of the postmodern city, a degraded hyperspace at once global and local. I conclude that the graft of lesbian fiction and postmodernist aesthetics should not necessarily be celebrated, or even taken for granted, but queried.

Like her fictional protagonists, who are often aspiring writers themselves, Schulman writes as if she had no models for writing lesbian fiction. Of course, she is not the first ambitious writer to write as if this were the case. In one sense, then, she implicitly distances herself from two older traditions of lesbian writing: the European tradition of yearning for island retreats, beginning with Sappho's Lesbos and extending to Monique Wittig's mythical islands; and the newer populist "tradition" of American lesbian-feminist romance and genre fiction, set in remote, idyllic, and pastoral places.

Schulman's lesbians reject the rural and the natural, and prefer urbanity. They live on the island of Manhattan, but they are not Amazons or lesbian separatists, and they do not inhabit this space alone. They are tied by webs of economics, race and ethnicity, class, and affection to the larger society. They work in pink ghetto jobs, go to families of origin for Jewish holidays and other gatherings, and they have alternative families in the AIDS and art activist communities. Schulman's subject is New York City itself, especially the Lower East Side, the historical meeting place of new and old waves of the poor, immigrants, political and artistic radicals, outcasts, and misfits; a neighborhood currently threatened by gentrification and homelessness. By inscribing the proletarian urban lesbian as intellectual and desiring subject into American fiction, Schulman transplants and transmutes the

Sapphic model from the upper-class salons of Paris into the grotty bars, tenements, ethnic restaurants, and lesbian clubs that line the streets of the East Village and the Lower East Side.

ISLANDS AND CITIES IN THE EURAMERICAN LESBIAN LITERARY TRADITION

While lesbians and lesbianism seem always to have had an affinity with islands, the nature of the relationship, particularly that between island and mainland, remains contested. Is every lesbian an island or none? Is the island a ghetto or a place where autonomy and connection are made possible?[6] Etymologically, the word island allows for both possibilities. Literally, an island is "a piece of land surrounded by water," but figuratively, it is "anything detached or isolated," from the Latin, *insula*.

Lesbian culture in general, but particularly its writing, has always been insular. The word "lesbian" itself, of course, by an epistemologically and linguistically fascinating process designed to put off real knowing[7], forges the connection between the island, the exiled poet, and the same-sex separatism of her reputed sexual practices at the same time that dictionaries render lesbians logically impossible.[8] The history of Euramerican lesbian writing is an island-hopping trajectory of desire from Sappho to Gertrude Stein to Monique Wittig to Nicole Brossard to Sarah Schulman, with the main stops on the itinerary the island-cities of Lesbos, Paris, Montreal, and New York. The use and abuse of Sappho as a model for female modernists for writing about lesbian desire and for imagining the connection between gender and writing itself has been explored by Elaine Marks, Susan Gubar, and Joan DeJean. Of these three critics, only Marks is primarily interested in how a contemporary lesbian writer and theorist such as Monique Wittig employs the Sappho model to revolutionize the possibilities of lesbian writing.

The symbolic geography connoted in and by the island location works negatively, in the case of the dominant culture, and for the most part positively in a lesbian symbolic. The insularity of lesbian culture, as the dictionary implies, renders it narrow: "of or like islanders, especially ignorant of or indifferent to other countries and their culture, narrow-minded." The implicit attitudes of the dominant culture suggest that lesbian culture, by definition, marginalizes itself because it is intrinsically separatist. Apparently isolated enough to be ignorant of the mainland, it deserves in turn to be ignored, or as Terry Castle put it, under-read. From the outset, judgment has been passed on lesbian culture: It keeps to itself, is unwelcoming of contact with the mainland, and has produced nothing that the mainland culture needs to know. So insular and insignificant is Lesbos that the very phrase "lesbian culture" is oxymoronic.

Similar problems accompany any discussion of the meaning of separatism. Separatism is in the eye of the beholder and can mean anything a writer wants it to mean. Separatists are perceived simultaneously as a vanguard and as cowards seeking safety in retreat, as crazed millennialists creating utopian outposts to the future, and as an economically and racist privileged elite who refuse to keep up with advanced theorizing. For example, the following three interpretations from the point of view of lesbian separatists, non-separatists, and lesbians who reject the term "lesbian" in favor of "queer," suggest something of the range and the instability of the term as it applies to lesbian culture. Those in the first group defend the practice, although admitting that its practitioners are a tiny holdout of true believers; the second group dismisses separatism as passé; the third finds anything lesbian and, by extension, feminist, particularly writing and theorizing, intrinsically separatist.

The lesbian separatist writers who defend it in the 1988 anthology, *For Lesbians Only: A Separatist Anthology*, argue that, although definitions have changed over the last fifteen years, separatism is still an urgent and central issue for lesbians and feminists. In 1991, lesbian-feminist social historian Lillian Faderman offered a more moderate view. On the one hand, separatism is narrow, bigoted, dogmatic, and has been consigned to the dustbin of history by the AIDS crisis; on the other, lesbians learned something by immersion in a women's culture and separatism has been useful strategically as a way of resisting the homophobia of the heterosexual women's movement and the sexism of gay liberation. Faderman concludes that it's no longer a hot topic.[9] Most interestingly, in the same year, queer theorists Lauren Berlant and Elizabeth Freeman constructed separatism so broadly that its reach extends to the "safe" spaces of Judith Butler's theorizing:

> Lesbian theory's solution to this dilemma [of masquerade] has been to construct imaginable communities...The female body has reemerged in the safe spaces of lesbian political theory...The blinking question mark beside the word *nation* in Jill Johnston's separatist *Lesbian Nation*; the erotogenic meta-

morphoses of the body, sex, and knowledge on the island of Monique Wittig's *The Lesbian Body;* and even the personal gender performances central to Judith Butler's sexual self-fashioning all reveal an evacuation of liberal nationality as we know it.[10]

According to Berlant and Freeman, if you are lesbian, especially if you are a writer/theorist, you are by definition a separatist. Separatists are no longer retreating to country communes; instead, they're writing theory. Or, more accurately, the books themselves are a form of separatism. Oddly enough, this remarkably totalizing (and condescending) definition, though it would include anti-separatist lesbian writers like Schulman, supports the separatist philosopher Marilyn Frye's argument that notions of separation are fundamental to all feminisms and are "there in everything from divorce to exclusive lesbian separatist communities, from shelters for battered women to witch covens, from women's studies programs to women's bars, from expansions of daycare to abortion on demand."[11]

Frye suggests that separation appears offensive and negative because denying men access to women is a form of insubordination. Separation attempts not only to control access but to undertake self-definition. Accordingly, lesbians as otherwise diverse as anti-identity political theorists like Butler, anti-separatist novelists like Schulman, and critics such as myself who attempt to imagine a lesbian literary history, are all separatists.[12] If nothing else, reading such divergent claims forces one to conclude that lesbian separatism, like other contemporary separatisms, while in one sense arouses fear and loathing, in other ways seems as unremarkable and as American as apple pie.

The insularity of lesbian culture has been connoted rather positively until very recently by lesbian writers, though there are significant differences between an American lesbian-feminist "tradition" and a French or Francophone radical lesbian one.[13] Frequently, American lesbian-feminists have been suspicious of or rejecting of the elitism or implicit racism of the Sappho model; lesbians writing in French do not express these concerns.[14] While Judy Grahn and Lillian Faderman have endeavored to uncover/rediscover the mythic or empirical origins of lesbian culture and pass on a tradition whose hallmarks are accessibility and realism in aesthetics and the creation of community through passionate friendships, French-speaking poets and mythmakers in France and Quebec such as Monique Wittig and Nicole Brossard have constructed a less accessible and anti-realist tradition which creates communities through writing. Indeed, Monique Wittig wrote that lesbianism is not just desire for one's own sex, but for "something else that is not connoted. This desire is resistance to the norm."[15] Brossard's formation is even bolder: "A lesbian who does not reinvent the word is a lesbian in the process of disappearing."[16]

THREE MODELS FOR LESBIAN WRITING: SAPPHIC, AMAZONIAN, AND ROMANTIC FRIENDSHIP

Some lesbian scholars have traced lesbian lineage through three different literally or metaphorically insular lines: Sapphic, Amazonian, and that of Romantic friends.[17] African-American lesbian critic Ekua Omosupe justly observes that the word "lesbian," when not inflected, refers only to white lesbian culture.[18] The philosophical, historical, and political problems bound up in these quests for origins ought to be undeniable to critics mindful of the lessons of post-colonialism as well as of deconstruction.[19] Nonetheless, lesbians, like other culturally disenfranchised groups lacking shared and valued identities and traditions, have tried to name, recover, uncover or, failing that, invent personages, events, and patterns by which to interpret and understand themselves. So, for example, while using the designation "pre- and post-" Stonewall to date events in recent gay and lesbian history is both Amerocentric and in any case inappropriate to the self-understandings of many lesbians, Stonewall's importance as a cultural landmark is unquestionable.

This discussion is not a brief for any one of these Sapphic, Amazonian, or Romantic friendship lines so much as it is an investigation of what is available for a contemporary American lesbian writer who needs a community of the word to trace her genealogy as a lesbian and an intellectual. Of the scholars and poets who have written about these lineages, some conflate the traditions or champion one as the most authentic line, but most revealingly, they ignore the ones with which they do not identify. What interests me most about attempts to trace lesbian literary lines is their insularity with respect to each other. Even when the logic of the argument for the importance of the Sappho, Amazon, or Romantic friendship models demands acknowledging its intertextuality, except for those tracing the Sapphic lineage most of these writers replicate avant-garde traditions by failing to cite the others. Each dreams up her lesbian lineage anew or rediscovers her in forgotten books, letters, and archives real or imaginary.

This anti-syncretic scholarship adds another layer of meaning to the island metaphor. That lesbians like and are like islands is something almost every lesbian knows but most lesbians, especially American ones, don't know how they know. Tellingly, in Monique

Wittig and Sande Zeig's *Lesbian Peoples: Material for a Dictionary*, a poststructuralist mythoethnography, the entry for Sappho is a blank page.[20] The reader may fill it in as she likes. In the absence of facts, invent the past you prefer.

In other ways, Wittig and Zeig invent lesbian history and pre-history as it ought to have been, according to late twentieth-century lesbian materialists. Though many entries can be read as whimsical additions to the cultural feminist fantasy of a glorious Amazonian past, careful reading suggests that Wittig and Zeig are sending up lesbian preoccupation with myths of origin and with the very notion that a transhistorical and transcultural lesbian lineage can be recovered and revived by tracing the most well-known models, that of Sappho and her school, of the Amazonian warriors, and of Romantic friends.

Not all scholars, even lesbian ones, appear to read Wittig with care. For example, in the longest and most densely researched (with almost no citations to lesbian scholarship, however, but that is the point) but oldest article in her recent book, *Perversions: Deviant Readings,* British media critic Mandy Merck argues that lesbian appropriation of the Amazon as cultural feminism's "signal motif" has been so entirely uncritical it manages somehow to be both literal-minded and historically ignorant of how the Amazon functioned in a misogynist patriarchal culture.[21] Some thirty pages into the argument of "The Amazons of Ancient Athens," Merck suddenly does a very muddled and unconvincing about-face, conceding that although the Amazonian past is "inappropriable" for contemporary feminist political struggles, the project itself is encouraging.

To illustrate the project's errors, Merck quotes the following passage from the preface to Wittig's novel, *The Lesbian Body*:

> Because we are illusionary for traditional male culture we make no distinction between the three levels [fictional, symbolic, actual]. Our reality is the fictional as it is socially accepted, our symbols deny the traditional symbols and are fictional for traditional male culture, and we possess an entire fiction into which we project ourselves and which is already a possible reality. It is our fiction that validates us.[22]

Merck reads Wittig literally, failing to understand that she is deconstructing the binary "fictional/real" and missing her point about the materiality of language and the constructedness of material reality: "It is not the fiction of female resistance which validates our struggles, but its reality."[23] Now whose scholarship is literal-minded and ignorant of history? Originally published in 1976, Merck's argument is anti-lesbian modernist or seemingly pro-postmodernist lesbian *avant la lettre*. By reprinting, in 1993, a 1976 article that lambastes lesbian scholarship as an ignorant misreading, Merck implicitly rejects almost two decades of lesbian research and theory as not worth discussing.

As evidence that Wittig's mythography can be read as complicating and refusing literal and insular readings of lesbian culture, here is an example—Wittig and Zeig's tongue-in-cheek entry for Amazons. It spins a lesbocentric tall tale about the rise, decline and re-creation of the lesbian peoples. Putting both matriarchy and patriarchy into a virtual "space off," this entry produces a triumphalist, universalizing narrative of lesbian culture. Originally universal, timeless, and culturally central, the lesbian peoples, inventors of language, cities, and so on, were driven into insular isolation, forced out of cities, not by the unnamed patriarchy but by the complicity and internal dissent of the mothers, the domesticated women. This isolation was eventually undone in the current Glorious Age, by lesbians who are, literally, everywhere, having thrown off their domestication. They have started to reclaim their centrality first by looking for islands, but as they grow stronger, they will reinhabit the cities of every continent.[24]

Perhaps the most ironic and subversive accomplishment of this piece of slyly deconstructive insular scholarship is that it is to be found where one least expects it. In public and university libraries, it is located not in the literature section among speculative fiction or poetry or in the social science scholarship on deviancy, but in the reference area, among the straight, that is, conventional geographical studies and atlases.

THE SAPPHO MODEL AND FRANCOPHONE LESBIAN WRITING

Lesbian and feminist critics do not agree about whether the Sappho model is useful for writers who do not want to be contained within an elitist and Eurocentric, specifically French, literary tradition. In 1979, literary critic Elaine Marks invented lesbian literary theory in her article, "Lesbian Intertextuality," by showing how what she calls the "Sappho model" connects sexual and textual practices from Lesbos to Paris.[25] Whether employed by women or by men, the Sappho model is a written, and in Marks's study, largely a French tradition. Marks shows how poets and novelists variously domesticated the lesbian, kept her inside, in the gynaeceum, and made her the object rather than the subject of writing, until very recently when contemporary lesbian writers like Wittig freed her.

In 1984, feminist critic Susan Gubar argued that Sappho was employed "if only fleetingly" during the early twentieth century by female modernist poets, not all of them lesbian, as a "fantasy precursor" of their "nonexistent or degraded literary matrilineage."[26] Later, Gubar claims, American lesbian writers rejected Sappho on lesbian-feminist political grounds.[27] In 1989, keeping a knowing but careful distance from both lesbian-feminist and feminist perspectives, Joan DeJean published an exhaustive study of how French writers and critics employed fictions of Sappho from the sixteenth to the early twentieth century. Unlike Marks or Gubar, DeJean's primary focus is on male writers whose hostile attraction to Sappho could be considered a form of literary cross-dressing or ventriloquism. Nonetheless, DeJean's findings suggest how contemporary lesbian readers and writers working outside the French tradition could still find empowerment in a revisionist Sappho model. Although DeJean indicates how a much smaller number of far less prominent female intellectuals used Sappho to empower themselves as writers, she concludes that since neither Sappho's writing nor her life are *conclusively* lesbian, contemporary readers could appropriate Sappho as the "archetypal lesbian writer," and "the ultimate post-structuralist."[28]

As different as these three critics are, they all underline the central role fantasies of Sappho have played in European literary history. In a sense, then, Sappho's influence transcends the bounds of her island: "From Martial's Bassa and Lucian's Megilla, model tribades of antiquity, to the lesbians of Diderot, Balzac, Proust, and Sartre, the female homosexual incarnating the Sappho model has moved from a small corner of the canvas to a central position."[29] Marks argues that Wittig revolutionized lesbian writing by undomesticating Sappho. In her formally and sexually subversive writing, with its hyperbole, repetitions, pronominal rebellion, and blatantly violent sexual imagery, Wittig brings the Sappho model back to her text, connects Lesbian verbal power with Amazonian physical strength, and thereby allows the lesbian writer to step outside of male culture. From the vantage point of 1979, Marks predicted that innovative lesbian-feminist writers will be the "most subversive voices of the century," "creat[ing] hyperbolic, sensuous fictions that illuminate possibilities for the woman as narrator and the woman as reader."[30]

Marks's actual formulation, that lesbian-feminist writers already "are, and will be" the most subversive—in their texts—is borne out in the writing practice of Nicole Brossard. In her poetry and fiction theory, the lesbian city-island becomes a continent: "*my continent woman...bringing me into the world.*"[31] Brossard's performative invocation of a lesbian continent exemplifies the lesbocentric way Francophone writers have universalized an insular culture. Brossard's text does what Wittig recommends in her essay, "The Point of View: Universal or Particular?": "A text by a minority writer is effective only if it succeeds in making the minority point of view universal, only if it is an important literary text."[32] Brossard's continent is a world of words, an intertextual construction of and by lesbian writers:

> my continent multiplied by those who have signed: Djuna Barnes, Jane Bowles, Gertrude Stein, Natalie Barney, Michèle Causse, Marie-Claire Blais, Jovette Marchesault, Adrienne Rich, Mary Daly, Colette and Virginia, the other drowned ones, Christina Perri Rossi, Louky Bersianik, Pol Pelletier, Maryvonne so attentive, Monique Wittig, Sande Zeig, Anna d'Argentine, Kate Millett, Jeanne d'Arc Jutras, Marie Lafleur, Jane Rule, Renee Vivien, Romaine Brooks. [33]

In Brossard's lesbian reappropriation of the Sappho model, even more than Wittig's, the lesbian is a thinker and a writer, and the city, as well as the island, is the place that inspires her. While the island allows more respite than does the city, neither is insular in the sense of narrow, because both encourage expansive thinking.

> The city-centre is homo-ideological, the city is homo-sexist; the island is utopian, the island is the place of replenishment. But what interests me in the city as well as on the island is that people are thinking. That is why in all my books, novels anyway, there is always a table. A writing table and/or a restaurant table where people are engaged in discussions while eating, drinking, smoking. Inside, outside around a table. In my work there is always a table and a street.[34]

ANTI-INTELLECTUALISM, THE AMAZONIAN MODEL, AND ANGLO-AMERICAN LESBIAN WRITING

Brossard and Wittig, writing in a Francophone lesbian literary tradition, emphasize lesbian intellectuality and aesthetic innovation, aspects correlated more with avant-garde urbanity than with sentimental retreat from patriarchy. If one compares Elaine Marks's essay to a similarly bold attempt by Catharine Stimpson, the differences between Francophone and Anglophone lesbian literary critical models are striking. Two years after Marks wrote about lesbian intertextuality, Stimpson's essay, "Zero Degree Deviancy: The Lesbian Novel in English," provided a map for English language lesbian fiction as Marks had done for French literature.

The differences in literary history evoked by Marks's and Stimpson's paradigms suggest that it is far more difficult for contemporary American lesbian writers to find a self-consciously literary lesbian tradition than it is for Francophone lesbians. For Americans in particular, there is no native Sapphic model. Even when Stimpson proposed another model for English language lesbian fiction, when fully worked out it is imaginable only as a French import, that is, in terms of Barthes's "zero degree" writing. Stimpson traces through English lesbian fiction a teleological and as yet incomplete model in which "lesbian romanticism," with its pattern of damnation, is succeeded by "lesbian realism," with its offer of the enabling escape.[35] Since neither mode allows a sense of humor and both are at least implicitly defensive about lesbianism, Barthes's "zero degree" of writing, with the possible exception of Bertha Harris's novels, is as yet impossible in English language lesbian fiction.

While Stimpson praises Harris as "the American equivalent of Monique Wittig," she does not explain who Wittig is, nor cite her in her notes.[36] By comparison with Marks, who predicts that lesbian-feminist voices will be the most subversive of the century, Stimpson hedges her bets; formal, or even more broadly speaking, literary subversion is not the ambition of the current crop of American lesbian-feminist writers. Nonetheless, within the realist-escape model, the attention of the "larger culture" may be gained in two ways, one formal, and the other literary historical. By being conventional in form and providing an easy read, lesbian fiction makes itself more accessible both for lesbian readers, tired from dealing with the larger culture's hostility, and for heterosexual readers, challenged by the book's lesbian content.[37]

Though these American writers might seek legitimacy by wrapping their work in the Sapphic and Amazonian mantle, they appropriate those myths primarily to construct an imaginary community of political women in solidarity. Read this way, their writing makes itself interesting to the larger world as the marker of a social experiment, not as a literary achievement. Somewhat dubious of the American cultural feminist tendency to embrace any and all Amazonian and matriarchal myths and call it "herstory," Stimpson elides the cultural differences between French and American lesbian literary traditions by merely noting that such myths "were popular in stylish lesbian circles in the earlier part of the twentieth century."[38]

JUDY GRAHN AND THE AMERICAN AMAZONIAN MODEL

American lesbians who stayed at home literally or metaphorically had and probably still have trouble imagining themselves into that elite and glamorous lesbian lineage. In her article, "A Meeting of the Sapphic Daughters," African-American novelist Ann Shockley rejects elitist Sapphic cults as implicitly racist.[39] As someone whose formally innovative writing did not fit Stimpson's model, lesbian avant-garde novelist Bertha Harris nonetheless recognized that many American lesbians who came to writing post-Stonewall seemed by reason of class or ethnicity excluded from the expatriate tradition:

> But I was poor and grubby; naive, emotional, sweaty with lowerclass need. I was short and peasantmade—and my ancestors, I learned, as I read my censored history, were rich or nearly rich; sophisticated, cool; longlimbed; and our family bloodline, the common identity among us, would always be nothing more, nothing less, than our common need for the word of consequence: will always be my acknowledgement of these women, despite all material differences between us, as my first ancestors.[40]

One thing that unites lesbian scholars of diverse orientations is that they have struggled for "that common need for the word" under far from ideal conditions. Merck calls herself a member of the British "lumpen intelligentsia"[41] who did her research over a period of several months "after work."[42] Judy Grahn, a working-class woman and an autodidact, began her research on Gay (she capitalizes the word) culture in 1964 by studying dictionaries she had to borrow from friends. The fear of political repression in the United States against gays and lesbians, inspired by rumors that government agents in New York City were confiscating gay writing, forced her to destroy her notes in 1965. Over the next two decades, she continued her research, being able to publish *Another Mother Tongue: Gay Words, Gay Worlds* only in 1984.[43] These material conditions for producing scholarship, which have changed very little except for a very few American scholars with tenure in a handful of elite universities, provide another compelling reason why lesbian culture is that which is not read or connoted.

In her chapter on the Amazons, Grahn jumps around between continents and islands, between pre-history, ancient history, and her own personal history. As part of her project of claiming a transhistorical and international Gay culture, Grahn universalizes the mythic figure of the Amazon. Crossing boundaries of time and space, Grahn includes in the Amazonian model not only the well-known European Amazons who are the subject of Merck's essay, but Amazons from Africa, India, China, the Middle East, and the writers and activists of the "Jewish Lesbian Nation" in the contemporary United States. Grahn includes herself in the Amazonian tradition, putting this imaginative scholarship to good use by letting it give her the courage to fight off a rapist.[44]

Guilty of the egregious sin of essentialism (as well as other theoretical faults), Grahn's work is unfashionable in current postidentitarian lesbian and gay studies. Unlike Grahn's, most lesbian and gay scholarship now routinely relies on a Foucauldian anti-essentialist and social-constructionist model of homosexuality which denies its existence outside of the major cities of western Europe before the eighteenth century, and in the case of lesbianism, before the end of the nineteenth. Accordingly, Grahn's scholarship, because it attempts to be mythopoetically compelling by creating a heroic and universal culture out of material and cultural abjection, has been banished to the island where unfashionable gay culture goes, unread and uncited by other lesbian scholars.

In her effort to be all-inclusive, Grahn attempts not only to discuss the contributions of gay male as well as lesbian culture but to argue that gay traditions are not just ancient but continuous. They transform and are transformed but they do not really perish. Accordingly, the Libyan Amazons were not just warriors but wanderers, and where they traveled they founded cities. The Libyan queen, Myrina, took her army up through Egypt to build cities on the islands of Greece. One of these cities, Mytilene, on the island of Lesbos, became, "a few centuries later," the home of Sappho.[45] Thus, Grahn melds together the Amazon and the Sapphic traditions: the warrior/poet, mythic figure/historical actor, and places her in a city on an island. That the search for origins and a supportive cultural community via the link to a symbolic lesbian geography masks the "paradox of a desire sustained only by the impossibility of fulfilling it"[46] is clear from the story of Renee Vivien's disillusionment with her dream of relocating to Mytilene. Vivien left the modern city-island of the Parisian lesbian community of artists and intellectuals, in despair over its engulfment by the patriarchal surround, and sought liberation and authenticity in Mytilene, only to find that the ancient city-island was no lesbian utopia.[47]

THE ROMANTIC FRIENDSHIP MODEL AND ANTI-URBANISM IN AMERICAN LESBIAN WRITING

As synthetic and as anti-separatist as Grahn is, and as given to universalizing lesbian and gay culture, she virtually isolates the tradition of Romantic friendship, which has been extensively studied by Lillian Faderman since 1981, in her first book, *Surpassing the Love of Men: Romantic Friendship between Women from the Renaissance to the Present* and continued in *Odd Girls and Twilight Lovers: A History of Lesbian Life in Twentieth-Century America*, 1991. Though Grahn devotes a few pages to the spinster, she generally means by the term a working-class woman who does manual labour for a living and bonds with other single women in a celibate lesbian way.[48] Grahn's spinster has little in common with the sort of women Faderman studies.

Faderman's Romantic friendship model constitutes a bourgeois tradition of intense female friendship that can be traced back to Europe in the Renaissance and then to European settlements in the United States. In it, the lesbian or more properly proto-lesbian couple, such as the famous Ladies of Llangollen, constitute a metaphorical island and provide the safety and succor of a stable relationship in a woman-hating world.[49] Whether the romantic friends are in real or imagined retreat from the masculine culture of cities, this model tends to be if not expressly anti-urban, then suburban, and to hold out the garden as an intermediary, if small and enclosed, space between the masculinist city and the country. In both Europe and America, it flourished as a normal and even elevating expression of genteel femininity until the late nineteenth century, when it was thrown into disrepute by the work of Freud and the sexologists, who made passionate friendship visible but as sexual deviancy. According to Faderman, this model was revived and reappropriated by American lesbian-feminists of the 1970s.[50] Perhaps because of the different political allegiances of Faderman and Grahn, they have more or less politely isolated the other to an island of her own, failing, once again, to cite each other's claims.

Neither Grahn's nor Faderman's Amazonian and Romantic friendship models of lesbian culture provide much in the way of inspiration for younger contemporary American lesbian writers who are inspired more by the city than the suburban or rural retreat and want to throw off the prescriptions—aesthetic, sexual, and political—of lesbian-feminism, especially in its separatist phase of the 1970s. Let me underline the extent of the rift by showing how two feminist texts of 1984, one critical and one fictional, variously consider the city.

Women Writers and the City: Essays in Feminist Literary Criticism, edited by Susan Merrill Squier, is the first anthology to focus on the ways women writers have imagined the city. Although many of the writers studied are lesbians, the ways in which lesbianism complicates or contradicts the virtually exclusive focus on gender is not problematized by the editor or the other essayists. Though the editor, in her introduction, admits that women have reacted positively as well as negatively to urbanity, the attitude of the Continental, British, and "Canadian" writers examined, according to the critics in Squier's collection is overwhelmingly anti-urban.[51]

For critics in Squier's anthology, whose analyses are indebted to American cultural feminism, the city/country or city/suburb dichotomy is imagined in ways that recreate traditional symbolic gender codes and oppositions between nature and culture. Urbanity, like maleness, is thought of as aggressive, public, intellectual, dynamic, and violent. Women and anti-urbanity are thought of as peaceful, domestic, spiritual, static, and safe.[52] In Squier's collection, only two of the four critics on American women writers suggest that they imagined the city somewhat positively, as providing an opportunity for heterosexual women to escape patriarchal constraints by providing healing and nourishment through community, spirituality, and learning. Even so, and most significantly exemplifying the growing rift in the 1980s between lesbian writers, Wendy Martin's essay on Adrienne Rich connects a separatist tendency in her lesbian-feminist vision with her growing alienation from cities and her ultimate decision to flee from Manhattan. Martin observes that Rich envisions Manhattan

> as a metaphor for economic exploitation and moral pollution; her poems reflect her increasing alienation from the racism, sexism, patriarchal capitalism which are expressed in the violence, pornography, economic oppression that she feels are characteristic of life in American cities.[53]

Rich's lesbian separatism, so Martin claims, should be seen as a feminist version of the older American tradition, the Puritan vision of the countryside as the safe place where the pure and the saved may form a community of the elect.

SARAH SCHULMAN'S FICTION AND AMERICAN "URBAN RADICAL WOMEN"

In an interview given in 1990, Schulman said each of her novels has been written as "a response to the other gay literature of its time."[54] Because Schulman uses urban lesbian radicals to provoke rethinking of the binary insularity/universality, her writing needs to be seen as a response to the ruptures in the aesthetic as well as the sexual and racial politics of American feminism in the mid-1980s. That is, Schulman writes in opposition not just to the Reaganite neoconservatism which pursued a "scorched earth" policy of massive underfunding and malignant neglect toward the cities of the northeastern United States, but to the symbolically coded anti-urban cultural politics of cultural feminism and lesbian-feminism. Ironically echoing Reaganite sensibilities, cultural feminists tended to be suspicious of cities because they were infamous for fostering avant-garde intellectual and sexual practices.

Her first novels were published by small lesbian or feminist presses in Florida and Seattle, Naiad Press and Seal Press. But Schulman's cast of bohemian artists and her obvious love for New York City's mean streets seem ill assorted with Naiad and Seal's commitment to producing positive fictional images of lesbians within the ever popular format of the coming out story and the girl-meets-girl romance. While Schulman's novels unapologetically assumed that the reader would be lesbian and have some familiarity with the cultural politics of American radical feminism from the 1960s on, they shamelessly parodied that culture and its taste for trashy genre fictions such as the romances and detective stories which were and are her lesbian and feminist publishers' mainstay.

Schulman's first novel appeared when American lesbian culture was in transition or crisis over the sex debates. After the Barnard conference, the relationship between American feminists and lesbians underwent a complex fractioning over issues of representation, especially sexual representation. The fragile cultural consensus between cultural feminists, especially those of the lesbian separatist variety, and feminist postmodernists, many of whom, as Catherine Stimpson argued, were lesbian, fell apart.[55]

Though feminist, lesbian, and now queer theorists have told and retold the story of the debates over the cultural politics of representation, they have focused their analyses mainly on the sex debates and given far less attention to their imbrication with race, and very little to aesthetics. All the areas of conflict had existed since the late 1970s and had played themselves out in other splits between lesbians and heterosexual feminists and between white feminists and women of color within the American feminist movement, particularly among movement and academic intellectuals. Though the sex debates were, well, sexy, they were not really new in the schismatic world of American feminism. What may have been new was that a minority of feminist intellectuals, many of them lesbians, had become culturally unintelligible to the mainstream.

Stimpson's examples of the aesthetic preferences of feminist postmodernists that so challenged other feminists are illuminating for understanding the cultural context in which Schulman published her novels. According to Stimpson, who is trying to be sympathetic, "[t]o a member of the feminist cultural consensus, postmodernists liked really strange, far-out cultural events. They preferred Gertrude Stein to Charlotte Brontë, Mary Kelly to Georgia O'Keeffe."[56] While Schulman might be right when she claims that the sex radicals won the fight over representation, the consequences in terms of political alliances and sexual practices have been discussed far more than what happened in terms of shifts in reading and writing practices. Whether or not all the lesbian intellectuals in the sex radicals camp were committed postmodernists, the consequences for lesbian fiction were clearly these: The sex got rougher and the reading got tougher.

SCHULMAN'S GENRE TROUBLE: *THE SOPHIE HOROWITZ STORY*

Sarah Schulman's fiction is a deliberate and audacious rejection of the anti-urbanism and the separatism of older and more established American lesbian-feminists like Adrienne Rich. In the same year Squier published her anthology, Sarah Schulman published her first novel, *The Sophie Horowitz Story*. The first of her three sexually explicit comic urban noirish fictions, it suggests that the pleasures and dangers of loving women, especially in the politically repressive 1980s, are intimately linked to loving city-life and loving writing.

Sophie is a failure as a detective and as an investigative reporter. Though she eventually locates Germaine Covington, a long-time underground lesbian radical of the 1970s, no one wants to know about it. Sophie is threatened with jail, as well as deceived and manipulated by women she considers friends. Finally, her feminist editors refuse to run her story because it's politically incorrect and too long for their readers' short attention span. When the protagonist is asked if her life is exciting, Sophie replies: "Sometimes I think I'd stay home all day and cry if I wasn't working on a project."[57]

The projects that Sophie fantasizes about as having commercial potential, unlike the unsuccessful narrative that becomes this novel, are modes of lesbian culture that will become celebrated as hallmarks of lesbian postmodernism in the late 1980s and 1990s: the lesbian detective story;[58] lesbian pornography, which she foresees in 1984 will have a ready market;[59] and even the first lesbian situation comedy.[60] Her elderly neighbor, the prolific formula fiction writer Mrs. Noseworthy (a.k.a. King James), nonetheless suggests that Sophie could aim higher: "Would you rather transcend the interchangeable facts of daily existence and everyday events to capture and address the higher moral questions of human commitment, desire and ability?"[61] Although this challenge is posed with a measure of sarcasm, now that Schulman's career is well under way, it has become clear that her aim is to transcend the limits of lesbian formula fiction.

Sophie Horowitz, the anti-heroic heroine, is a young and struggling writer for the *Feminist News,* where she writes a column called "On the Right and Left," which makes enemies all over the political spectrum. Even the way she performs her ethnicity, marked by her name and her fondness for Jewish food and Yiddish expressions, makes it clear that she is a secular Jew who is not at home in mainstream American Judaism. Sophie is a cynic and an outsider to all the communities she passes through as she writes about them. While she says she has abandoned any search for roots because of Jewish orthodoxy's misogyny and homophobia, she also rejects cultural assimilation into the American mainstream. In one hilariously irreverent scene, Sophie and another Jewish lesbian, researching a story on the connection between women and orthodoxy, find their place in Judaism, making love behind the curtain that separates the sexes.

At the time Schulman published her first novel, she was at work at a second book, to be entitled *When We Were Very Young: Radical Jewish Women on the Lower Eastside 1879–1919,* for which she received a 1984–85 Fulbright award to study Jewish history in Brussels. Although this book was never published, an extract from it appeared in 1986 in *The Tribe of Dina: A Jewish Women's Anthology.*[62] The essay, like Schulman's novels themselves, is in the form of a walking tour whose purpose is to show contemporary feminist readers how radical Jewish women's political and cultural activities forged links across class, race, and ethnicity, as well as sexualities. This densely populated and polyglot neighborhood, with its tenements, settlement houses, cafes, theaters, factories, brothels, and markets, became a "form of female network, [and] thus provided the locus of the community,"[63] connecting prostitutes, trade unionists, garment workers, Yiddish writers, anarchists, socialists, suffragists, and members of a proletarian avant-garde.

In 1984, what lesbian journalist and sex radical Susie Bright has called the year of the "lustful lesbian,"[64] Schulman published her first novel with Naiad Press. The fit between author and publisher was imperfect. Schulman was unusually graphic and adept at writing about "politically incorrect" lesbian sex; Naiad, a publishing house specializing in producing Harlequin romances for a middlebrow lesbian audience, was well known for producing tepid "vanilla sex," as it was known at that time, in which the reader had to wade through the first hundred or so pages before getting to the "good parts," the sex scenes in which body parts and processes were vaguely and romantically encoded in terms of shells, waves, petals, and other natural things.

As if in illustration of Stimpson's claims in "Zero Degree Deviancy" about lesbian readers' demands that lesbian fiction wrap potentially challenging ideas in an easy reading format, Schulman, especially at first, seduced lesbian readers into *thinking* by writing engagingly about sex. The first paragraph of *The Sophie Horowitz Story* announces that the reader is in for all-girl action, with no slow romantic build-up leading immediately from coming out to couple-building, monogamy, and a house in the suburbs. These are sexually active dykes, out in all senses of the word, in the city, and strong enough to risk visibility as desiring subjects.[65]

IN A KITSCH STATE OF MIND: *GIRLS, VISIONS AND EVERYTHING*

In Sarah Schulman's second novel, *Girls, Visions and Everything,* her protagonist, Lila Futuransky, poses a question which haunts all thinking about lesbian literary history, but especially underscores how thin the tradition of American lesbian writing seemed even in the mid-1980s. "Lila often asked herself why she tried to write lesbian fiction when she never read any."[66] In point of fact, Schulman herself is a frequent reviewer of lesbian fiction for *Lambda Book Reports.* If one remembers Schulman's claim that she writes in response to the current state of gay literature, then it would seem that she thought of *Girls, Visions and Everything* as emerging from a lesbian void.

Lila, like all Schulman's heroines and like the author herself, who has supported herself as a waitress and typist, is an underpaid and underemployed office worker. Her "real job," however, is writing. In search of artistic models and community, Lila becomes part of the loosely knit lesbian community that creates plays and performance art at the East Village club, The Pyramid. The in-crowd calls the place "The Kitsch-Inn," because of its aesthetic, about which Lila has doubts. While there was a lesbian club of that name, Schulman's club also resembles the WOW Cafe, a tiny but very influential lesbian "community built around a theatre."[67]

Jill Dolan was the first to write about the aesthetic and political implications of the venue. By creating a lesbian spectatorial community, WOW seemed to offer almost utopian possibilities for subverting heterosexist representational codes. Although Teresa de Lauretis critiqued Dolan for conceiving of "the" lesbian spectator as a unified and non-contradictory subject for whom sexuality was the master category and other differences were occluded, by writing about WOW, word spread that these performers were playing an important part in developing audiences for a new and more theoretically sophisticated lesbian culture.

Linking the campy butch-femme dynamic operative in WOW performance to the "pro-sex" side in the sex wars, Dolan defended their highly controversial (at that time) usage as offering in the context of lesbian desire the potential for changing gender-coded structures of power.[68] Kate Davy made even stronger claims about how WOW's comic appropriations of popular culture were intended to be and were unreadable by heterosexual audiences.[69] In addition, in the new headnotes for the version of her essay "Toward a Butch-Femme Aesthetic" printed in *The Lesbian and Gay Studies Reader*, Case claims that these performances "escape the kinds of theoretical assimilation that currently make queerness welcome even as it erases the individual presence of gays, and particularly, lesbians."[70]

By contrast with the large claims of Dolan, Davy, and Case, Sarah Schulman's protagonist, Lila Futuransky, is far more cautious about and less impressed with the deliberately tacky aesthetic of The Kitsch-Inn. Lila, no stranger to rejection from lesbian publishers, nonetheless describes herself as a novice in the kitsch state of mind.[71] She doesn't quite fit in anywhere. Although this "dyke about town" claims she is not the marrying kind, she is also unlucky in love. The novel starts with her being stood up for her date with the flirtatious performer, Helen Hayes, who resembles controversial performance artist Holly Hughes. As a result, she finds herself getting involved in an on-again off-again relationship with a factory worker and costume designer named Emily Harrison. While Lila hopes that this time she can stick with things long enough so there will be a chance of having "girls, visions and everything," the only way she, a proletarian lesbian intellectual, can imagine her situation, real and fantasized, is in terms of Jack Kerouac's macho adventuring in *On the Road*.[72]

In the novel's central passage, Lila reflects about her double and contradictory vision of lesbians as victims and survivors, and speculates that cultural survival demands that they figure out how to make lesbians popular.

> Lila had often considered the question of marketing lesbian popularity. She looked at other groups of outcasts who had managed to make a name for themselves…After considering various historical examples, she concluded that the most successful model was that of the beats…The thing was, they had made a phenomenon of themselves. They made themselves into the fashion, each one quoting from the other, building an image based not so much on their work as on the idea that they led interesting lives. Lila firmly believed that was exactly what lesbians needed to do. Why not make heroes out of Isabel Schwartz and Helen Hayes, and make The Kitsch-Inn the new mecca? Let kids from all over America pack their bags, sneak out at night and flock to the East Village to hang out with the lesbians.[73]

The trajectory of *Girls, Visions and Everything* implies that lesbian coupling and domesticity is chosen by default in the absence of other larger creative possibilities. If you can't make good art, maybe you can stay home and make good sex. As is typical of Schulman's fiction, there is no happy ending. Lila eventually brings off the Worst Performance Festival at The Kitsch-Inn, and it is, predictably, very bad. In spite of its silliness, it gets good reviews. Unlike the lesbian critics cited above, Lila is dissatisfied with The Kitsch-Inn's narrow anti-aesthetic.[74] "Which was better, the sad truth or the fun deception?"[75] Her discontent seems consonant with theater critic Erika Munk's claims that performance art is "famously resistant to dealing with the outside world; its politics, when present at all, not only spring from autobiographical impulses but remain limited by them. Constricted themes, narrow skills, and inflated, needy egos plague this kind of theatre."[76]

In what seems to her the absence of an available and usable lesbian literary tradition, Lila falls back on reading and re-reading Jack Kerouac's *On the Road*. Believing that she shares Jack's mystical view of women, Lila nonetheless feels that Jack fails to tell her what to do with them once she has one, namely Emily. As she nears the end of the narrative, Lila wonders whether she too should take a trip or whether, being a woman, her trip is domestic and internal. She is growing older and perhaps it is time to grow up and settle down.[77] With this realization, she turns her book and her identification with Jack Kerouac over to her friend Isabel, another writer. Lila weeps as she rejects Isabel's version of the urban lesbian dream. "Lila, you can't stop walking the streets and trying to get under the city's skin because, if you settle in your own little hole, she'll change so fast that by the time up wake up, she won't be yours anymore...Don't do it buddy."[78]

TRAUMA, NOT RECOVERY: *AFTER DELORES*

If *Girls, Visions and Everything* is a downward trajectory ending in tears as coupling up takes the place of urban adventuring, then Schulman's next and, so far, most realized work of fiction takes her protagonist even further into despair. In *After Delores,* the streets are filled with junkies, gentrification is taking over the Lower East Side, and "the lesbian community" has dispersed.[79] There is no feminist or lesbian cultural center or hang-out comparable to the *Feminist News* or The Kitsch-Inn. From novel to novel, Schulman uses the island cityscape in increasingly self-conscious ways to suggest her protagonists' sense of being caught between the dominant culture and the circumscribed limits of an abject and seemingly pre-literary lesbian culture.

Of course, how Schulman uses the city as site of a lesbian literary quest can be read in different ways. In *The Safe Sea of Women: Lesbian Fiction 1969–1989*, critic Bonnie Zimmerman finds that by the third novel, both the size of Schulman's city and her fictional power has diminished. Having abandoned the outward movements of the picaresque hero, Schulman's protagonists have become preoccupied with inner questing, to the point of immobilizing despair.[80] Rather than applauding Schulman for her literary ambition in taking on a lesbian literary tradition, Zimmerman finds an imaginative decline in her oeuvre as it becomes more critical of the new lesbian subcultures emerging on the Lower East Side. Rejecting Schulman's trajectory into more and more self-consciously literary as well as cultural concerns, Zimmerman instead singles out for critical praise "the most notably original form of the lesbian novel to emerge in the late 1980s...the story of recovery from a traumatic experience..."[81]

But that is exactly the point of *After Delores:* The nameless, totally abject narrator, an alcoholic coffee-shop waitress, does not and cannot recover from her traumatic loss. Though it is precisely at an Alcoholics

Anonymous meeting that she makes the final connection that allows her to solve the mystery that appears to drive the plot of the novel, the narrator is as alienated by AA as she is everywhere else and thus has no wish to stop drinking. At a time when many segments of the American lesbian-feminist comunity were preoccupied with Twelve-step programs and recovery from all forms of addiction, including addiction to love and sex, and were reading lesbian detective stories that showed courageous amateur sleuths solving crimes and restoring justice, Schulman published her first novel with a mainstream press and parodied the vicarious satisfactions lesbian detective fiction offered readers.

Though the narrator successfully figures out who killed Punkette, a young go-go dancer, and kills her killer, the quest for knowledge and revenge is meaningless. The narrator's motives as well as her "victory" are deprived of all significance by the only person who knows about them. "You weren't going through all this to find some man. You are just a lonely person who had absolutely nothing better to do."[82]

Being nothing, "after Delores," the narrator, who describes herself as a reactive person, becomes fixated on the lives of those around her and re-triangulates the unhappy relationship Punkette had with Charlotte and Beatriz, an actress and director who are caught up in mind-games and brutal though thrilling sex. By contrast with all the other characters, Punkette is the only person in the novel who doesn't have a double identity, though her real name, Marianne Walker, is far more prosaic than the one the narrator gives her. Punkette, who is just five or six years younger than the narrator, belongs to a new generation of urban proletarian lesbians. The narrator meets her only once before Punkette is swiftly removed from the scene by death. Nonetheless, the narrator feels she is the "most real" character, because, "in the middle of sordid business, she still had faith in love."[83]

While in some ways the narrator resembles the typical hard-boiled avenger of detective fiction who is "played for a sucker" by a femme fatale in a deceitful game "which poses a threat to his [sic] very identity as a subject,"[84] she is so immobilized by melancholia that she hardly seems to have the detective's energy for honoring his debt. Having killed the cab driver who murdered Punkette, the narrator seems not to have restored order so much as to have lost her subjectivity entirely: "I wasn't even there. I was a floating sensation."[85]

There are no positive images of lesbians in this novel and no enabling escapes into the vital lesbian urban subculture Schulman had described in the two previous novels. In this, Schulman's first novel written for mainstream audiences, she does no special pleading for lesbians, and doesn't come through on the last novel's wish to make lesbians "popular." *After Delores* is no celebration of the glamor and romanticism of an outlaw lesbian culture that would be marketed by the popular press as "lesbian chic."

Though the novel relies less on one-liners, and the dialogue and monologues are written in longer spurts and in sometimes memorably poetic prose, the narrator, unlike Schulman's earlier heroines, is not a writer. Her head lives in the sixties, and she owns just one book, Patti Smith's poetry. "The only thing that happened in the last two decades that made any sense to me at all."[86] There is no lesbian culture to sustain the narrator. Though, like Schulman's other protagonists she is a hanger-on in the world of alternative lesbian theater, that world is presented as tawdry and unfulfilling. Her quest has provided her with no sense of belonging or meaning. There is only absence and alienation.

UNIVERSAL OR NARROW? *PEOPLE IN TROUBLE*

Sally Munt wanted to claim Sarah Schulman as a lesbian postmodernist, but acknowledged that Schulman's novel, *People in Trouble*,[87] is a puzzling regression into expressive realism of the morally earnest lesbian-feminist sort.[88] It has, however, some important twists. Not only is the novel a heavily didactic lesbian entry into the new category of AIDS fiction, its most developed character is a heterosexual male. Though the novel's setting is not so tightly focused on the Lower East Side as in her previous books, Schulman uses city locations perhaps even more effectively to connect social with sexual stratification in order to force rethinking of the binary universal/narrow.

As in the rest of her fiction, Schulman displays cynicism toward the 1980s imperative to couple up and nest. Her couples live in rather unhappy triangles. This time around, the triangle is composed of Peter and Kate, married yuppie East Village artists whose radical art is a substitute for radical politics, and Molly, a much younger lesbian who turns her marginal living as a ticket-taker in a cinema into involvement with an AIDS-activist group called Justice. Starting with an epigraph from Marx—"It is not the consciousness of men that determines their being, but their social being that determines their consciousness"— Schulman contextualizes the tawdry drama of Kate and Molly's affair as the novel's primary contradiction: "Here we are trying to have a run-of-the-mill illicit lesbian love affair," Molly said, "And all around us people are dying and asking for money."[89]

Schulman's focus on stratification within New York City is unusual. She does not stress the older patterns of racial and class segregation that have always effectively separated the city's white elite from the much larger darker-skinned underclass. Schulman emphasizes neighborhoods like the Lower East Side that until recently have been a mosaic of ethnic, artistic, and political minorities, but are increasingly being gentrified by privileged whites returning to the city from suburban areas.

In novel after novel, characters remark on the loathesome spread of gentrification in artsy areas of lower Manhattan, particularly Soho and Tribeca. Here the chief villain is Ronald Horne, a real estate mogul modeled after Donald Trump, who has a fiendishly clever idea of targeting and then expropriating apartments inhabited by gay men and people of color who develop the AIDS virus. Homophobia and gentrification will team up to bring about the destruction of Manhattan's gay and Black ghettos. So, rather than separation, the pattern that interests Schulman most in *People in Trouble* is overlap or layering. Molly is far more troubled than Peter or Kate by the knowledge that "New York is a death camp for thousands of people, but they don't have to be contained for us to avoid them. The same streets I have fun on are someone else's hell."[90]

While none of the three members of the triangle is in a so-called "high-risk" group, Schulman has chosen the configuration to represent different degrees of vulnerability to the crisis. One's social standpoint, which seems more or less the same as identity, seems to determine identifications, though some movement seems possible. As a white heterosexual male, Peter sees himself as a member of the "general population," rather than as one of the "people in trouble." His wife occupies a liminal space, and Molly, as a lesbian, is simultaneously at lowest risk personally and the most caught up with the survival of "her people." Molly's is the vanguard position because, according to Schulman, who in the Loewenstein interview sounds in this regard very much like an old-style lesbian-feminist, her oppression conveys an epistemological and moral advantage.[91]

As Schulman admits, this is less a novel about AIDS than about the connection between social neglect and homophobia.[92] One of her characters remarks, echoing Schulman's own sentiments, that apart from survivor accounts and journalism, all AIDS novels are unsatisfactory. In trying to write about AIDS, Schulman continues her practice of attempting to push the boundaries of lesbian literature by responding to what is missing in the fiction being written by her contemporaries.

While she may have been the first "out" lesbian novelist to write about AIDS, that is less interesting than the fact that she writes as a lesbian intellectual who is unimpressed with aesthetic responses to the crisis.

Like some lesbian and gay theorists who have considered the ways in which both homosexuality and AIDS constitute challenges to the very notions of representation and intelligibility, Schulman is aware that fiction as a form is rendered insignificant by the enormity of the AIDS epidemic.[93] She is, however, less urgently concerned with the formal and epistemological issues AIDS has created for artists than with the need for collective political action. James, a gay activist working for Justice, has researched the literature of disaster and found it wanting: "The challenge is to turn it from an overwhelming personal void into a group effort, to try to help others avoid the same fate."[94]

Rather than a novel about AIDS, then, Schulman has written a novel about AIDS activism, from the point of view of an activist artist, that suggests how much art and artists fail people in trouble. Not only is homophobia a less difficult subject to depict than AIDS itself, but Peter's complacent sense of safety and entitlement as a heterosexual male artist offers satiric possibilities for an essentially comic novelist like Schulman. When he finally meets Molly, he informs her that he has a problem with her "separatism," with her wanting to "run-around in gay-this and gay-that." His more "universal" view is that men too are people and people are all the same.[95]

If Peter provides an easy target for Schulman's satire, his wife Kate is depicted even more caustically. Schulman seems unimpressed by recent theoretical claims about proliferating sexualities, and in particular with the epistemological and political possibilities of bisexuality, if that is an accurate description of Kate's perspective. Kate is not so much bisexual as she is *not* lesbian. In spite of the hot sex she enjoys with Molly and her closeness to gay men dying of AIDS, Kate's beliefs about lesbians are identical with Peter's. Lesbians are narrow, live in ghettos, hate men, and aren't sufficiently intellectual enough to be artists. Agitated by a conversation with Molly's ex-lover Pearl, Kate denies she is gay because she likes men: "I want to be universal."[96] To validate her position, she calls her dealer, and asks whether he thinks of her as a lesbian: "Absolutely not...You're an artist. You need a wide range of perverse experiences."[97] Fired up with perverse experiences, Kate begins to cross-dress and to take her art in a more obviously political direction. Dumped by Molly, who decides she'd rather be loved by one of her own people, Kate achieves the universality she craves. Quite unintentionally, her artwork brings about the death by "flaming collage" of a real estate baron. As a result, Kate's installation, "People in Trouble," makes her famous in the art world. She is invited all over the world to start fires.

Molly, by contrast, remains poor and obscure, but because she is still capable of responding to the beauty of the city, she tries to "remember the truth and not just the stories."[98] That Schulman makes the distinction and that she prefers the former makes it hard to read this novel as an example of lesbian postmodernism. As does the preachy ending, which hammers home the point about the limitations of art, storytelling, and even speech. Though like all Schulman's heroines, Molly ends up a single lesbian, she is far from alone. Molly joins the demonstrators.[99]

EMPATHY: A PSYCHODRAMA WITH POLITICAL IMPLICATIONS

Schulman does, however, keep working the edge, attempting to produce a politically engaged but nonprogrammatic lesbian fiction in the face of the twin absences in contemporary American lesbian cultural politics of a vital progressive movement and of an available literary tradition. In *Empathy,* her latest and most ambitious novel, Schulman stretches the genre conventions of the lesbian romance and detective fiction to work with and against Freudian and popular narratives about the origins and meaning of lesbian desire.

Empathy is hysterical text about hysterics. Two of its three main characters are Anna O. and Dora, Freud's most famous hysterics, the first of whom formulated what became his "talking cure" and the second of whom became a feminist heroine for a later generation of feminist psychoanalytic critics. Hysterics, too, are people in trouble; they suffer from reminiscences as well as from excessive "virile" identifications they do not consciously understand.

The novel's epigraph comes from a passage of Freud's "A Case of Homosexuality in a Woman," in which he traces the "masculine" intellectuality of lesbians to a determination to spite their fathers. Accordingly, lesbians and lesbian desire are only intelligible, in the Freudian narrative, in relation to men, specifically to patriarchs. The "masculine" intellectuality of the adult lesbian is the symbolic attainment of her childish wish to have her father's child. The lesbian who seems to be a man actually hates men or vice versa; she cannot be a woman who loves women. She is not central to or even in her own narrative, though in her unhappiness she disturbs the (heterosexual) narrative with which she must engage because it is the only one available.

Empathy is a psychodrama with political implications, the discourse and narrative of hysteric, whose "emotional crises [are] accompanied by theatricality."[100] As in the psychoanalytic understanding of hysteria, Anna seeks to be understood by the attempt to construct an intelligible (lesbian) narrative out of "private theater."[101] The exterior playmaking and theatrical setting figuring so importantly in Schulman's previous novels are replaced here by interior monologues, imaginary dialogues, and scenes from plays.

The most important events in *Empathy* take place in the split psyche of the main character, Anna O., a lesbian whose alter ego is masculine, the post-Freudian "street corner" psychiatrist, Doc. Anna and Doc, both of whom are out of touch with American pop culture, have been involved in a triangular relationship with the cruel and beautiful "woman in white leather," who, like America herself is "equally self-centered and malleable."[102] Anna and Doc seem somewhat more comfortable with modernist culture and structuralist theories than they do with postmodernist artifacts like *People* magazine, Pop-tarts, and the recovery movement.

Like Schulman's other protagonists, Anna is a Jewish lesbian office worker living on the Lower East Side. Like the others, too, she lives in abjection. Alienated by homophobia from her parents, who are both psychoanalysts, and shattered by the breakup of an affair with the unnamed but Madonna-like "woman in white leather," who denies that she is a lesbian, Anna engages in imaginary consultations with Doc. Her objective is to validate her existence and restore her self-esteem by being allowed to visit her ex-lover's mother, a recognition that lesbians in real life rarely attain.

As in other Schulman novels, the protagonist is a lesbian who is attracted to women who want to be straight or bisexual. Their ambitious transgression on the rights of heterosexual men to have exclusive and unlimited access to straight women makes the affairs difficult and short-lived and hence provides a way of avoiding containment within the lesbian romance plot. Because these "femmey" women refuse to identify as lesbians, they mark the more butch or masculine lesbian who loves them as the genuine deviant, and their remonstrations against her take the form of rejecting the narrowness of lesbian life for the universality of heterosexuality.

In one hallucinatory encounter the woman in white leather tells Anna that she realized she's not a lesbian anymore because women can't be heroes or have fun together.[103] The "realizations" are linked together by the absence of a culturally intelligible lesbian narrative that makes lesbians and lesbian desire thinkable. In the everyday, as well as a psychoanalytic sense of the word, what is missing is empathy.

Schulman employs the concept in several different and sometimes confusing ways. Sometimes in this novel, as well as in everyday usage, "empathy" is used interchangeably with "sympathy," the experience of sharing the same feeling with another person.[104] The two words, however, point in different directions, empathy toward a recognition of the otherness of the other and sympathy toward similarity based on shared feelings. Not only does the ex-lover fail to have empathy with Anna in the self-psychology sense of listening to her in order to gain access to the inner world of another human being recognized as an other; she also refuses to empathize with her in the more orthodox Freudian sense of identifying with her as a lesbian.[105] If identification produces subjectivity, then the woman in white leather refuses to constitute herself as a lesbian subject and dismisses Anna as narrow for doing so. According to the woman in white leather, lesbians can't be heroic or have fun because lesbian desire is unimaginable:

> "Fun…is when you get what you've always imagined. When you've always known what you want and then you get it. With a woman you can't have this because you've never imagined what you've wanted. There's no gratification. No gratification at all."
> "This is so brutal," Anna said. "Why is this happening to me?"
> "Don't give up so easily. You're too weak."
> "There's something very important that I don't understand. How can I be a woman and still be happy?"
> "Shut up," the woman said. "Don't tell me what to do."[106]

Doc, who more than anything hates interruptions and thinks of failures to listen as almost capital moral offenses, has also been silenced by the woman in white leather. After listening to Anna, Doc recognizes that she too suffers from empathy. She believes in good and evil and, like the narrator of *People in Trouble,* she feels socially responsible.

In a less insistent but perhaps more successful way than in *People in Trouble,* the inner world is constructed as a subset of the outer one. Homophobia and American imperialism both are failures of empathy. The lack of empathy as a centrifugal identification that characterizes homophobia is connected to the larger denial of social and political responsibility or centripetal identification that led, on January 16, 1991, to American involvement in and glorification of the Gulf War.[107] Just as the AIDS crisis complicates Molly and Kate's affair in *People in Trouble*, the Gulf War queers the happy ending of this novel.

In the final confrontation scene between Anna and the woman in white leather, Freud's inability to understand lesbian sexuality except by way of its relation to men and specifically to male homosexuality, is problematized as a failure in empathy that Anna has tried to make up for by being Doc. When her ex-lover demands to know why Anna is dressed "as a man," as Doc, she replies that it is because otherwise she can't get "sympathy," or rather "empathy." Lesbians can only be understood as man haters or imitation men:

> I was trying to prove that I was not something that could actually never exist...The end result was that I, Anna O., could not exist. I was nothing. I only existed relationally. I only existed in relation to men. I'm sick of being a reflection. How many times do I have to come out? And do I always have to do it anecdotally? When it's not a story, but a constant clash of systems.[108]

The woman in white leather remains unimpressed with Anna, who has still not managed to be perceived as heroic or fun. Like some queer theorists who believe that they have made the leap into a condition beyond identity, the ex-lover complains that Anna is obsessed with her homosexuality. Doc interjects, "What about yours?" The question sets off a virtual reprise of the original hallucinatory quarrel that started the novel. "That's why you left me...because I wasn't a big enough *dyke*." "No," Doc answers for Anna, "I left you because you don't listen."[109] For the woman in white, as for other narcissistic clients of the Doc's, this remark insinuates the ultimate transgression, that Anna might compare herself with her, that is, hint at or even imagine an empathic relationship between them, which could in turn have moral and political implications. Schulman imagines two outcomes for the confrontation: In the more dramatic, Doc shoots the woman in white leather; in the other, the final lack of empathy (in the sense of a capacity to imagine the non-relational existence of lesbians) is verbalized in the seemingly nonsensical dialogue between Doc/Anna and the woman in white leather which ends their ontological entanglement. Not comprehending Doc's statement that he hasn't been himself lately, the woman asks, "Why, because you've been alone?" "No," he answers, "because I've been without you."[110]

With the woman in white leather out of the way, and Doc no longer needed, Anna is free in a sense to exist as a lesbian and to find love with Dora, who not only listens to her but desires her as a woman. But Schulman's notion of empathy won't allow her to let the story end happily as a lesbian romance between Freud's most famous hysterics. She can't resist didacticism and she can't let her readers or Anna forget the political world.

In finding Dora, Anna finds not only love but a new understanding of morality, politics, and subjectivity. She integrates her selves, her split psyche, by becoming a multiplicity. Some of those worlds are real and relate to the changed global political context brought about by the Gulf War. Some are real but smaller and are based in the unresolved past of Anna's homophobic family. And others are purely fantasies. Accordingly, Anna is depicted in the final dramatic intertext about her family's Passover seder as still struggling against their homophobia, but being somewhat more articulate at providing an alternative account of her lesbianism to her father: "Despite what Freud says, the reason I am a lesbian is not because of wanting to hurt you. It's not about you in any way. I really love you, Pop, and I'm a lot like you and being a lesbian is about me. Okay?"[111] Like the woman in white leather, her analyst father's hearing is selective: "I'm glad to hear that you love me. Sometimes I'm not too sure."[112] If the scene with her family is another piece of "private theatre," so too is the discovery of Dora finally revealed as a similar device, in this case, a cinematic fantasy. The last sentences in the novel resemble those of Schulman's earlier novels which resist the closure and the enclosure of lesbian romance: "Anna came out of the movie and found it had rained. The sidewalk was wet."[113]

CONCLUSION

In her last two novels, with their epigraphs and reworkings of Freud and Marx, Schulman has clearly announced the scope of her literary ambitions. Having parodied or escaped the formal constraints of lesbian genre fiction, as well as many of the conventions of lesbian romanticism and realism, Schulman seems to be taking the American lesbian novel in a new and more self-consciously literary direction. Those who have followed Schulman's development so far, however, not only disagree about whether she has become a better writer; they also disagree about whether she is to be thought of primarily as a lesbian or as a universal writer.

What might seem to push her work in the direction of universality is a superficial reading of the new prominence male characters and concerns seem to have in her fiction, such as her decision to include a heterosexual but not entirely villainous male like Peter as the most developed character in *People in Trouble,* and her affectionate if not idealized portrayal of a primarily gay male activist group modeled on ACT UP. Even more obvious is the fact that the most sympathetic character in *Empathy* is Doc, the "man" within Anna O. Schulman, however, is not making her writing more universal by writing about men, but pushing the possibilities of lesbian fiction by putting lesbians and men together in the same fictional space, something that the previous generation of lesbian-feminists writers who were primarily engaged in demonstrating that enabling escapes from heterosexuality were indeed possible, had no reason to be interested in. Schulman provokes readers, especially non-lesbians, to rethink the binary universal/narrow (heterosexual male/lesbian), by having these two kinds of characters, one the unmarked norm and the other the marked yet invisible minority, interact. This amounts not so much to a rejection of lesbian insularity, to what Peter calls Molly's separatism, but an undermining of his pathetic claims to universality.

Similarly, care needs to be taken in drawing universalizing conclusions about the meaning of changes in Schulman's writing about sex. Admittedly, since Schulman began to publish with E.P. Dutton, her writing no longer seems so "limited" by exclusively lesbian subcultural concerns, such as the freeing up of ways of writing about sex in the aftermath of the sex wars. But this way of looking at Schulman tends to use the observation that she is writing less frequently about the physical details of lesbian sex acts to support the conclusion that she is less of a lesbian and more of a universal writer. Schulman dismisses such "praise" as homophobia: "Reviews that I now get say things like 'This isn't a gay book, this is a universal book.' That's called a good review; because if it was a gay book, there'd be something wrong with it."[114] This line of thinking ignores developments in lesbian writing such as the much greater availability of lesbian porn, which in turn owes something to Schulman's earlier accomplishments themselves, and places the emphasis on "larger" cultural issues such as the often heard claim that as fiction becomes postmodern, distinctions between elite and popular art become blurred to the point of erasure.

Seeking cultural legitimacy for Schulman's fiction by claiming her as a lesbian postmodernist runs the risk of normalizing her writing by lending it the prestige of the virtually universal discourse of postmodernity, whose nature is itself notoriously impossible to pin down. So, for example, in Sally Munt's essay, "'Somewhere over the rainbow…': Postmodernism and the Fiction of Sarah Schulman," various leading but sometimes contradictory indicators of "postmodernism" become the arbiter, the alternative master narrative, by which Schulman's writing is to be judged. Though Munt provides a sympathetic reading of Schulman, her attempt to bring her work under the umbrella of postmodernism is not persuasive, not only because her argument is circular (she assumes what she sets out to prove), but because she admits that the evidence of the later novels suggests that a postmodern analysis fails to do justice to her writing.[115]

Based on shifts in her novels away from parody and the ever-increasing skepticism about avant-garde art and performance as substitutes for politics, as well as the explicit and caustic comment by the narrator in *Empathy* that "Marxism had been replaced by postmodernism,"[116] it seems that Schulman's relationship with postmodern aesthetics is ambivalent to say the least. The relationship between lesbianism and postmodernism can no more be celebrated without anxiety and skepticism than can the earlier marriages of convenience between feminism and Marxism or feminism and postmodernism.

Moreover, recent cultural history tends to repeat itself in this case too. If Joan Nestle is right in claiming that lesbian-feminism was a butch-femme relationship in which feminism was the respectable partner who cleaned up the other's act,[117] then lesbian postmodernism might seem to offer the same de-deviantizing cultural authority. Valuing Schulman's accomplishments only to the degree that her work seems to take the postmodern turn implies that her writing has no significant lesbian prehistory of its own and no claims on readers' interests except insofar as it can be shown to resemble the increasingly canonical works of postmodern fiction's male exemplars. As I have argued here, Schulman's fiction is not so easily or so profitably contained within newly and ironically universalizing narratives of "lesbian postmodernism," but is better addressed as a critical engagement with notions of lesbian insularity, in particular the struggle to find literary predecessors in the Sappho model which could enable a non-separatist but anti-assimilationist contemporary American lesbian writing.

CHAPTER 6

QUE(E)RYING PEDAGOGY:
TEACHING THE UN/POPULAR CULTURES

> *"We have all the answers,"* Dostoevsky said, *"it is the questions we do not know."*
> —Qtd. by Shoshana Felman and Dori Laub, *Testimony: Crises of Witnessing in Literature, Psychoanalysis, and History*

If institutionalization is the answer for lesbian and gay studies in North American universities, what is the question? If, broadly speaking, the pedagogical concerns of the older scholarship seem framed by defusing homophobia[1] and increasing tolerance and visibility for sexual minorities, how does the newer antihumanist, feminist, and poststructuralist theorizing of, by, and about lesbian and gay cultures reflect an awareness of the need to que(e)ry pedagogy? My tentative and personally guilty answer is: so far, not very much.

Working within and against the discipline of education, Mary Bryson and Suzanne de Castell have, however, thrown down the gauntlet to everyone who claims to teach queerly. They are issuing a challenge to scholars to show that a queer pedagogy is "still" possible, observing parenthetically that, in the canonical *The Lesbian and Gay Studies Reader*, in "666 pages and 42 chapters spanning a wide range of intellectual domains, [there is] not a single entry that deals explicitly with the educational implications or applications of these new discourses."[2] The argument of this chapter is positioned at an oblique, psychoanalytic angle from theirs, and my conclusion might appear to be only slightly less pessimistic, but my reasons for reaching it are rather different. Where we come into greater alignment is in my contention that the rush to get institutionalized will only postpone the question of what the best lesbian and gay studies scholarship puts into question.

The few scholars who have broached these issues as questions rather than answers realize that if lesbian and gay studies does what some queer theorists say it could do—question and interrupt the operation and reproduction of heteronormativity and other normalizing/pathologizing discourses—then the traditional humanist project of schooling and its entire pedagogical agenda is dead. As a result, the pedagogical stakes of que(e)rying pedagogy are high, not just for conservatives, but for those on the other end of the political spectrum who have deep investments in the liberatory possibilities of reform studies such as women's studies, cultural studies, and other minority studies. Que(e)rying pedagogy, even and especially in those areas, according to educational theorist Deborah Britzman, means

> thinking differently about what discourses of difference, choice, and visibility mean in classrooms and in our own education, as well as thinking about structures of disavowal within education, or the refusals—whether curricular, social, or pedagogical—to engage a traumatic perception that produces difference as a disruption, as an outside to normalcy.[3]

In Michael Warner's often cited review article of the complex relationship of queer theory to feminism, postmodernism, psychoanalysis, cultural studies, and most of all lesbian and gay studies, "From Queer to Eternity: An Army of Theorists Cannot Fail," one particularly insightful comment about the relationship between queer theory and pedagogy has been overlooked. Though Warner proceeds deconstructively in his analysis generally—and correctly, in my opinion—refusing to define queer theory in conventional academic terms as a field, a disipline, a subject matter, a canon, a methodology, or a set of theoretical subjects presumed to know, he does admit that queer theory is "a way of teaching culture."[4] I want to ask, in more than a superficial procedural sense, "How?"

I teach women's studies and lesbian studies courses in the largest women's studies program in what's rumored to be the most politically progressive university in Canada. Faculty at my large urban university front radical magazines, go to all the right, that is, *left* demonstrations, and there are so many socialist feminists that we used to have monthly dinners until the group got so large we couldn't find a restaurant big enough to seat us all. The student body is the most multiethnic in the country, and groups and coalitions of people of color, feminists, gays, lesbians, and bisexuals, and other minorities are vocal and visible. Nonetheless, based on my teaching experiences and research about the extent of homophobia in women's studies classes,[5] my sense is that my university is as predictably homophobic as other otherwise progressive North American university environments. Until very recently, most of the numerous lesbian and gay faculty have been too scared to come out and there have been no explicitly labeled gay and lesbian studies courses; in the spring of 1994, however, students occupied the president's office and demanded an end to homophobia on campus and the introduction of a gay and lesbian studies program.

I mention these banal facts of my cultural geography because institutional setting plays a crucial but unattended and surprisingly reductionist role in lesbian and gay studies literature in constructing the horizon of expectations about its pedagogical possibilities. While a reader of the literature may deduce that disciplinary, discursive, and political considerations, for example investments or disinvestments in feminism, anti-racism, poststructuralism, and a reform studies model, factor strongly in how the field is being constructed, questions have yet to be asked about what we hope to learn and teach differently (and better) if or when institutionalization comes.

Instead of asking questions about how theoretical developments and controversies such as the one over universalizing or minoritizing approaches might inform and affect pedagogical practices, most contributors to the literature so far have fixated on giving answers about whether or not to institutionalize. The assumption seems to be that if only we had the right institutional configuration, whether it's the more modest notion of adding a course to an established curriculum or the more grandiose dream of free-standing, degree-granting programs, we could get beyond homophobia and the way would be clear to do the interesting theoretical work. This focus on institutionalization postpones and displaces questions about what we want lesbian and gay studies to do and whether the field, if it is a field, should be framed as a discourse about minorities designed to promote tolerance and understanding in the general public or as a discourse that unsettles everyone's assumptions about those very categories and who or what is implicated in them.

If institutionalization is the solution, what is the problem? According to most accounts, on the east and west coasts of the United States, in the elite and therefore best progressive schools, liberal attitudes to sexual minorities prevail, lesbian and gay studies are being institutionalized by the best and the brightest theorists, and everything is groovy. Everywhere else, that is, in the cultural hinterlands where many of us are doing this work, homophobia prevails, and theories and practices are a generation or so out of date. If you're not lucky enough to be at Santa Cruz or Princeton, then opportunities for anti-homophobic education seem limited. "They" are the theoretical vanguard and "we" are the foot soldiers slogging behind them, trying to catch up. It seems that our pedagogical situations are reversed, however, with the ones that the strategists imagined for the military avant-garde. They were "the special troops who advanced before the main body of the army into enemy lines, serving as shock troops to disrupt the enemy's forces, and, usually with great loss to themselves, insuring the success of those who followed."[6]

This fantasy, a form of California dreamin', like the one of the queer theorist I related earlier whose Radical Think Tank in the Pacific Northwest solved the problem of canonicity,[7] overlooks the work that pedagogy does. It also plays down the possibilities that antihomophobic transformation might occur without benefit of free-standing gay and lesbian studies programs, prestigious centers, and the presence of theoretical superstars who teach to the converted. It overlooks the quietly subversive work that a generation of students and teachers have accomplished by raising impertinent questions in the classroom, by slyly getting texts and essay topics on the syllabus, and humbly learning from their theoretical and pedagogical disasters how to teach and learn about gay and lesbian issues.[8] The fantasy that looks only toward benign institutional change from the top down and intellectual legitimation by a theoretical vanguard overlooks the cognitive and political shifts that can occur in everyday though highly charged encounters between students and teachers, and in seemingly unlikely institutional settings, such as composition classes taught by straight teaching assistants at Indiana University.[9]

First things first. Even in progressive institutions and where conditions for doing theory are somewhat favorable, homophobia rules the classroom and instructors must expect to encounter it. When I talk about gay and lesbian issues in my women's and gender studies classes, I'm likely to be met with walkouts or uncomfortable silences, occasional boos and hisses, and questions on the order of the one Sarah Schulman's lesbian speaker has to field in *The Sophie Horowitz Story:*

"Do you do it with animals?"[10] As much as I love animals, I'd prefer not to engage with the usual homophobic ignorance and install myself in the pedagogical fantasy I call "Beyond Antihomophobia 101." There, my students ask questions a little bit more like the ones I read in the literature about the disciplining of gay and lesbian studies, like the ones Ed Cohen poses:

> If we accept the assessment that this genealogical coincidence between "sexuality" and "identity" is the effect of a "modern" Western regime of power which implicates human bodies in and as the sites of its discursive (re)production, then how are we to understand the consequences of a politics that grounds itself in/on a "sexual identity"? Or, in other words, to the extent that "sexuality" and "identity" are both predicated upon a constellation of power relations that naturalize their own historical contingency by making themselves knowable as fixed qualities of somatic differentiation, what limitations do the political articulations of "sexual identity" unwittingly import?[11]

How do I get there from here? In my pedagogical fantasy, there's no name-calling or stoney silences and students don't giggle, cover their eyes, or walk out when I show films about lesbians and gays. They've got a language to talk about sexuality, they're not afraid to display an interest by showing up for the lecture on lesbian love poetry or Jeffrey Weeks in about the same numbers as the ones on other subjects. They don't normalize heterosexuality and pathologize everything else, and the English majors talk about gay and lesbian texts in our small discussion groups in the same detached and critically informed way they consider the other material on the syllabus. Right. Ed Cohen, Michael Warner, et al.—will you please tell me, as I await (and even work for) the coming of a fully funded, free-standing gay and lesbian studies program, how to get myself and my students beyond Antihomophobia 101?

The routine traumas I experience when I teach gay and lesbian subject matter in my progressive institution make the fantasy very attractive. The uneven developments which obtain between the sophistication of poststructuralist queer theory and the crude, rude, and raw realities of my classrooms make me envious and frustrated. Because I haven't been able to teach gay and lesbian studies without "the unleashing of unpopular things,"[12] I am compelled to theorize about my own failures and to speculate about what I've read or heard about those of others. This chapter attempts to bring questions of theory and practice together by doing a symptomatic reading of scenes of pedagogical failure taken from accounts of teaching gay and lesbian material. My intent is not to praise or blame teachers or students. I don't think that queer pedagogy is difficult or maybe even impossible because teachers are bad or students are homophobic. My concern is to uncover the cognitive work that needs to be done and can be done to get beyond Antihomophobia 101 with or without benefit of institutionalization.

Though there are many contenders in this category, Richard Mohr's rebarbative yet acutely observant and personally unsparing account of his first experience, in 1981, of teaching a gay issues course within the philosophy department at the University of Illinois is the most disturbing one in the literature. Entitled "Gay Studies in the Big Ten: A Survivor's Manual," it's not entirely clear who or what survived this trauma or what, if anything, Mohr learned from the experience or did differently in his many subsequent offerings of gay studies courses.[13]

Mohr's account makes for uncomfortable reading because it is framed by his profoundly cynical attitudes to American post-secondary education, especially to the hope that reform studies might inspire political transformation. If my discussion of his discussion seems scathing, I would stress that Mohr's preferred pedagogical persona is that of the curmudgeon, not a gay Mr. Chips. One of my favorite essays by him, "The Ethics of Students and the Teaching of Ethics: A Lecturing," begins, "I hate students. They are not the death of spirit, they are its malaria."[14] Unlike most contributors to gay and lesbian studies, Mohr rejects the more optimistic views of students' capacities for learning that are generally favored by feminist and other progressive pedagogies. No Paolo Freire he, both Mohr and his class come off rather badly. Unlike much of the writing in this genre, there is no note of triumph or self-congratulation, and although in a coda he mentions that as a result of his course, one "uptight suburban" woman set up a support group for gay runaways, he seems quite surprised by this development. There are none of the usual paeans to students who took risks and struggled to unlearn their homophobia.[15]

Based on his own self-presentation, Mohr appears to be an incompetent and insensitive teacher and his students are dim-witted homophobes. He runs a teacher-centered classroom, engages in pseudo-Socratic dialogue with students—a class of people he despises—and regards the university neither as a knowledge factory nor a consciousness-raising group, but as a four-year long cotillion designed primarily to marry off the white middle-class to each other.[16] Mohr's cynical yet unfashionable theoretical and pedagogical beliefs make it easier to read his account against the grain, so that the pedagogical chaos he describes can be instructive and provocative rather than merely sympathized with, as in other accounts of homophobia in the classroom.

Mohr's class could be read as a guide of what not to do, but because he doesn't explicitly reflect on the theoretical understandings that guide his pedagogical practices, he doesn't state how he connects his theories about sexual and other identities—they're fixed, very fixed—with the process of knowledge production. In a short intersession class composed, according to his remarkable categories, of 1/3 white suburban females, 1/3 black football players, and less than 1/3 gay students (one was lesbian; none of the gays were racially identified), he managed to offend and alienate everyone.

In his first class, Mohr showed a documentary film which he thought would get the work of consciousness-raising over with. He opened discussion by asking what in the film had made anyone uncomfortable, therefore guaranteeing that homophobic responses would not only be produced, but that they would frame the discussion, and in many ways the entire course.[17] The straight women said it made them sick. In trying to defend gay rights by making an analogy with the Black civil rights struggle, he unleashed a wave of crude homophobic slurs and then nearly incited a race riot. The first day ended with "everyone yelling and the class...on the verge of out-of-control."[18] In his "most successful class" at the end of the course, he asked insulting questions of an invited lesbian separatist academic, who told him to "fuck off" because he was "too stupid to understand," which led the whole class to break into spontaneous applause.[19]

Though much of what characterized this class, such as the teacher's puzzled and disappointed expectation that most of the class would be gay and literate about gay cultures, and the disastrous and almost violent response to the first showing of a film, are routine occurrences in accounts of lesbian and gay studies, Mohr, also typically, was unprepared for what transpired. His account of this historic class from hell ends with a flat and sardonic citation of his "triumph" over his cultural geography: "And so gay studies came to this sleepy Republican university in a little Republican town in the tired Republican state of Illinois."[20]

Sometimes, more by virtue of what didn't take place or failed to happen, even an account like Mohr's can suggest how to carry out a theoretical practice that would get beyond the normalizing and pathologizing pedagogies framed by homophobia. These accounts show how teachers, given a forced opportunity to learn from classroom debacles, might rethink their pedagogical practices. They could make them more consistent not only with general poststructuralist claims about the liberatory possibilities of unfixing identities and increasing identifications, but also engage more specifically with persuasive and powerful critiques of the ways heteronormativity constricts everyone's capacity to learn.

In the growing genre of writing about the disciplining of gay and lesbian studies, most of the literature, even *Tilting the Tower: Lesbians Teaching Queer Subjects*, edited by Linda Garber,[21] consists of experiential narratives about how lesbians and gays survive as teachers and students. Equally popular are "how to" accounts of setting up activist groups and coalitions, centers, workshops, and courses, such as are collected in the Gay and Lesbian Studies Issue of *The Journal of Homosexuality*, edited by Henry L. Minton.[22] These descriptions and prescriptions are mainly tales of individual and institutional heroism or villainy.

Unhappy stories of education outnumber the happy stories in this only seemingly new outpost of the educational literature, which actually goes back at least as far as Plato's "Apology." The assumption underlying and impelling this recent writing is that if only we could get the right institutional setting (it must exist somewhere, probably in California, in or around San Francisco), the right teachers (gay and out) and the right students (ditto), and the right curriculum (theoretically and politically correct), then the hopes that gay and lesbian studies evoke, as have all the other older but not so groovy reform disciplines, will be realized. It's sometimes hard to believe that Michael Warner's subtitle—"An Army of Theorists Cannot Fail"—is entirely ironic.[23] This chapter rereads unhappy stories about teaching gay and lesbian studies to question the logic underlying these assumptions and to suggest that what is routinely ignored in them (along with serious discussion of the political climate in which we teach) is the process by which knowledge is produced, or pedagogy itself.

Not surprisingly, given this orientation toward the praising or blaming of heroic or villainous individuals and the reliance on embattled but eventually triumphant liberal humanist common sense, what's greatly under-represented in the literature so far is discussions about the pedagogies—the processes by which learners come to know and teachers show how they learn—that inform these practices. By pedagogy, I do not so much mean checklists, "how to" guidelines, and other narratives about techniques and methodologies, although these can be useful, but analyses of how knowledges are produced and resisted.

There is already an abundance of literature in gay and lesbian studies about how to run an antihomophobia workshop, how to come out to students, how students can organize for lesbian and gay studies, and how to set up and devise curricula for courses in a variety of disciplines and institutional settings. But very little has been written about the philosophies of teaching that presumably inform these activities, or about their historical and ideological relationship to other and older pedagogies, such as feminist and critical pedagogies from which they have arisen as critiques.[24] Only a few authors have taken up closely related issues, such as the differing theoretical paradigms that have informed gay and lesbian studies;[25] or the question of what lesbian and gay studies might learn from the successes and failures of women's studies and other ethnic studies;[26] or the threats that a new theoretical and largely white male elite's drive to institutionalize *gay and* lesbian studies will erase the intellectual and political accomplishments of a generation of women working in feminist and lesbian studies.[27] This situation is as remarkable, it seems to me, as it is contradictory, occurring as it does at a time of crucial theoretical shifts in understanding about the relationships among sexuality, identity, and knowledge.

While Eve Kosofsky Sedgwick has forced a rethinking in many quarters of the theoretical and political limitations of the so-called "minoritizing" approach to the study of hetero/homosexualities, the consequences for pedagogical practices of the theoretical shift toward universalizing discourses and proliferating sexualities have hardly been seriously addressed.[28] Among the more obvious and more potentially encouraging pedagogical shifts in understanding and practice that readings of Sedgwick's work supports are the realizations that everyone has a stake in gay and lesbian studies and that anyone can and should teach and learn from a perspective that is antihomophobic. Far less obvious and potentially more disturbing insights suggest that common sense assumptions about the work of education no longer obtain; chief among them, and most cherished perhaps, is the "domino effect," the assumption that ignorance is a passive lack that can be replaced with knowledge, which will in turn replace hatred with tolerance.[29]

In spite of these theoretical shifts in understanding of what could constitute gay and lesbian studies, most of the published narratives and how to accounts treat teaching and learning about gays and lesbians as more or less "special events." This is most apparent and most disturbing in the many accounts of attempts to add or otherwise integrate lesbian material into women's studies classes.[30] Furthermore, the social situation in which the teaching and learning occurs does not lend itself to a "universalizing" framework. That is, the occasion is almost always external or at best peripheral to the everyday business of the university or the classroom. Outside agitators, whether students or professors, experts from somewhere else, guinea pigs from the gay and lesbian hotline, or trained facilitators are brought in to do the antihomophobia workshop, the guest lecture, "the" lesbian lecture in a women's studies course, the segment of a gender studies, ethnic studies, or other course devoted to gay and lesbian themes.

The entire course devoted to gay and lesbian studies (whatever that might mean) and named as such in the calender is still rather uncommon at the undergraduate level. There are probably no more of them in all of North America than one could count on the fingers and toes of one body (my attempts to tabulate them via various gay and lesbian and women's studies electronic billboards came up with rumours that there was a class or a program somewhere rather than much in the way of hard facts). Though the grapevine and other hype machines suggest otherwise, the institutionalization of gay and lesbian studies is as yet mainly a matter of smoke and mirrors.

For example, the Toronto Centre for Lesbian and Gay Studies, an entity often cited in the literature, and with which I have been involved, has—by design—no university attachments, to date offers no courses let alone degree-granting programs, and employs no teachers. The Centre, at the insistence of its visionary-activist founder, Michael Lynch, decided that it could do the most advanced work by locating itself outside academic institutions. It publishes a newsletter (irregularly), offers lectures on "popular" and accessible topics (occasionally), and awards small prizes in memory of Michael Lynch (pin money). Another high visibility/low budget enterprise run by another visionary-activist, Martin Duberman, is The Center for Lesbian and Gay Studies at the City University of New York (CLAGS). CLAGS puts on regular high-profile conferences and seminars, produces a newsletter, and is the recipient of a Rockefeller grant which for the next few years will provide one year's support for new scholars. That's it. The center has a tiny budget, can make no appointments of its own and runs no free-standing academic program.

In terms of attaining secure, permanent institutional sites with all the academic paraphernalia of secretaries, line budgets, teaching positions, and administrators, gay and lesbian studies is a generation behind women's studies and other ethnic studies and is struggling toward the moment of institutionalization—not without lots of internal dissent—in a time of deep vertical cuts to university budgets and social and political backlash. Those are the realities, and that is why the hopes tied up in institutionalization and theoretical gentrification are key components of the pedagogical fantasy of "Beyond Antihomophobia 101," and why it is so widespread, so appealing, and so unhelpful to most of us who are attempting to teach gay and lesbian texts at the undergraduate level.

For most of us, teachers and students alike, are caught in a theoretical and political bind: We exist in institutions which are covertly if not overtly homophobic, where there are few if any out lesbian and gay teachers or students and where it's very difficult to get courses with some gay and lesbian content on the books. When the courses are offered, they are taken by students for all manner of reasons, among them, "it fit into my timetable." As the literature on teaching about gay and lesbian issues indicates, the vast majority of these students are not themselves gay and out, and therefore, not surprisingly, they are illiterate about, if not hostile to, gay and lesbian cultures. The poignant and paradoxical fact is that this typical student demographic profile exists at the same time that, for many of us who read, think, and write about the intersection of sexuality/identity/knowledge, the limits of teaching and learning about homosexuality in terms of "homophobia," tolerance, and other minoritizing discourses have never seemed so clear.

This is the social context in which I want to ask questions about the possibilities and limits of gay and lesbian pedagogy. What do you do while you're waiting for gay and lesbian studies to come to your (red) neck of the woods; while women's studies (one sessional lecturer and two part-timers) is struggling for survival and not very eager to make room for lesbian studies; while your university undertakes a study which reveals, like all the others, that gays, lesbians, and bisexuals are harassed, victimized, and otherwise endangered in all their encounters with everyday life in your academy, and yet most of the faculty and staff say that they know no gays on campus, that there is no problem, so there's no need for antihomophobia workshops, which would just waste university money, and anyway, the Bible condemns sodomy?[31] Deconstructing heteronormativity is the most urgent question for lesbian and gay, or more accurately, antihomophobic education, and it is a question of and for pedagogy rather than one about whether or not to demand to be "institutionalized." The word's unfortunate double-meaning ruefully suggests that this legitimizing "solution" might be double-edged and not quite the panacea that some claim it to be.[32] If my memory serves me, avant-gardes that became institutionalized, such as the high modernists, never recovered from the experience.

Leaders of workshops on unlearning homophobia, writers of reports on curricular transformation, and feminist, gay and lesbian teachers routinely refer to the need to break the silence on gay and lesbian issues in the university classroom. Actually, the notion of "silence" is misleading and ultimately not all that helpful to those who are curious about how to imagine, let alone to practice, a pedagogy that would not be merely gay and lesbian, but would be antihomophobic, even queer.[33]

Homophobia, heterosexism, and a fascination with gays and lesbians are already screaming their presence in our classrooms, perhaps most oddly but not entirely unexpectedly in those classrooms devoted to women's studies, gender studies, and gay and lesbian studies. Attending to homophobic discourse, learning how to question and reply to it without getting caught within its limited and destructive focus, is, I would argue, currently the first and the most logical step in que(e)rying pedagogy.[34] Because it can be done by anyone, teacher or student, gay or straight, without the aegis of institutionalized gay and lesbian studies, it can be employed anywhere, in any discipline. At the same time, because figuring out how to do it requires a cognitive reframing of the heteronormative binary, heterosexual-us/homosexual-them, this approach allows the exciting theoretical breakthroughs of queer theory to be practiced in places where most of the professors, let alone the students, wouldn't likely follow the drift of Ed Cohen's questions. Of course, there's a catch. Reframing that binary is very hard work. Even recognizing its presence is far from easy.

One short essay, "Breaking the Silence: Sexual Preference in the Composition Classroom," stands out in the literature because of the close attention the authors pay to pedagogy as a process of knowledge production in which it's possible to interrupt homophobic logic and make cognitive shifts away from fixed identities and limited identifications. The authors, Allison Berg, Jean Kowaleski, Caroline Le Guin, Ellen Weinauer, and Eric A. Wolfe, who were at the time teaching assistants and all of them straight-identified, detail how, with the best of intentions, they were complicit in creating a course from hell that almost rivals Mohr's.[35] Unlike him, however, they seem to have learned how they inadvertently structured the segment of the course on "sexual preference" as a way of teaching using terms of homophobia that objectified gays and lesbians and normalized heterosexuals. They analyze how they framed a question about homosexuality in a writing assignment in such a way as to remove themselves and what they assumed was the heterosexual majority from consideration by pathologizing everybody else. They innocently asked the students to:

> Describe a conversation with someone either of your own or another sexual preference (lesbian, male homosexual, bisexual,

asexual, heterosexual) on the issue of homosexuality. Give as many salient details as you can about this conversation, particularly how attitudes about homosexuality were expressed.³⁶

The teachers, naturally enough, received responses that ranged from "violence to disgust" and made the classroom even less safe for sexual minorities.³⁷ When the lecturer in turn delivered an angry lecture in which he condemned the students' responses as unacceptable expressions of homophobia that amounted to fascism, the students erupted, the class became polarized as everyone blamed everyone else, and hostility, alienation, and betrayal reigned.³⁸ Though the authors use the outdated phrase "sexual preference" and do not reference the theoretical work of Sedgwick and others who have problematized minoritizing approaches to antihomophobic education, their analysis of what shifted in their understanding of their pedagogical practice is entirely consistent with those poststructuralist and queer theoretical insights.

On the premise that failures can be instructive, I believe much can be learned from careful analysis of failed opportunities, two of them mine, to question and interrupt homophobic discourse in the classroom. I use my reading of student questions I or other teachers deflected to make space for a critique of the two chief but implicit assumptions structuring most discussions of lesbian and gay studies pedagogy to date; namely, that the "right" gay and lesbian books will teach themselves, and that the presence of the "right" identities in the classroom, of "out" gay and lesbian teachers and a sufficient number of similar students, will undo the trauma of homophobia.

Calling this state of affairs "homophobia," has itself become more and more conceptually and practically problematic.³⁹ Although still used as the principal term of reference organizing and framing liberal humanist interventions such as antihomophobia workshops and university-sponsored studies of living and working conditions for their gay, lesbian, and bisexual minority members, homophobia and the strategies commonly used for confronting it are at best instruments of a new social etiquette and at worst a recuperation of heterosexuality as an implacable norm.

Homophobia not only psychologizes but centers the "malady" from the point of view of the presumed normal heterosexual. Not surprisingly, it has given rise to its twin, "heterophobia," a repellent but understandably outraged attempt to wrest back conceptual control to the status quo, on a parallel with "reverse discrimination." Predictably, when a normal and unquestioned state of affairs, stretching from ignoring to murder, becomes the focus of inquiry thereby implying that things ought to be different, traumas of various kinds result. Though making the unspeakable speak creates difficulties for sexual minorities as well as for the ostensible "general population," the distress of the latter is the usual focus of concern in both antihomophobia workshops as well as in the university- sponsored studies.

Out gay and lesbian teachers, good intentions, and a more inclusive curriculum are desirable but they are not sufficient to do this work. It takes intellectual, political, and emotional courage to withstand and work through the trauma that predictably results whenever the smooth operation of the normal/pathological binary is questioned and interrupted. Because heterosexism and illiteracy about gays and lesbians are the norm in university culture, and antihomophobic educational practice does not yet have the moral authority attached to it that anti-sexist and anti-racist pedagogy do, teacher accounts, my own included, about teaching a session, a section or an entire course in gay and lesbian texts, are not happy stories.

It is my contention, however, that these accounts, painful though they may be to read, have something instructive to tell us, something that goes beyond the easy ascription of teacher or student heroism, villainy, or incompetence. They suggest that the humanist assumptions underlying all reform pedagogies, chief among them that the provision of knowledge about despised and marginalized groups will simultaneously empower them and decrease the bad conduct of dominants, need to be rethought if not rejected outright. They problematize feminist and other radical pedagogical expectations that classrooms can and ought to be "safe havens" for stigmatized minorities. Finally, while these accounts cast doubts on the expectations that classrooms will become liberated zones, my reading of them is not meant to support the cynical dismissal of progressivist hopes for educational change as necessarily utopian.

Rather, I want to use these accounts to encourage teachers and theorists to think about what can be learned and made productive from encountering the limits of (humanist) pedagogy. My reading of these narratives is informed by the startling and even disturbing claim of Shoshana Felman and Eve Sedgwick that ignorance, the desire to ignore, is actively produced and maintained rather than a mere absence or passive state.[40] Ignorance, especially perhaps homophobic ignorance, is thus not only less than amenable to pedagogical replacement with antihomophobic knowledge, but becomes more insistent when gay and lesbian material threatens to be introduced into the classroom. Recognizing the active operations of the desire to ignore and learning to expect its predictable present absence are absolutely crucial to understanding what happens or fails to happen when gay and lesbian material is brought into the classroom.

The only reasonably sure way to avoid the trauma that results when unpopular things are unleashed is to take the "emperor's new clothes approach" to the teaching of gay and lesbian texts. This is a tried and true method for defusing tension around homophobia in many women's studies classes. For example, in one group interview with women's studies students, straight, bisexual, and lesbian, I was told many anecdotes which suggest that seemingly more inclusive curricula do not in themselves guarantee that these texts will be taught. More than one student mentioned a course on women writers taught by a feminist professor, with lesbian material on the syllabus, in which the discussion allotted to two lesbian novels about lesbians written by openly lesbian writers took place without their subject matter being addressed. Forty-five minutes of one fifty- minute class on Jane Rule's *Desert of the Heart* was devoted to discussing the difficulties of obtaining divorces, until a lesbian asked when the class was going to discuss the novel. Her question was met with silence and the class broke up.[41]

A most instructive treatment of how to avoid teaching lesbian textuality may be found in Gail B. Griffin's lyrical account of her development as a women's studies teacher, *Calling: Essays on Teaching in the Mother Tongue*. Griffin's class in women's literature was so intrigued by Alice Walker's *The Color Purple* that they insisted on extending the discussion for several days. In an effort to conclude the discussion, Griffin asked the class whether the ending satisfied them. It did not, because the class was baffled and disappointed by Celie's continuing lack of desire for her transformed husband, Albert. Griffin's perception that this had been a "wonderful interchange" shifted uneasily in the last few minutes of the last class.[42] The continuing silence of the class's four lesbian students jarred Griffin into noticing that she and the rest of the class had apparently forgotten to mention that Celie's real love, Shug, is another woman. What seems like a candid confession about how she allowed heterosexism to subvert the teaching of a potentially "subversive" text is coyly re-enacted in her account of the incident, in which Griffin once again makes lesbians and lesbianism unspeakable and invisible. Still unwilling to write out what she refers to as the "L-word," Griffin displays an impoverished understanding of lesbian sexuality/textuality:

> Now, *The Color Purple* is a most subversive novel. It makes a homosexual relationship so inescapably, irrefutably superior to

any heterosexual choice, so absolutely healthy, vital, and liberating, that only the most rigid of homophobes can possibly resist it. Although genitals appear specifically and prominently in its pages, it is so little about genital sexuality that the issue is virtually moot. For this reason, however, the novel can be dangerous. You can, in fact, get away with teaching *The Color Purple* without ever mentioning the L-word. I had, I realized, just done so. Acceptance had slid into avoidance.[43]

What begins as an ironic self-critique of what she failed to say in several hours of discussion segues into an extremely puzzling because unwarranted self-celebration of her success at giving voice to and for her lesbian students. In the four euphemistic sentences Griffin generously doles out in the last minute of the last class, she points out that Celie "chose" another woman to love. Still no "L-word" there either. As in the students' interview material I discussed above, Griffin teaches lesbian texts by not teaching them. "Silence. And the class ended."[44]

The four "L-word" students are abjectly grateful that they don't have to take the risk and the consequences of educating the class and their teacher themselves. When the class is over, and it's safe to speak because no one else is listening, they offer thanks: "We were sitting there listening and wondering if anybody was going to say it or would we have to do it, and I was trying to get up the nerve, and you saved us."[45] From what? Apparently from the trauma of discussing lesbianism in a women's studies classroom.

Having failed not just to address her students' and her own heterosexism, Griffin also fails to teach lesbian culture. Leaving them as uneducated about lesbians as they were when they entered her class, Griffin blithely concludes her account of how she gave voice to her lesbian students by appropriating for herself Adrienne Rich's paean to teachers who "made a difference." While on the evidence of her own narrative Griffin egregiously failed, even refused, to give her students, straight and non-straight, information about lesbian culture, she nonetheless lauds herself for being one of those antihomophobic educators who "gave you the books/who let you know you were not alone ...You have a people."[46]

If Gail Griffin is no heroine of antihomophobic pedagogy, neither am I. Like the colleague I alluded to above, my poststructuralist feminism involves "reading for the absence," and for years I have integrated lesbian material, as well as material by other groups of women who are frequently excluded or tokenized, into all my courses. Nonetheless, I feel that I fail over and over again to deliver on the promises of an antihomophobic pedagogy, that is, one which questions and interrupts the operation of the binary heterosexual/homosexual so as to produce something more interesting than tolerance. It always feels like the first time to me, and I hope to do better next time, that is, to work with my class toward a thorough and convincing deconstruction of the binary so that they get a sense of how it operates in our social and cultural texts, all the while keeping the trauma of doing this work from being completely overwhelming for me and the class.

My most dramatic failure to do this work occurred when I deflected an angry rhetorical question of a feminist student in an upper-level women's autobiography course. Thirty female students, nearly all of them white and straight English majors, were concluding their discussion of the anthology of writing by radical women of color, *This Bridge Called My Back*.[47] The tense but polite classroom atmosphere was interrupted by the voice of an angry and agitated white student who indignantly asked: "When are we going to start reading and talking about normal women?" There was an audible gasp from the whole group.

Startled, angry, and fearful about how my course and, by extension, myself were being positioned by the student, I pretended not to know what she was getting at. I did not give her question a potentially and provocatively Lacanian reply: "But we already are!" Rather than reversing her question and giving it back to her in a displaced form, allowing "that which is said by one [to be perceived and articulated as] being already the reply,"[48] I gave an informal lecture on "difference" and binary oppositions. Thus, that year's most important question remained unprobed and unworked through. I gave the students and myself a temporary reprieve in dealing with homophobia and racism as well as lost an opportunity to investigate how to rethink representational and reading practices. The theories I live and write by weren't making it into my classroom.

The reprieve was, however, bought at a high price; though the presence of "unpopular things," in this case racial, sexual, and class difference, was always pervasive in my classroom, they were not quite "unleashed." Instead, it was a protracted standoff. The "normal" women held onto their subject positions, circled their wagons, and kept the "others" at bay. The Others felt, well, Othered. This course became a tour of the dreaded and exotic Other. On student evaluations, many of the women complained that the course was not really a course on women's autobiographies but was about "Blacks and lesbians." I was repeatedly faulted for allowing the "Black and lesbian" students (4 out of 35, however you count) to dominate discussions.

Because that student's question kept nagging me, the next year I attempted to address it through designing a new course with a colleague who specializes in anti-racism and post-colonialism. We, the white lesbian and the straight woman of color, pledged not to do the "samo" of women's studies—take Mary Wollstonecraft as feminism's originary moment, lead up to the triumph of the white women's movement, and tack on a one week p.s. at the end about women of color and lesbians. Our course would deconstruct the normal/deviant, center/margin binary as it operates in women's studies courses whose chief focus is gender rather than the production of social difference. After some objections from the department, this multi-sectioned lecture and tutorial course was put on the books, retitled by them, "An Introduction to Gender Studies." My colleague and I were assigned two graduate student teaching assistants to lead tutorial groups, a white gay male and a straight white female, neither of whom had taught "political" courses before.

Along with all the predictable glitches which occur when teaching anything the first time, sickness forced me to miss the first semester. In my absence, my tutorial was taken over by a graduate assistant with no teaching experience and my colleague restructured the course. Since she had to do all the lecturing, she taught what she knew best. The first semester lectures were exercises in close reading, and focused primarily on how racial and gender differences are inscribed in pseudo-universalizing discourses. Racism and sexism were treated as effects of difference rather than vice versa, and, though texts by Audre Lorde figured prominently, almost no attention was paid to sexuality.

My first day back, I learned from a variety of sources that my tutorial was in crisis. Unpopular things had been threatening. After one explosion about racism, the ideologically polarized group of fifteen women and men of diverse races, classes, and ethnicities, all of them ostensibly heterosexual, largely refused to talk to each other. Both the original tutorial leader and the group were defensive, keen to assign blame somewhere. Since the unstructured format of the first semester's tutorial had no chance of working as long as the silent treatment was in effect, I decided to have the students bring three questions in each week and work on them in small groups. While this format was an improvement, the crisis in my tutorial made me seriously doubt whether good intentions and a transformed curriculum in and of themselves would give me a better shot at replying to the assumptions about knowledge and identity which informed my former student's angry question about normalcy.

Her question took on an added resonance when I learned that the students in my tutorial had developed an official and punishing discourse about difference based on their understanding of the lectures. The critique of pseudo-universals had been taken to mean that one must not generalize—never, about anything. They also learned that one can speak only from and apparently about one's own subject position. They were prohibited from speaking for others and believed they must identify themselves according to their visible and obvious marks of difference, that is, by race and gender. Class and sexuality, being less patently visible, went unremarked. Our course on "gender, race, and class" had constructed a modified version of what Michael Warner calls "Rainbow Theory" in his introduction to *Fear of Queer Planet*. We were missing a few colors—like pink and purple—but we had constructed a "fantasized space where all embodied identities could be visibly represented as parallel forms of identity."[49] The white males tried to remember that they must always preface their remarks by indicating that they were speaking only as "white males." They nervously joked about how illegitimate and awful they were as white males. The jokes were unfunny, involving as they did an unpleasant mixture of guilt and resentment.

The students' interpretations of the official discourse, or set of prohibitions in "Introduction to Gender Studies" effectively put identities on trial. The tutorial was immobilized by naturalizing assumptions that racial and other differences are fixed and obvious rather than constructed and fluid, as well as by the assumption that people are discriminated against because they are *already* different rather than vice versa.[50] The tutorial felt like a courtroom where students had learned how to testify as victims or perpetrators of racism and sexism. Given the limited options, they struggled to assert and maintain positions of purity and innocence as victims of oppression or reluctantly and ashamedly admitted their complicity and privilege as perpetrators.

It took me a little longer to understand that, although the students had been discouraged from speaking for others, they took this caveat to apply only to race and gender, the categories of visible social difference that had been showcased and reified in the lectures. As a result, homophobic discourse about gays and lesbians, who were apparently unrepresented in the tutorial group, had become the release valve for prohibited speech. Ridicule and contempt for "fags," and to a lesser extent, for lesbians, were easily and unselfconsciously expressed by almost all of the students. When it finally came time according to the restructured syllabus to discuss gay and lesbian texts as gay and lesbian texts, the students' assumptions about the obviousness and visibility of identity markers had been reinforced by our course's apparent reification of identities. That meant that the hunt was on to make a check-list of the visible characteristics and behavior traits of that unrepresented identity group. Against our intentions, our course was predicated pedagogically on a form of what Edward Said called "Orientalism": we conferred "on the other a discrete identity, while also providing the knowing observer with a standpoint from which to see without being seen, to read without interruption."[51] Our course had apparently confirmed what they already knew—that homosexuals were a despised, and despicable, quasi-ethnic minority whose distinguishing characteristics were not sexual practices so much as a certain style or set of mannerisms.

Because of my absence, lesbian (and gay) material was introduced, as it is (when it is at all) in most women's studies classes, only in the final weeks of the year, when the class was reaching or had already reached its saturation point about diversity groups. For me, it felt like a re-run of "when are we going to start reading and talking about normal women?" As a result, the lecture hall and some of the tutorials became scenes of trauma in Felman's clinical rather than moralistic sense. We concocted, mainly unintentionally, scandalous situations without a cure, wherein events in excess of our frames of reference produced a radical condition of exposure and vulnerability.[52] A lecture I gave on the denaturalizing aspects of Freud's thinking about sexuality was greeted with audible sounds of disbelief and disgust.

Like Richard Mohr, the openly gay white male teaching assistant decided to let a film do the initial consciousness-raising about homophobia. Like my colleague and I, he too made a fetish out of what he had added to the curriculum. The gay-themed and gay-directed commercial film he had chosen to show our class, *Parting Glances*, was a personal favorite, something he knew almost by heart and had come to regard as a sacred text. In many ways, the film seemed a safe choice for a "first time" cinematic encounter with sexual difference. It was a chaste, middlebrow, realist text about innocuous gay white yuppies that presented gays as just like straights.

With no introduction, the lights went down, the film came on, and the students began to act as students predictably do in teacher stories about showing that first film, whatever it is, in gay and lesbian studies classes. That is, they gasped, they clung to their friends, they covered their eyes, and let out loud "yucchs." A few walked out. As in Griffin's account of how not to teach *The Color Purple*, there was

"Silence. And the class ended." Actually, as bad as it was, it could have been worse, as Mohr's account indicates.

The teaching assistant was devastated, but hid his feelings enough so as to field questions with his tutorial when the film ended. Because he was out to his students, he was treated as a native informant, in Lacan's terms, "the subject assumed to know." An implicit believer in humanist pedagogy, he did not object to the way their questions had positioned him, nor to their commonsensical assumptions that "knowledge...can be supported or transported by one alone." The "question-and-answer" session was the opposite of dialogical because neither teacher nor students recognized that everybody present, straight, nonstraight, and anti-straight, was implicated in the information he was imparting.[53]

This amiable and popular teacher was asked and for a while tried to answer their questions, as posed: "Why do all gay men love opera? Do they all have classy apartments in New York City? How come they're all white and rich? Why is the one who plays the female role messier than the other guy? Why did the director stereotype those gays so much?" Eventually he was so traumatized he could no longer speak. He gave up and put his head in his hands. After a tense silence, when he was able to speak again, he told the students that he couldn't answer any more of their questions just then because they made him feel like the "Other" and that felt terrible.

The teaching assistant named himself as the Other in a way in which our students by then were familiar, that is, in the sense of the marginalized and excluded subaltern as the feminist and post-colonialist theorists we read in our course used the concept, rather than as Lacan's "true Other," "who gives the answer one does not expect," and in whose knowledge is constituted "the return of a difference."[54] Though each of these senses of the Other does not preclude the other, the teaching assistant, perhaps because he too was under the sway of Rainbow Theory, did not think that the teaching of un/popular cultures requires the pedagogue to play the other in the Lacanian sense too. In any case, he did not think to question their questions. And so, as in Griffin's class, this painful exercise, not exactly a "wonderful interchange" in any but the most ironic sense, came to an end. Once again, "Silence. And the class ended."

This disturbing experience became another humanist moment. Perhaps the students learned something about good behavior toward and increased empathy for minorities, but it's just as likely that they concluded that they shouldn't ask questions that disturb the teacher.

Because of the course's emphasis on the visibility and obviousness of identities, especially marked identities, an opportunity for analysis of the production of knowledge about all identities was once again lost.[55]

My tutorial that week was no better and almost as surreal. Rather than treat me, the course director, an out and obvious lesbian, as a native informant, the students used the structuring device of our group, the asking of three student-generated questions about the text of the week, in this case the film, to discuss: "How do you recognize a lesbian?" The question terrified me, perhaps because it reminded me of others constructed along the same lines; to wit, how do you recognize a witch, a Jew, a communist, an alien from outer space. The question intrigued the students, so much so that the other two questions were immediately dropped and utterly forgotten in the gleeful and excited discussion that followed—a discussion in which all of the students were actively engaged. Lisa M. Walker's perceptive article, "How To Recognize a Lesbian: The Cultural Politics of Looking Like What You Are," was a few months away from publication, but her observations about her ambivalence concerning the trope of lesbian visibility would have helped me with my own confusion in light of the classroom crisis that erupted that day:

> I do not wish to diminish the fact that the impulse to privilege the visible often arises out of the need to reclaim signifiers of difference that dominant ideologies have used to define minority identities negatively. But while this strategy of reclamation is often affirming, it can also replicate the practices of dominant ideologies that use visibility to create social categories on the basis of exclusion. The paradigm of visibility is totalizing when a signifier of difference becomes synonymous with the identity it signifies. In this situation, members of a given population who do not bear that signifier of difference or who bear visible signs of another identity are rendered invisible and are marginalized within an already marginalized community.[56]

Before I could intervene and turn the question back to the questioner, asking why they wanted or needed to know how to recognize a lesbian, and were they interested in learning how to recognize heterosexuals, the group answer, arrived at collectively, was announced: she is short, wears glasses, and is flat-chested. Pretty common visual markers, two of which are routinely ascribed to "feminists," but in that group, the only woman possessing all three characteristics was me. Suddenly, a dissenting voice shot out; a female student, an out lesbian in other classes, but closeted in our "unsafe" tutorial, began to demand that they produce evidence for their claim. Taller than me, voluptuous, and gifted with good vision, she did not fit the description. Nonetheless, she too deflected the question. Instead of coming out and asking: "Ain't I a lesbian,?" her counter-claim led the discussion down predictable paths about the errors of stereotyping. Yet again, deflected questions produced "Silence. And the class ended."

In retrospect, the traumatic questions posed to the gay male teaching assistant and to me in our tutorials seem not only structurally identical, but wholly predictable outcomes, even measures of a cruel success in terms of our course's presentation of the logic of difference and normalcy. As with the pluralist and humanist notions of "diversity"—or difference as already unproblematically "there," only awaiting inclusion and representability on the syllabus and in the front of the classroom—by the end of the year, "hom(m)osexuality" too had been rendered visible and intelligible.[57] That is, "homosexuality" was rendered in terms of heterosexuality or sameness. My colleague and I had successfully taught our students how to "read for the absence" of gays and lesbians in a way that did not implicate themselves and therefore did not teach them "how to recognize heterosexuality" either.

And yet, the most instructive and endlessly deflected question was yet to be posed in our course. On the final exam, whose questions were collectively put together by the entire teaching team and distributed ahead of time in the last class, we asked the students to tell us how the course had challenged their understandings of gender, race, class, or sexuality. The correct answer to this question was valued at 10% of the final grade. And of course, we got it. Over and over again, members of one or another dominant group told us in unconvincingly vague abstractions how they had learned to tolerate minorities.

How they were implicated in their reading practices was a question they never addressed, since we had not posed it. In our fairly progressive institution, we experienced and committed "radical teachers" unwittingly taught our students to give us the answers they thought we expected rather than the ones Lacan solicited from his seminar, the ones that might structure a lesbian and gay studies that could conceivably get beyond Antihomophobia 101: "Let everybody tell me, in his [sic] own way, his [sic] idea of what I am driving at. How, for him [sic], is opened up—or closed—or how already he [sic] resists, the question as I pose it."[58] If Michael Warner's concise definition of queer theory as a way of *teaching* culture is as promising and disruptive as I believe it could be, then that means that the accent has to fall on the participle. It's a verb form, not a noun, especially not if the noun in question is "institutionalization."

NOTES

CHAPTER 1. The Making of an Un/popular Culture

1. Penelope Engelbrecht, "'Lifting Belly Is a Language': The Postmodern Lesbian Subject," *Feminist Studies* 16 (Spring 1990): 110–111.

2. Arlene Stein, ed., *Sisters, Sexperts, Queers: Beyond the Lesbian Nation* (New York: Plume, 1993).

3. Katie King, "The Situation of Lesbianism as Feminism's Magical Sign: Contests for Meaning and the U.S. Women's Movement, 1968–1972," *Communications* 9 (1986): 66.

4. Adrienne Rich, "Compulsory Heterosexuality and Lesbian Existence," in Henry Abelove, Michèle Aina Barale and David M. Halperin, eds., *The Lesbian and Gay Studies Reader* (New York: Routledge, 1993), 227.

5. King, "The Situation of Lesbianism as Feminism's Magical Sign," 65.

6. Rich, "Compulsory Heterosexuality," 227.

7. Elizabeth Wilson, "Forbidden Love," in *Hidden Agendas: Theory, Politics and Experience in the Women's Movement* (London: Tavistock, 1986), 173.

8. Catharine R. Stimpson, "Nancy Reagan Wears A Hat: Feminism and its Cultural Consensus," in *Where the Meanings Are: Feminism and Cultural Spaces* (New York: Methuen, 1988), 179–196.

9. Ann Ferguson, "Patriarchy, Sexual Identity, and the Sexual Revolution," in "Viewpoint" by Ann Ferguson, Jacquelyn N. Zita, and Kathryn Pyne Addelson, "On 'Compulsory Heterosexuality and Lesbian Existence': Defining the Issues," *Signs* 7 (Autumn 1981): 160.

10. *Ibid.*, 160, 164, 166.

11. *Ibid.*, 164.

12. Janice G. Raymond, "Putting the Politics Back Into Lesbianism," *Women's Studies International Forum* 12 (1989): 152.

13. Joan Nestle, "Butch-Femme Relationships: Sexual Courage in the 1950s," *A Restricted Country* (Ithaca, NY: Firebrand Books, 1987), 105–106.

14. Lillian Faderman, *Odd Girls and Twilight Lovers: A History of Lesbian Life in Twentieth-Century America* (New York: Columbia University Press, 1991), 251.

15. Ibid., 268–269.

16. Ibid., 269–270.

17. Ibid., 269.

18. Jeffrey Weeks, *Sexuality and Its Discontents* (London: Routledge, 1985), 217, 234.

19. Gayle Rubin, "Thinking Sex: Notes for a Radical Theory of the Politics of Sexuality," in Carole S. Vance, ed., *Pleasure and Danger: Exploring Female Sexuality* (New York: Routledge, 1984), 282.

20. Ibid., 310.

21. Ibid., 287.

22. Ibid., 297.

23. Ibid., 307.

24. Ibid., 309.

25. Gayle Rubin, "The Traffic in Women: Notes on the 'Political Economy' of Sex," in Rayna R. Reiter, ed., *Toward an Anthropology of Women* (New York: Monthly Review, 1975), 197–210.

26. Stimpson, "Nancy Reagan Wears a Hat," 189.

27. For one of the most concise treatments of what the discursive and disciplinary shift required and what its political consequences have been for feminism, Stimpson quotes the art critic Lisa Tickner:

> "It was psychoanalysis that permitted an understanding of the psychosocial constructions of sexual differences in the conscious/unconscious subject. The result was a shift in emphasis from equal rights struggles in the sexual division of labor and a cultural feminism founded on the reevaluation of an existing biological or social femininity to a recognition of the processes of sexual *differentiation*, the instability of gender positions, and the hopelessness of excavating a free or original femininity beneath the layers of patriarchal oppression." Stimpson, "Nancy Reagan Wears a Hat," 189–190.

28. Stimpson, "Nancy Reagan Wears a Hat"; Teresa de Lauretis, "Upping the Anti (sic) in Feminist Theory," in Marianne Hirsch and Evelyn Fox Keller,

eds., *Conflicts in Feminism* (New York: Routledge, 1990), 225–270; Sue-Ellen Case, "Introduction," in Sue-Ellen Case, ed., *Performing Feminisms: Feminist Critical Theory and Theatre* (Baltimore: Johns Hopkins University Press, 1990); Elizabeth A. Meese, *(Ex)Tensions: Re-Figuring Feminist Criticism* (Urbana, IL: University of Illinois Press, 1990).

29. Judith Roof, "Lesbians and Lyotard: Legitimation and the Politics of the Name," in Laura Doan, ed., *The Lesbian Postmodern* (New York: Columbia University Press, 1994), 47–66.

30. Emma Pérez, "Irigaray's Female Symbolic in the Making of Chicana Lesbian Sitios y Lenguas (Sites and Discourses)," in Laura Doan, *The Lesbian Postmodern* 104–117; Ruthann Robson, "Embodiment(s): The Possibilities of Lesbian Legal Theory in Bodies Problematized by Postmodernisms and Feminisms," *Law and Sexuality: A Review of Lesbian and Gay Legal Issues* 2 (1992): 37–80.

31. Sheila Jeffreys, *The Lesbian Heresy: A Feminist Perspective on the Lesbian Sexual Revolution* (North Melbourne, Australia: Spinifex, 1993); Raymond, "Putting the Politics Back Into Lesbianism."

32. See note 8 in chapter 5 for Frye's analysis in her essay "To See and Be Seen: The Politics of Reality," in *The Politics of Reality: Essays in Feminist Theory* (Trumansburg, NY: The Crossing Press, 1983), 160.

33. Ekua Omosupe, "Black/Lesbian/Bulldagger," *differences* 3 (Summer 1991): 108.

34. Gloria Anzaldúa, "To(o) Queer the Writer—Loca, escritora y chicana," in Betsy Warland, *In Versions: Writings by Dykes, Queers and Lesbians* (Vancouver: Press Gang, 1991), 249–251.

35. Bertha Harris, "What We Mean to Say: Notes Toward Defining the Nature of Lesbian Literature," *Heresies* (Fall 1977): 5.

36. *Ibid.*, 6.

37. Monique Wittig, *The Straight Mind and Other Essays* (Boston: Beacon Press, 1992), 32, 102.

38. Judith Butler, *Gender Trouble: Feminism and the Subversion of Identity* (New York: Routledge, 1990); Barbara Christian, Ann Du Cille, Sharon Marcus, Elaine Marks, Nancy K. Miller, Sylvia Schafer, and Joan W. Scott, "Conference Call," *differences* 2 (Fall 1990): 52–108.

39. Radicalesbians, "The Woman-Identified Woman," in Anne Koedt, Ellen Levine, and Anita Rapone, eds., *Radical Feminism* (New York: Quadrangle, 1973), 240.

40. Michael Warner, "From Queer to Eternity: An Army of Theorists Cannot Fail," *Village Voice Literary Supplement* (June 1992): 19.

41. Butler, *Gender Trouble;* Sue-Ellen Case, "Toward a Butch-Femme Aesthetic," in Henry Abelove, Michèle Aina Barale, and David M. Halpern, eds., *The Lesbian and Gay Studies Reader* (New York: Routledge, 1993), 294–306; Catharine R. Stimpson, "Afterword: Lesbian Studies in the 1990s," in Karla Jay and Joanne Glasgow, *Lesbian Texts and Contexts: Radical Revisions* (New York: Columbia University Press, 1990), 377–382.

42. Patricia White, "Female Spectator, Lesbian Specter: The Haunting," in Diana Fuss, ed., *inside/out: Lesbian Theories, Gay Theories* (New York: Routledge, 1991), 142–172.

43. John Storey, *An Introductory Guide to Cultural Theory and Popular Culture* (Athens, GA: University of Georgia Press, 1993), 125–153.

44. Maria Maggenti, "Wandering Through Herland," in Arlene Stein, ed., *Sisters, Sexperts, Queers: Beyond the Lesbian Nation,* 254.

45. Donald G. Marshall, *Contemporary Critical Theory: A Selective Bibliography* (New York: Modern Language Association, 1993).

46. Raymond Williams, *Keywords* (London: Flamingo, 1983), 87.

47. James Clifford, "Introduction: Partial Truths," in James Clifford and George Marcus, eds., *Writing Culture: The Poetics and Politics of Ethnography* (Berkeley: University of California Press, 1986), 19.

48. Fredric Jameson, "On 'Cultural Studies,'" *Social Text* 34 (1993): 35.

49. *Ibid.,* 33.

50. Danae Clark, "Commodity Lesbianism," in Henry Abelard, Michèle Aina Barale, and David M. Halperin, eds., *The Lesbian and Gay Studies Reader,* 199.

51. Camille Paglia, *Sexual Personae: Art and Decadence from Nefertiti to Emily Dickinson* (New York: Vintage, 1990), 117.

52. Jameson, "On 'Cultural Studies,'" 35.

53. Terry Castle, *The Apparitional Lesbian: Female Homosexuality and Modern Culture* (New York: Columbia University Press, 1993); Ann Ferguson, "Is There a Lesbian Culture?," in Jeffner Allen, ed., *Lesbian Philosophies and Cultures* (Albany, NY: State University of NewYork Press, 1990), 63–88; Gabriele Griffin, ed., *Outwrite: Lesbianism and Popular Culture* (London: Pluto Press, 1993).

54. Alisa Solomon, "Queer Culture: A Celebration—and a Critique," *Village Voice,* 21 June 1994, 4.

55. Williams, *Keywords,* 91.

56. "Michael Coren's Diary," *Frank,* 7 July 1994, n.p.

57. But see, for example, Ann Powers's "Queer in the Streets, Straight in the Sheets," *Village Voice,* 29 June 1993, 24, 30–31, and the withering rather than outraged responses from lesbian readers that followed in the next week's letters to the editor about Powers's comic as well as homophobic misunderstandings of lesbian sexuality.

58. Camille Roy, "Speaking in Tongues," in Arlene Stein, ed., *Sisters, Sexperts, Queers: Beyond the Lesbian Nation,* 10.

59. Tom Morris, "Life's a Pimp," *The Guardian,* 19 April 1994, 10.

60. Marleen Barr, "Food for Postmodern Thought: Isak Dinesen's Female Artists as Precursors to Contemporary Feminist Fabulators," in Libby Falk Jones and Sarah Webster Goodwin, eds., *Feminism, Utopia and Narrative* (Knoxville, TN: University of Tennessee Press, 1990); Suzanne Clark, *Sentimental Modernism: Women Writers and the Revolution of the World* (Bloomington: Indiana University Press, 1991); Molly Hite, *The Other Side of the Story: Structures and Strategies of Contemporary Feminist Narrative* (Ithaca, NY: Cornell University Press, 1989).

61. Charles Russell, *Poets, Prophets, and Revolutionaries: The Literary Avant-Garde From Rimbaud to Postmodernism* (New York: Oxford University Press, 1985), 251.

62. Robson, "Embodiment(s): The Possibilities of Lesbian Legal Theory in Bodies Problematized by Postmodernisms and Feminisms."

63. Jean Walton, "Sandra Bernhard: Lesbian Postmodern or Modern Postlesbian," in Laura Doan, *The Lesbian Postmodern,* 252.

64. Laura Doan, *The Lesbian Postmodern.* See full citation, Note 29.

65. Linda J. Nicholson, ed., *Feminism/Postmodernism* (New York: Routledge, 1990).

66. Katie King, "Producing Sex, Theory, and Culture: Gay/Straight Remappings in Contemporary Feminism," in Marianne Hirsch and Evelyn Fox Keller, eds., *Conflicts in Feminism* (New York: Routledge, 1990), 82–101.

67. *Ibid.,* 83.

68. Eve Kosofsky Sedgwick, *Epistemology of the Closet* (Berkeley: University of California Press, 1991), 11.

69. *Ibid.,* 27. Sedgwick's treatment of feminist theory in *Epistemology of the Closet* is casual and out of date, relegated in any case mainly to citations of names in footnotes. Lesbian theory is treated as a subdivision of gay theory and is regarded as relevant to her project only to the degree that it separates gender from sexuality and links lesbian concerns with those of gay males (*Ibid.,* 33, 37, 39). In her later overview of lesbian and gay studies, "Gender Criticism," in Stephen Greenblatt and Giles Gunn, eds., *Redrawing the Boundaries: The*

Transformation of English and American Literary Studies (New York: Modern Language Association, 1992), lesbian theory gets the same treatment. In an article almost thirty pages long, the work of Cherríe Moraga and Audre Lorde merits two lines, though she praises their work for being "the most formally innovative writing now being done in gender and sexuality theory" ("Gender Criticism," 294).

70. Sedgwick, *Epistemology of the Closet*, 1, 9, 59.

71. Butler, *Gender Trouble: Feminism and the Subversion of Identity*, 128.

72. *Ibid.*, 137–141. Unfortunately, Butler, Sedgwick, and another queer theorist, Diana Fuss, author of *Essentially Speaking: Feminism, Nature and Difference* (New York: Routledge, 1989) and editor of one of the most important anthologies in lesbian and gay studies, *inside/out: Lesbian Theories, Gay Theories* (New York: Routledge, 1991), are all rather uninterested in most contemporary contributors to the development of lesbian theory. In her first book, Fuss claims that the major problem of lesbian theory is its failure to theorize male homosexuality; she is silent about the work of most lesbian theorists, and under that heading names lesbian activists and creative writers rather than academics and scholars (*Essentially Speaking*, 100, 111).

73. Teresa de Lauretis, "Queer Theory: Lesbian and Gay Sexualities. An Introduction," in Teresa de Lauretis, ed., *Queer Theory*, special issue of *differences* 3 (Summer 1991): xvii. In her introduction, de Lauretis explains that she was inspired to call this theorizing "queer" in reference to a New York conference she participated in in 1989 entitled "How do I Look? Queer Film and Video," rather than by the political action group, Queer Nation (xvii).

74. *Ibid.*, iv.

75. *Ibid.*, iv–vi.

76. *Ibid.*, iv.

77. *Ibid.*, iii.

78. Teresa de Lauretis, "Eccentric Subjects: Feminist Theory and Historical Consciousness," *Feminist Studies* 16 (1990): 135–138.

79. Englebrecht, "'Lifting Belly is a Language"; Robson, "Embodiment(s): The Possibilities of Lesbian Legal Theory in Bodies Problematized by Postmodernisms and Feminisms."

80. Roof, "Lesbians and Lyotard."

81. Tessa Boffin and Jean Fraser, eds., *Stolen Glances: Lesbians Take Photographs* (London: Pandora, 1991); Pat Califia, *Macho Sluts* (Boston: Alyson, 1988); Laura Doan, *The Lesbian Postmodern*.

82. Lily Burana, Roxxie, and Linnea Due, eds., *Dagger: On Butch Women* (San Francisco: Cleis Press, 1994).

83. Judith Halberstam, "F2M: The Making of Female Masculinity," in Laura Doan, *The Lesbian Postmodern*, 216.

84. Maggenti, "Wandering Through Herland," 245–256; Steven Seidman, "Identity and Politics in a 'Postmodern' Gay Culture: Some Historical and Conceptual Notes," in Michael Warner, ed., *Fear of a Queer Planet: Queer Politics and Social Theory* (Minneapolis: University of Minnesota Press, 1993), 105–142; Arlene Stein, "The Year of the Lustful Lesbian," in *Sisters, Sexperts, Queers: Beyond the Lesbian Nation*, 13–34; Robin Wiegman, "Introduction: Mapping the Lesbian Postmodern," in Laura Doan, *The Lesbian Postmodern*, 1994), 12.

85. The process and its implications are explored by Gloria Anzaldúa, *Borderlands/La Frontera: The New Mestiza* (San Francisco: Spinsters, 1987), l; Mary Meigs, "Falling Between the Cracks," in Betsy Warland, ed., *In Versions: Writings by Dykes, Queers and Lesbians* (Vancouver: Press Gang, 1991), 105–116; Minnie Bruce Pratt, *Rebellion: Essays 1980–1991* (Ithaca, NY: Firebrand Books, 1991).

86. Roof's citational practices in her later essay, "Lesbians and Lyotard: Legitimation and the Politics of the Name," are both different and similar; she cites many of the most important lesbian theoretical texts, not in the interest of showing developments in the discourse, but as a way of arguing against the formulation of a lesbian postmodern.

87. Susan Bordo, "Review Essay: Postmodern Subjects, Postmodern Bodies," *Feminist Studies* 18 (Spring 1992): 174.

88. Alison Hennegan, "On Becoming a Lesbian Reader," in Susanna Radstone, ed., *Sweet Dreams: Sexuality, Gender and Popular Fiction* (London: Lawrence & Wishart, 1988), 165–190; Jean E. Kennard, "Ourself Behind Ourself: A Theory for Lesbian Readers," in Elizabeth A. Flynn and Patrocinio P. Schweickart, eds., *Gender and Reading: Essays on Readers, Texts, and Contexts* (Baltimore: Johns Hopkins University Press, 1986), 63–80.

89. Aislin, *Where's the Trough? And Other Aislin Cartoons* (Toronto: McClelland and Stewart, c1985), 14.

90. Heather Findlay, "Freud's 'Fetishism' and the Lesbian Dildo Debates," *Feminist Studies* 18 (Fall 1992): 563–579; Erica Rand, "We Girls Can Do Anything, Right Barbie? Lesbian Consumption in Postmodern Circulation," in Laura Doan, *The Lesbian Postmodern*, 189–209; June L. Reich, "Genderfuck: The Law of the Dildo," *Discourse* 1 (Fall 1992): 112–127.

91. Deborah P. Britzman, "Decentering Discourses in Teacher Education: Or, The Unleashing of Unpopular Things," *Boston University Journal of*

Education 173 (1991): 60–80; and "Is There a Queer Pedagogy? Or, Stop Reading Straight," *Educational Theory* 45 (Spring 1995): 151–166.

92. Sedgwick, *Epistemology of the Closet*, 21, 60; Jacquelyn N. Zita, "Lesbian and Gay Studies: Yet Another Unhappy Marriage?," in Linda Garber, ed., *Tilting the Tower: Lesbians Teaching Queer Subjects* (New York: Routledge, 1994), 258–276.

93. J. Laplanche and J-B Pontalis, *The Language of Psychoanalysis*, trans. Donald Nicholson-Smith (London: Karnac, 1988), 465.

CHAPTER 2. Paper Lesbians and Theory Queens

1. Heather Zwicker, "Queer Readings" (paper presented at the 1994 Learned Societies Conference, Lesbian and Gay Studies, Calgary, Alberta).

2. Aislin, *Where's the Trough? And Other Aislin Cartoons* (Toronto: McClelland and Stewart, c1985), 14.

3. In the Summer 1992 special issue of the journal *October* focusing on "The Identity in Question," Butler noted that the conference goers' intimacy or lack of intimacy with "Judy/Dr. Judith Butler" itself became a way of problematizing identity ("Discussion," 113–114). Butler carries on this intertextual self-citation in the preface to her most recent book, *Bodies That Matter: On the Discursive Limits of Sex* (New York: Routledge, 1993), by complaining that questioners who address her by the diminutive, "Judy," attempt to patronize, (re)constitute, and unpredictably appropriate her variously as unruly child or feminine film star *(Bodies That Matter*, ix–x). Conspicuously uncited in this bracketed part of the book are the events and personages in academic culture which produced Butler as a theoretical diva with a large following of fans and her own fanzine. How should one cite her? Moreover, in the published discussion of a paper by Butler not included in *October*, Butler announces a change in her theorizing of performativity which also seemed to address as if by anticipation the zine's author, Miss Spentyouth's, citational practices in the "Spring Fever of 1993":

> it seems important to me to rethink performativity, as Derrida suggests, as citationality, for the invocation of identity is always a reinvocation, ...and there is promise in the iterability of the signifier...I do not profess a subject who generates its performances...what I did suggest was that it is only through the citing of a norm, a citing which instantiates and institutes the norm, that a subject is produced. So the subject is an effect of a citational practice. Whereas I did write in *Gender Trouble* about parodic and subversive performance, I explicitly did not refer to subversion in this context, because *Paris Is Burning* has forced a rethinking of my notion of parodic subversion, for clearly some forms of parody are not subversive (110–112).

4. Alison Hennegan, "On Becoming a Lesbian Reader," in Susannah Radstone, ed., *Sweet Dreams: Sexuality, Gender and Popular Fiction* (London: Lawrence & Wishart, 1988), 165–190; Jean E. Kennard, "Ourself Behind Ourself: A Theory for Lesbian Readers," 63–80.

5. Victoria A. Brownworth, "Parochialism and Polarization: The Politics of Lesbian and Gay Reading," *Lambda Book Report* 3 (March/April 1993): 10–11.

6. Ellen Louise Hart, "Literacy and the Lesbian/Gay Learner," in Caroline Sidaway, M. Eugenia Rosa, Ellen Louise Hart, Sarah-Hope Parmenter, and Anza Stein, *The Lesbian in Front of the Classroom: Writings by Lesbian Teachers* (Santa Cruz, CA: HerBooks, 1988), 39.

7. Terry Castle, *The Apparitional Lesbian: Female Homosexuality and Modern Culture* (New York: Columbia University Press, 1993), 18.

8. Lillian Faderman, *Odd Girls and Twilight Lovers: A History of Lesbian Life in Twentieth-Century America* (New York: Columbia University Press, 1991).

9. Michel de Certeau, *The Practice of Everyday Life,* trans. Steven F. Rendall (Berkeley: University of California Press, 1984), 174.

10. *Ibid.*, xix.

11. *Ibid.*, xxi.

12. *Ibid.*, xxiv.

13. Jonathan Culler, *On Deconstruction: Theory and Criticism after Structuralism* (Ithaca, NY: Cornell University Press, 1982), 81.

14. Wolfgang Iser, *The Act of Reading: A Theory of Aesthetic Response* (Baltimore: Johns Hopkins University Press, 1978), x.

15. Paul de Man, *Blindness and Insight: Essays in the Rhetoric of Contemporary Criticism* (New York: Oxford University Press, 1971), 107.

16. Paul de Man, "The Resistance to Theory," in *The Resistance to Theory* (Minneapolis: University of Minnesota Press, 1986), 20.

17. Shoshana Felman, *Jacques Lacan and the Adventure of Insight: Psychoanalysis in Contemporary Culture* (Cambridge: Harvard University Press, 1987), 90.

18. Sarah Schulman, *My American History: Lesbian and Gay Life During the Reagan/Bush Years* (New York: Routledge, 1994), 247–252, and "Questions," *Lambda Book Report* 4 (July/August 1994): 49.

19. Michael Warner, "From Queer to Eternity: An Army of Theorists Cannot Fail," *Village Voice Literary Supplement* (June 1992): 18.

20. de Man, "Resistance to Theory," 5.

21. Bonnie Zimmerman, *The Safe Sea of Women: Lesbian Fiction 1969–1989* (Boston: Beacon Press, 1990), 15.

22. Katie King, "The Situation of Lesbianism as Feminism's Magical Sign: Contests for Meaning and the U.S. Women's Movement, 1968–1972," *Communications* 9 (1986): 65.

23. *Ibid.*

24. *Ibid.*, 87.

25. *Ibid.*, 88.

26. Zimmerman, *The Safe Sea of Women*, 14.

27. King, "The Situation of Lesbianism as Feminism's Magical Sign," 68.

28. Elizabeth L. Kennedy and Madeline D. Davis, *Boots of Leather, Slippers of Gold: The History of a Lesbian Community* (New York: Routledge, 1993).

29. See Deborah Britzman's poststructuralist feminist critique in her essay "Beyond Innocent Readings: Educational Ethnography as a Crisis of Representation," in William Pink and George Noblitt, eds., *The Futures of the Sociology of Education* (New Jersey: Hampton Press, 1995), 133–156. The phrase "innocent reading" comes from Althusser, 1979: "There is no such thing as an innocent reading, we must ask what reading we are guilty of… ," as cited in Ellen Rooney, *Seductive Reasoning: Pluralism as the Problematic of Contemporary Literary Theory* (Ithaca, NY: Cornell University Press, 1989), 37.

30. Sheila Jeffreys, "Butch and Femme: Then and Now," in Lesbian History Group, ed., *Not a Passing Phase: Reclaiming Lesbians in History 1840–1985* (London: The Women's Press, 1989), 158–187.

31. Kennedy and Davis, *Boots of Leather, Slippers of Gold*, 395.

32. Jeffreys, "Butch and Femme: Then and Now," 187.

33. Kennedy and Davis, *Boots of Leather, Slippers of Gold*, xv.

34. Lillian Faderman, *Surpassing the Love of Men: Romantic Friendship and Love between Women from the Renaissance to the Present* (New York: William Morrow, 1981).

35. Kennedy and Davis, *Boots of Leather, Slippers of Gold*, 9, 328.

36. George Chauncey, Jr., "Christian Brotherhood or Sexual Perversion? Homosexual Identities and the Construction of Sexual Boundaries in the World War I Era," in Martin Bauml Duberman, Martha Vicinus, and George Chauncey, Jr., eds., *Hidden from History: Reclaiming the Gay and Lesbian Past* (New York: New American Library, 1989), 313.

37. Kennedy and Davis, *Boots of Leather, Slippers of Gold*, 2.

38. *Ibid.*, 201, 211.

39. *Ibid.*, 229, citing Marilyn Frye, "Lesbian 'Sex,'" in Jeffner Allen, ed., *Lesbian Philosophies and Cultures* (Albany, NY: State University of New York Press, 1990), 305–316.

40. Britzman, "Beyond Innocent Readings" (forthcoming).

41. Kennedy and Davis, *Boots of Leather, Slippers of Gold*, 6.

42. Teresa de Lauretis, "Film and the Visible," in Bad Object-Choices, ed., *How Do I Look: Queer Film and Video* (Seattle: Bay Press, 1991), 223–224.

43. Lawrence Chua, "We Ought To Be in Pictures," *Village Voice Literary Supplement* (June 1992): 25; Lisa Duggan, "Scholars and Sense," *Village Voice Literary Supplement* (June 1992): 27; Warner, "From Queer to Eternity," 19.

44. Compare Lisa M. Walker's critique of the paradigm of visibility in lesbian theory in "How to Recognize a Lesbian: The Cultural Politics of Looking Like What You Are," *Signs* 18 (Summer 1993): 866–890.

45. Teresa de Lauretis, "Sexual Indifference and Lesbian Representation," *Theatre Journal* 40 (1988): 177.

46. de Lauretis, "Film and the Visible," 242.

47. *Ibid.*, 240. See also Lisa M. Walker, "How to Recognize a Lesbian: The Cultural Politics of Looking Like What You Are."

48. de Lauretis, "Film and the Visible," 268.

49. Chua, "We Ought To Be in Pictures"; Duggan, "Scholars and Sense"; Warner, "From Queer to Eternity."

50. Judith Roof, *A Lure of Knowledge: Lesbian Sexuality and Theory* (New York: Columbia University Press, 1991).

51. Castle, *The Apparitional Lesbian*, 2.

52. *Ibid.*, 12.

53. Eve Kosofsky Sedgwick, *Between Men: English Literature and Male Homosocial Desire* (New York: Columbia University Press, 1985), 2–3.

54. Teresa de Lauretis, *The Practice of Love: Lesbian Sexuality and Perverse Desire* (Bloomington: Indiana University Press, 1994), 115–116, 192–193.

55. Castle, *The Apparitional Lesbian*, 71.

56. Lee Edelman, *Homographesis: Essays in Gay Literary and Cultural Theory* (New York: Routledge, 1994), 244.

57. Judith Halberstam, "F2M: The Making of Female Masculinity," in Laura Doan, *The Lesbian Postmodern*, 226.

58. Sheila Jeffreys uses the same convention in her recent book, *The Lesbian Heresy: A Feminist Perspective on the Lesbian Sexual Revolution* (North Melbourne, Australia: Spinifex, 1993), 18, and for the same reasons, but, unlike me, she unequivocally rejects all postmodernist lesbian theorizing as well as queer theory.

59. Castle, *The Apparitional Lesbian*, 90.

60. Roof, *A Lure of Knowledge*, 168.

61. Castle, *The Apparitional Lesbian*, 244, 250.

62. Sue-Ellen Case, "Tracking the Vampire," *differences* 3 (Summer 1991): 1–20, cited in Castle, *The Apparitional Lesbian*, 244.

63. Jacques Derrida, "Limited Inc.," *Glyph* 2 (1977): 162–254.

64. Henry Abelove, Michele Aina Barale, and David M. Halperin, eds., *The Lesbian and Gay Studies Reader* (New York: Routledge, 1993).

65. For example, Jeffrey Escoffier, "Generations and Paradigms: Mainstreams in Lesbian and Gay Studies," *Journal of Homosexuality* 24 (1992): 7–26; and Jacquelyn N. Zita, "Lesbian and Gay Studies: Yet Another Unhappy Marriage?," in Linda Garber, ed., *Tilting the Tower: Lesbians Teaching Queer Subjects* (New York: Routledge, 1994), 258–276.

66. Julia Creet, "Daughter of the Movement: The Psychodynamics of Lesbian S/M Fantasy," *differences* 3 (Summer 1991): 135–159.

67. Abelove, Barale, and Halperin, eds., *The Lesbian and Gay Studies Reader*, xvii

68. For example, Julie Abraham on Terry Castle in Julie Abraham, "A Case of Mistaken Identity?," *Women's Review of Books* (July 1994): 36–37.

69. For example, Steven Seidman, "Identity and Politics in a 'Postmodern' Gay Culture: Some Historical and Conceptual Notes," in Michael Warner, ed., *Fear of a Queer Planet: Queer Politics and Social Theory* (Minneapolis: University of Minnesota Press, 1993), 111–112.

70. For example, Diana Fuss, *Essentially Speaking: Feminism, Nature and Difference* (New York: Routledge, 1989), 46–47, 111.

71. For example, Eve Kosofsky Sedgwick on Moraga and Lorde in Sedgwick, "Gender Criticism," in Stephen Greenblatt and Giles Gunn, eds., *Redrawing the Boundaries: The Transformation of English and American Literary Studies* (New York: Modern Language Association, 1992), 294.

72. Judith Butler, *Gender Trouble: Feminism and the Subversion of Identity* (New York: Routledge, 1990).

73. Donald G. Marshall, *Contemporary Critical Theory: A Selected Bibliography* (New York: Modern Language Association, 1993).

74. Michel de Certeau, *The Practice of Everyday Life*, trans. Steven F. Rendall (Berkeley: University of California Press, 1984), 188.

75. Miss Spentyouth, *Judy!* 1, Spring Fever, 1993.

76. Its outrageous cathexis was to Noam Chomsky. See *Alphabet Threat*, Number 3 (1993), produced in Sacramento, California.

77. Judith Butler, *Bodies That Matter: On the Discursive Limits of "Sex"* (New York: Routledge, 1993).

78. Andrew Ross, "New Age Technoculture," in Lawrence Grossberg, Cary Nelson, and Paula Treichler, eds., *Cultural Studies* (New York: Routledge, 1992), 553.

79. Larissa MacFarquahar, "Putting the Camp Back into Campus," *Lingua Franca* (September/October 1993): 6–7.

80. de Certeau, *The Practice of Everyday Life*, 176.

81. Miss Spentyouth, *Judy!*, 1.

82. Linda Garber, ed., *Tilting the Tower: Lesbians Teaching Queer Subjects* (New York: Routledge, 1994).

83. Miss Spentyouth, *Judy!*, 8.

84. The definition of "hypertrophic reading" from de Certeau, *The Practice of Everyday Life*, xxi.

85. Castle, *The Apparitional Lesbian*, 4.

86. *Ibid.*, 148.

87. *Ibid.*, 238.

CHAPTER 3. Back to the Future with *Dykes To Watch Out For* and *Hothead Paisan*

1. Andrea Juno and V. Vale, *Angry Women* (San Francisco: Re/Search Publications, 1991).

2. *Ibid.*, 4.

3. The *Hothead Paisan* zines are published quarterly by Giant Ass Publishing, P.O Box 214, New Haven, CT 06502. The first issue was published in February 1991.

4. Diane DiMassa, *Hothead Paisan: Homicidal Lesbian Terrorist* (Pittsburgh: Cleis Press, 1993), 21.

5. Alison Bechdel, *Dykes To Watch Out For* (Ithaca, NY: Firebrand Books, 1986), *More Dykes To Watch Out For* (Ithaca, NY: Firebrand Books, 1988), *New, Improved! Dykes To Watch Out For* (Ithaca, NY: Firebrand Books, 1990), *Dykes To Watch Out For: The Sequel* (Ithaca, NY: Firebrand Books, 1992), and *Spawn of Dykes To Watch Out For* (Ithaca, NY: Firebrand Books, 1993).

6. Bechdel, *Spawn of Dykes To Watch Out For*, 7–9.

7. DiMassa, *Hothead Paisan: Homicidal Lesbian Terrorist*. See previous citation. n.p.

8. M. Thomas Inge, *Comics as Culture* (Jackson: University Press of Mississippi, 1990), 142.

9. Pagan Kennedy, "P.C. Comics," *The Nation* 19 (March 1990): 386.

10. Compare the insightful but heterosexually challenged article about "The Popular Pleasures of Female Revenge (Or Rage Bursting in a Blaze of Gunfire)," by Kirsten Marthe Lentz, *Cultural Studies* 7 (October 1993): 374–405.

11. Tee Corinne, "Comics By Women," *Country Women Magazine* 29 (1977): 25

12. S. Bryn Austin and Pam Gregg, "A Freak Among Freaks: The Zine Scene," in Arlene Stein, ed., *Sisters, Sexperts, Queers: Beyond the Lesbian Nation*, 81–95; Henry Jenkins, III, "Star Trek Rerun, Reread, Rewritten: Fan Writing as Textual Poaching," *Critical Studies in Mass Communication* 5 (1988): 85–107; Constance Penley, "Feminism, Psychoanalysis, and the Study of Popular Culture," in Lawrence Grossberg, Cary Nelson and Paula A. Treichler, eds., *Cultural Studies*, 479–500; and Matias Viegener, "There's Trouble in that Body: Queer Fanzines, Sexual Identity and Censorship," *Fiction International* 22 (1992): 123–136.

13. Lynda Hart, *Fatal Women: Lesbian Sexuality and the Mark of Aggression* (Princeton: Princeton University Press, 1994), dedication page.

14. Nancy Bereano of Firebrand Books, telephone conversation with author, July 20, 1990.

15. J. Laplanche and J-B Pontalis, *The Language of Psychoanalysis*, trans. Donald Nicholson-Smith (London: Karnac, 1988), quoted in Penley, "Feminism, Psychoanalysis, and the Study of Popular Culture," 493.

16. Bess Tuna, "Hothead Paisan: Our Favorite Lesbian Terrorist interviewed by Bess Tuna on KBRAT (plus a real interview with Diane and Stacey, artist and publisher) by Fish," *Brat Attack* 3 (1993): 27.

17. Robert Hough, "Seizing Books: Degrading Customs," *The Globe and Mail*, 12 February 1994, D5.

18. DiMassa, *Hothead Paisan*, Issue 3 (August 1991), Issue 9 (February 1993).

19. Dianne DiMassa, *Hothead Paisan*, Issue 2 (May 1991): 46.

20. Dianne DiMassa, *Hothead Paisan*, Issue 5, (February 1992): 83–85.

21. Corinne, "Comics by Women," 25.

22. Peter Bürger, *Theory of the Avant-Garde*, trans. Michael Shaw (Minneapolis: University of Minnesota Press, 1994), 57–59.

23. Stephen Perkins, "Subspace Zines: International Zine Show," *Alternative Press Review* (Winter 1994): 22.

24. Alison Bechdel, telephone conversation with author, July 27, 1990.

25. Alison Bechdel, telephone conversation with author, July 27, 1990. Bechdel's comments here describe what she discusses in the script she uses when she presents a slide show to public audiences about the creation of her characters.

26. Diana Fuss, *Essentially Speaking: Feminism, Nature and Difference* (New York: Routledge, 1989), 103.

27. DiMassa, *Hothead Paisan: Homicidal Lesbian Terrorist*, 19.

28. *Ibid.*, 144.

29. *Ibid.*, 11–13.

30. *Ibid.*, 43.

31. Tuna, "Hothead Paisan: Our Favorite Lesbian Terrorist interviewed by Bess Tuna on KBRAT (plus a real interview with Diane and Stacey, artist and publisher) by Fish," 30.

32. Charles Russell, *Poets, Prophets, and Revolutionaries: The Literary Avant-Garde From Rimbaud to Postmodernism* (New York: Oxford University Press, 1985), 28.

33. DiMassa, *Hothead Paisan: Homicidal Lesbian Terrorist*, 9.

34. Diane DiMassa, *Hothead Paisan*, Issue 1 (February 1991): 22.

35. Diane DiMassa, *Hothead Paisan: Homicidal Lesbian Terrorist* (Pittsburgh: Cleis Press, 1993).

36. Bechdel, telephone conversation with author, July 27, 1990. See note 25.

37. Elizabeth A. Meese, *(Sem)erotics: Theorizing Lesbian: Writing* (New York: Columbia University Press, 1992), 20.

38. Bechdel, telephone conversaton with author, July 27, 1990. See note 25.

39. Bette Gordon, quoted in Andrew Ross, *No Respect: Intellectuals & Popular Culture* (New York: Routledge, 1989), 201.

40. Regenia Gagnier, "Between Women: A Cross-Class Analysis of Status and Anarchic Humor," *Women's Studies* 15 (1988): 138.

41. Russell, *Poets, Prophets, and Revolutionaries*, 4.

42. Bechdel, "Theory and Practice," in *New, Improved! Dykes to Watch Out For*, 20.

43. Catharine R. Stimpson, "Zero Degree Deviancy: The Lesbian Novel in English," in *Where the Meanings Are: Feminism and Cultural Spaces* (New York: Methuen, 1988), 97.

44. Bechdel, "The Rule," in *Dykes To Watch Out For*, 22.

45. Bechdel, "The VCR," in *More Dykes To Watch Out For*, 52.

46. *Ibid.*

47. *Ibid.*

48. Alison Bechdel, "Serial Monogamy," in Margaret Reynolds, ed., *The Penguin Book of Lesbian Short Stories* (London: Viking, 1993), 357–367.

49. DiMassa, *Hothead Paisan: Homicidal Lesbian Terrorist*, 53–60.

50. *Ibid.*, 26.

51. Valerie Solanis, "Excerpts from the SCUM (Society for Cutting Up Men) Manifesto," in Robin Morgan, ed., *Sisterhood Is Powerful* (New York: Vintage, 1970), 577.

52. DiMassa, *Hothead Paisan: Homicidal Lesbian Terrorist*, 44–45.

53. See for example, Maria Maggenti, "Wandering Through Herland," and Eva Yaa Asantewaa, "Sister to Brother: Women of Color on Coming Together with Men," in a special issue of *Outweek* 40 (April 4, 1990): 40–49.

54. Bourdieu, quoted in Ross, *No Respect*, 59.

55. See, for example, Sue-Ellen Case's "Introduction," in Sue-Ellen Case, ed., *Performing Feminisms: Feminist Critical Theory and Theatre* (Baltimore: Johns Hopkins University Press, 1990), 40–53; Sue-Ellen Case, "Toward a Butch-Femme Aesthetic," in Henry Abelove, Michèle Aina Barale, and David M. Halpern, eds., *The Lesbian and Gay Studies Reader*, 294–306; Teresa de Lauretis

"Sexual Indifference and Lesbian Representation," *Theatre Journal* 40 (1988): 148–155; and Jill Dolan, "In Defense of the Discourse: Materialist Feminism, Postmodernism, Poststructuralism...and Theory," *TDR* (Fall 1989): 58–71.

56. de Lauretis, "Sexual Indifference and Lesbian Representation," 155.

57. Teresa de Lauretis, *The Practice of Love: Lesbian Sexuality and Perverse Desire* (Bloomington: Indiana University Press, 1994)

58. Case, "Toward a Butch-Femme Aesthetic," 305.

59. Jill Dolan, "'Lesbian' Subjectivity in Realism: Dragging at the Margins of Structure and Ideology," in Sue-Ellen Case, ed., *Performing Feminisms: Feminist Critical Theory and Theatre* , 40–53.

60. Russell, *Poets, Prophets, and Revolutionaries*, 36.

61. Nicole Brossard, *The Aerial Letter*, trans. Marlene Wildeman (Toronto: The Women's Press, 1988), 122.

62. See Kate Davy, "Constructing the Spectator: Reception, Context, and Address in Lesbian Performance," *Performing Arts Journal* 29 (1986): 43–52, a position refined in "Reading Past the Heterosexual Imperative: Dress Suits to Hire," *TDR* (Spring 1989): 153–170; Jill Dolan "The Dynamics of Desire: Sexuality and Gender in Pornography and Performance," *Theatre Journal* (May 1987): 156–174; later self-critiqued in "Breaking the Code: Musings on Lesbian Sexuality and the Performer," *Modern Drama* 32 (March 1989): 146–158.

63. DiMassa, *Hothead Paisan: Homicidal Lesbian Terrorist*, 169–170.

64. Bechdel, "Down to the Skin: A Mildly Erotic Epilogue," in *More Dykes to Watch Out For*, 82–108.

65. Jacques Derrida and Marie-Françoise Plissart, "Right of Inspection," *Art & Text* 32 (Autumn 1989): 12.

66. Lucy Lippard, *Get the Message?: A Decade of Art for Social Change* (New York: Dutton, 1984), 118.

67. Russell, *Poets, Prophets, and Revolutionaries*, v.

68. Bürger, *Theory of the Avant-Garde*, 57–59; Andreas Huyssen, *After the Great Divide* (Bloomington: Indiana University Press, 1986), 159–177; and Russell, *Poets, Prophets, and Revolutionaries*, 270.

69. Julia Kristeva, "Postmodernism?," in Harry R. Garvin, ed., *Romanticism, Modernism, Postmodernism, Bucknell Review* (Lewisberg, PA: Bucknell University Press, 1980), 140.

CHAPTER 4. Toward a Butch-Femme Reading Practice: Reading Joan Nestle

1. See the entry for Alison Bechdel in the "Notes on the Authors," in Margaret Reynolds, ed., *The Penguin Book of Lesbian Short Stories* (London: Viking, 1993), 424.

2. JoAnn Loulan, *The Lesbian Erotic Dance: Butch Femme Androgyny and Other Rhythms* (San Francisco: Spinsters, 1990), 42–44.

3. Katie King, "Audre Lorde's Lacquered Layerings: The Lesbian Bar as a Site of Literary Production," in Sally Munt, ed., *New Lesbian Criticism: Literary and Cultural Readings* (New York: Columbia University Press, 1992), 55.

4. Samuel R. Delany, "Street Talk/Straight Talk," *differences* 3 (Summer 1991): 35, 38.

5. Joan Nestle, "Butch-Femme Relationships: Sexual Courage in the 1950s," in *A Restricted Country* (Ithaca: Firebrand Books, 1987), 100–109.

6. *Ibid.*, 104.

7. Joan Nestle, *A Restricted Country*. See previous note.

8. See Judith Butler, *Gender Trouble: Feminism and the Subversion of Identity* (New York: Routledge, 1990); Teresa de Lauretis, *The Practice of Love: Lesbian Sexuality and Perverse Desire* (Bloomington: Indiana University Press, 1994); and Judith Roof, *A Lure of Knowledge: Lesbian Sexuality and Theory* (New York: Columbia University Press, 1991).

9. King, "Audre Lorde's Lacquered Layerings," 56; Nestle, *A Restricted Country*, 11.

10. Clare Whatling, "Reading Awry: Joan Nestle and the Recontextualization of Heterosexuality," in Joseph Bristow, ed., *Sexual Sameness: Textual Differences in Lesbian and Gay Writing* (New York: Routledge, 1992), 226.

11. Nestle, "Butch-Femme Relationships: Sexual Courage in the 1950s," 103.

12. Joan Nestle, *The Persistent Desire: A Femme-Butch Reader* (Boston: Alyson Publications, 1992), 18.

13. Among the most influential texts in English language feminist and lesbian theorizing of subjectivity were the following: Catherine Belsey, *Critical Practice* (London: Methuen, 1980); Michel Foucault, "The Subject and Power," in Brian Wallis, ed., *Art After Modernism: Rethinking Representation* (New York: Godine, 1984), 417–34; Kaja Silverman, *The Subject of Semiotics* (New York:

Oxford University Press, 1983); Julian Henriques, Wendy Hollway, Cathy Urwin, Couze Venn, and Valerie Walkerdine, eds., *Changing the Subject: Psychology, Social Regulation and Subjectivity* (London: Methuen, 1984); Nancy K. Miller, "Changing the Subject: Authorship, Writing, and the Reader," in Teresa de Lauretis, ed. *Feminist Studies/Critical Studies* (Bloomington: Indiana University Press, 1986); Paul Smith, *Discerning the Subject* (Minneapolis: University of Minnesota Press, 1988); Teresa de Lauretis, "Sexual Indifference and Lesbian Representation," *Theatre Journal* 40 (1988): 155–177; Sue-Ellen Case, "Toward a Butch-Femme Aesthetic," in Henry Abelove, Michèle Aina Barale, and David M. Halpern, eds., *The Lesbian and Gay Studies Reader*, 294–306; Teresa de Lauretis, "Eccentric Subjects: Feminist Theory and Historical Consciousness," *Feminist Studies* 16 (Spring 1990): 115–150.

14. Monique Wittig, "The Mark of Gender," in *The Straight Mind and Other Essays* (Boston: Beacon Press, 1992), 80–81, and *The Lesbian Body*, trans. David Le Vay (New York: Bard, 1976).

15. Sue-Ellen Case, "Toward a Butch-Femme Aesthetic," 295.

16. Sue-Ellen Case, "Introduction," in Sue-Ellen Case, ed., *Performing Feminisms: Feminist Critical Theory and Theatre* , 12–13.

17. de Lauretis, *The Practice of Love*, 4–8.

18. de Lauretis, "Sexual Indifference and Lesbian Representation," 155.

19. Compare Case, "Toward a Butch-Femme Aesthetic"; Kate Davy, "Constructing the Spectator: Reception, Context, and Address in Lesbian Performance," *Performing Arts Journal* 29 (1986): 43–52; and Jill Dolan, "In Defense of the Discourse: Materialist Feminism, Postmodernism, Poststructuralism...and Theory," *TDR* (Fall 1989): 58–71; and Jill Dolan, "'Lesbian Subjectivity in Realism: Dragging at the Margins of Structure and Ideology," in Sue-Ellen Case, ed., *Performing Feminisms: Feminist Critical Theory and Theatre*, 40–53.

20. Jane Gallop, *Reading Lacan* (Ithaca: Cornell University Press, 1985), and *Thinking Through the Body* (New York: Columbia University Press, 1988).

21. Nestle, *A Restricted Country*, 159.

22. Elizabeth A. Meese, *(Sem)erotics: Theorizing Lesbian: Writing* (New York: Columbia University Press, 1992).

23. Elizabeth A. Meese, "Theorizing Lesbian: Writing—A Love Letter," in Karla Jay and Joanne Glasgow, eds., *Lesbian Texts and Contexts: Radical Revisions* (New York: University Press, 1990), 70–88.

24. *Ibid.*, 71.

25. Cherríe Moraga and Gloria Anzaldúa, eds., *This Bridge Called My Back: Writings By Radical Women of Color* (Watertown, MA: Persephone Press, 1981).

26. Audre Lorde, *Zami: A New Spelling of My Name* (Freedom, CA: The Crossing Press, 1983), and *Sister Outsider* (Trumansburg, NY: The Crossing Press, 1984).

27. de Lauretis, "Sexual Indifference and Lesbian Representation," 164.

28. *Ibid.*

29. Smith, *Discerning the Subject*, 118.

30. *Ibid.*, 72.

31. Patricia Waugh, *Feminine Fictions: Revisting the Postmodern* (New York: Routledge, 1989).

32. Smith, *Discerning the Subject*, 150.

33. *Ibid.*, 40.

34. *Ibid.*, 79.

35. *Ibid.*, 108.

36. Notable examples include Sedgwick, "A Poem is Being Written," *Representations* 17 (19987): 110–143; and Gallop, *Thinking Through the Body*.

37. Cornel West, "The New Cultural Politics of Difference," in Russell Ferguson, Martha Gever, Trinh T. Minh-ha and Cornel West, eds., *Out There: Marginalization and Contemporary Cultures* (New York: New Museum of Contemporary Art, 1990), 29.

38. Biddy Martin, "Lesbian Identity and Autobiographical Difference[s]," in Bella Brodzki and Celeste Schenke, eds., *Life/Lines: Theorizing Women's Autobiographies* (Ithaca, NY: Cornell University Press, 1988), 82.

39. Biddy Martin, "Sexual Practice and Changing Lesbian Identities," in Michèle Barrett and Anne Phillips, eds., *Destabilizing Theory: Contemporary Feminist Debates* (Stanford, CA: Stanford University Press, 1992), 117.

40. *Ibid.*, 115.

41. See his "Ethnic Identity and Post-Structuralist Difference," *Cultural Critique* 6 (1987): 199–220.

42. Gayatri Chakravorty Spivak, "Feminism and Deconstruction, Again: Negotiations," *Outside in the Teaching Machine* (New York: Routledge, 1993), 128.

43. *Ibid.*, 130.

44. *Ibid.*, 128.

45. *Ibid.*, 129.

46. Meese is citing Janice G. Raymond, *A Passion for Friends: Toward a Philosophy of Female Affection* (Boston: Beacon Press, 1986), 4.

47. Meese, "Theorizing Lesbian: Writing—A Love Letter," 83.

48. Roger Fisher and William Ury, *Getting to Yes: Negotiating Agreement Without Giving In* (London: Penguin, 1981), xii, 4, 12.

49. Carolyn Steedman, *Landscape for a Good Woman* (New Brunswick, NJ: Rutgers University Press, 1987), 110.

50. Elizabeth Wheeler, "Bulldozing the Subject," *Postmodern Culture* (May 1991): 5–17.

51. The best exception to this is a moment in Radhakrishnan's essay, "Negotiating Subject Positions in an Uneven World," in Linda Kauffman, ed., *Feminism and Institutions* (London: Basil Blackwell, 1989), 288, where he is in dialogue with Elizabeth Meese's reading of the conflicting subject position in Gordimer's Rosa Burger; nonetheless, his reliance on Edward Said's notion of "unevenness" is somewhat problematic for feminist, let alone lesbian readers, because of the relationship between evenness/unevenness and filiation/affiliation, with the pair's sexist and heterosexist connotations. Compare his telling qualification/redundancy, "normative heterosexism."

52. Couze Venn, "The Subject of Psychology," in Julian Henriques, Wendy Hollway, Cathy Urwin, Couze Venn, and Valerie Walkerdine, eds., *Changing the Subject: Psychology, Social Regulation and Subjectivity* (London: Methuen, 1984), 151.

53. West, "The New Cultural Politics of Difference," 31.

54. Butler, *Gender Trouble*, 14.

55. West, "The New Cultural Politics of Difference," 35.

56. Nestle, *A Restricted Country*, 9.

57. *Ibid.*, 29.

58. *Ibid.*, 30.

59. *Ibid.*, 31.

60. *Ibid.*, 33.

61. Lorde, *Zami: A New Spelling of My Name*, 226.

62. Nestle, *A Restricted Country*, 36.

63. R. Radhakrishnan, "The Changing Subject and the Politics of Theory," *differences* 2 (1990): 148.

64. Nestle, *A Restricted Country*, 175.

65. Julia Swindells, "Liberating the Subject? Autobiography and 'Women's History': A Reading of the Diaries of Hannah Cullwick," in Personal Narratives Group, ed., *Interpreting Women's Lives: Feminist Theory* (Bloomington: Indiana University Press, 1989), 24–25.

66. Ibid., 26.

67. Ibid., 38.

68. Steedman, *Landscape for a Good Woman*, 22.

69. Nestle, *A Restricted Country*, 10. See Elizabeth Meese's use of the idea of the gift in *(Ex)Tensions: Re-Figuring Feminist Criticism* (Urbana, IL: University of Illinois Press, 1990), 46–49, though she does not explain how negotiation and gift-giving and gift-reception relate to each other; Biddy Martin also discusses the trope of the gift in Nestle in "Sexual Practice and Changing Lesbian Identities."

70. Nestle, *A Restricted Country*, 11.

71. Ibid., 116.

72. Lillian Faderman, *Odd Girls and Twilight Lovers: A History of Lesbian Life in Twentieth-Century America* (New York: Columbia University Press, 1991), 174.

73. Ibid., 158–159.

74. Janice G. Raymond, "Putting the Politics Back Into Lesbianism," *Women's Studies International Forum* 12 (1989): 151.

75. Nestle, *A Restricted Country*, 158–159.

76. Smith, *Discerning the Subject*, 77.

77. Fredric Jameson, *The Political Unconscious: Narrative as a Socially Symbolic Act* (Ithaca, NY: Cornell University Press, 1981), 102.

78. Nestle, *A Restricted Country*, 107–108.

79. Ibid., 108.

80. Ibid., 107.

81. Ibid., 11.

82. Margaret Hunt, "A Fem's Own Story: An Interview with Joan Nestle," in Christian McEwen and Sue O'Sullivan, eds., *Out the Other Side: Contemporary Lesbian Writing* (London: Virago Press, 1988), 239, 242.

83. Raymond, "Putting the Politics Back Into Lesbianism," 151.

CHAPTER 5. Sarah Schulman: Urban Lesbian Radicals in a Postmodern Mainstream

1. "The Lesbian Avengers," excerpts from *The Lesbian Avenger Handbook*, in Sarah Schulman, *My American History: Lesbian and Gay Life During the Reagan/Bush Years* (New York: Routledge, 1994), 279–313.

2. Endorsement by Fay Weldon for Sarah Schulman's *Empathy* (New York: Dutton, 1992).

3. Sally Munt, "'Somewhere Over the Rainbow…': Postmodernism and the Fiction of Sarah Schulman," in Sally Munt, ed., *New Lesbian Criticism: Literary and Cultural Readings* (New York: Columbia University Press, 1992), 33–50.

4. Terry Castle, *The Apparitional Lesbian: Female Homosexuality and Modern Culture* (New York: Columbia University Press, 1993), 90.

5. Sarah Schulman, *Girls, Visions and Everything* (Seattle: Seal Press, 1986), 16.

6. Micheline Grimard-Leduc, "The Mind-Drifting Islands," in Sarah Hoagland and Julia Penelope, eds., *For Lesbians Only: A Separatist Anthology* (London: Onlywomen Press, 1988), 493.

7. Marilyn Frye, *The Politics of Reality: Essays in Feminist Theory* (Ithaca, NY: The Crossing Press, 1983), 158, 160.

8. This is Frye's argument in her esssay "To See and Be Seen," in *The Politics of Reality*, 160:

> The use of the word 'lesbian' to name us is a quadrifold evasion, a laminated euphemism. To name us, one goes by way of a reference to the island of Lesbos, which in turn is an indirect reference to the poet Sappho (who used to live there, they say), which in turn is itself an indirect reference to what fragments of her poetry have survived a few millenia of patriarchy, and this in turn (if we have not lost you by now) is a prophylactic avoidance of direct mention of the sort of creature who would write such poems or to whom such poems would be written…assuming you happen to know what is in those poems written in a dialect of Greek over two thousand years ago on some small island somewhere in the wine dark Aegean Sea. This is a truly remarkable feat of silence.

9. Lillian Faderman, *Odd Girls and Twilight Lovers: A History of Lesbian Life in Twentieth-Century America*, 237–240.

10. Lauren Berlant and Elizabeth Freeman, "Queer Nationality," *boundary 2* (Spring 1992): 174–175. Though Berlant and Freeman admitted that Queer

Nation, the subject of their celebration, was effectively dead at the time they wrote, in 1991, their paper was reprinted in *Fear of a Queer Planet*, 1993, without emendation, as if the demise had not occurred. What happened to the performative politics such as "Queer Nights Out" they praise so highly for offering ways of dismantling apparatuses organizing sexual practices into 'facts' of sexual identity, especially given the fact that Queer Nation folded because of (the usual boring old) unresolved divisions over gender, race and class? And with things like the Queer Shopping Network gone, what happens to their argument?

11. Marilyn Frye, "Some Reflections on Separatism and Power," in Sarah Hoagland and Julia Penelope, eds., *For Lesbians Only: A Separatist Anthology*, 62.

12. See my anti-separatist argument about lesbian ethics, co-written with Martha Saunders, "Realizing Love and Justice: Lesbian Ethics in the Upper and Lower Case," *Hypatia* (Fall 1992): 148–171.

13. The notion of national and nationalist categories is admittedly a problematic one. The very notion of placing women, especially lesbians, in such categories, which can be "genealogical illusions" even when lesbians themselves do it, is brilliantly critiqued by Elaine Marks in "'Sapho 1900': Imaginary Renee Viviens and the Rear of the Belle Epoque," *Yale French Studies* 75 (1988): 175–189.

14. Penelope Engelbrecht, "'Lifting Belly Is a Language': The Postmodern Lesbian Subject," *Feminist Studies* 16 (Spring 1990): 110; Susan Gubar, "Sapphistries," *Signs* 10 (Autumn 1984): 59.

15. Monique Wittig, "Paradigm," in George Stambolian and Elaine Marks, eds., *Homosexualities and French Literature* (Ithaca, NY: Cornell University Press, 1979), 114.

16. Nicole Brossard, *The Aerial Letter*, trans. Marlene Wildeman (Toronto: The Women's Press, 1988), 122.

17. Note the asymmetry of the three names; the third lacks the mythic as well as cosmopolitan aura of the Lesbos-Paris-New York-Montréal trajectory.

18. Ekua Omosupe, "Black/Lesbian/Bulldagger," *differences* 3 (Summer 1991): 108.

19. Judith Roof, *A Lure of Knowledge: Lesbian Sexuality and Theory* (New York: Columbia University Press, 1991), 127.

20. Monique Wittig and Sande Zeig, *Lesbian Peoples: Material for a Dictionary* (New York: Avon, 1978).

21. Mandy Merck, "The Amazons of Ancient Athens," in *Perversions: Deviant Readings* (London: Virago Press, 1993), 121.

22. Merck, "The Amazons of Ancient Athens," 161, citing Monique Wittig, *The Lesbian Body*, trans. David Le Vay (New York: Bard, 1976), 161. In *Lovhers*, trans. Barbara Godard (Montréal: Guernica, 1986), 17, Nicole Brossard is even more hyperbolic: "In reality, there is no fiction."

23. Merck, "The Amazons of Ancient Athens," 161.

24. Wittig and Zeig, *Lesbian Peoples: Material for a Dictionary*, 5.

25. Elaine Marks, "Lesbian Intertextuality," in George Stambolian and Elaine Marks, eds., *Homosexualities and French Literature: Cultural Contexts/Critical Texts*, 353–377.

26. Gubar, "Sapphistries," 62, 46.

27. *Ibid.*, 59.

28. Joan DeJean, *Fictions of Sappho 1546–1937* (Chicago: University of Chicago Press, 1989), 20, 21.

29. Marks, "Lesbian Intertextuality," 361. Marks's contention about the centrality of (female) homosexuality lends credence to Eve Sedgwick's claim in *Epistemology of the Closet* (Berkeley: University of California Press, 1990), 1, 9, that the homo/hetero definition has moved from a marginal to a central position in all areas of Western knowledge and culture.

30. Marks, "Lesbian Intertextuality," 370.

31. Brossard, *Lovhers*, 106.

32. Monique Wittig, "The Point of View: Universal or Particular?," in *The Straight Mind and Other Essays* (Boston: Beacon Press, 1992), 64.

33. Brossard, *Lovhers*, 108.

34. Louise Cotnoir, Lise Guevremont, Claude Beausoleil, and Hugues Corriveau, "Interview with Nicole Brossard on *Picture Theory*," trans. Luise von Flotow-Evans, *Canadian Fiction Magazine* 47 (1983): 126.

35. Catharine R. Stimpson, "Zero Degree Deviancy: The Lesbian Novel in English," in *Where the Meanings Are: Feminism and Cultural Spaces* (New York: Methuen, 1988), 105.

36. *Ibid.*, 109.

37. *Ibid.*, 108–109.

38. *Ibid.*, 108.

39. Ann Allen Shockley, "A Meeting of the Sapphic Daughters," *Sinister Wisdom* 9 (Spring 1979): 54–59.

40. Bertha Harris, "The More Profound Nationality of their Lesbianism: Lesbian Society in Paris in the 1920s," in Phyllis Birkby, Bertha Harris, Jill Johnston, Esther Newton, and Jane O'Wyatt, eds., *Amazon Expedition: A Lesbian Feminist Anthology* (Albion, CA: Times Change, 1973), 78–79.

41. Merck, "The Amazons of Ancient Athens," vii.

42. Ibid., 2.

43. Judy Grahn, *Another Mother Tongue: Gay Words, Gay Worlds* (Boston: Beacon Press, 1984).

44. Ibid., 163-201, 185–201.

45. Ibid., 170–172.

46. Roof, *A Lure of Knowledge*, 127.

47. Elyse Blankley, "Return to Mytilene: Renee Vivien and the City of women," in Susan Merrill Squier, ed., *Women Writers and the City: Essays in Feminist Literary Criticism* (Knoxville: University of Tennessee Press, 1984), 58–63. In "'Sapho 1900'," 189, Marks rejects Gayle Rubin's lesbian feminist claiming of Vivien as a lesbian ancestor, calling it a misreading inspired by the will to classify. Though I have no wish to prescribe or proscribe "real" and "inauthentic" lesbians, Marks would probably be hostile to this project of placing Schulman within lesbian literary traditions as well.

48. Grahn, *Another Mother Tongue*, 112–113.

49. *Lillian Faderman, Surpassing the Love of Men: Romantic Friendship and Love between Women from the Renaissance to the Present* (New York: William Morrow, 1981), 74–75, 85.

50. Ibid., 20.

51. Sherrill Grace's article, "Quest for a Peaceable Kingdom: Urban/Rural Codes in Roy, Laurence, and Atwood," in Squier, ed., *Women Writers and the City*, 193–209, elides the differences between English Canada and Quebec; she says nothing about Brossard and her love affair with the city; she does devote two pages to Gabrielle Roy's bleak portrait of Montréal.

52. See Sherrill Grace's list in "Quest for a Peacable Kingdom," 201, and by contrast, Susan Saegert's feminist urban studies deconstructionist approach to these claims in "Masculine Cities and Feminine Suburbs: Polarized Ideas, Contradictory Realities," *Signs* 5, Supplementary (1980): S96–97.

53. Wendy Martin, "Another View of the 'City Upon the Hill': The Prophetic Vision of Adrienne Rich," in Squier, ed., *Women Writers and the City*, 249.

54. Andrea Freud Loewenstein, "Troubled Times: Interview with Sarah Schulman," in Betsy Warland, ed., *InVersions: Writing by Dykes, Queers & Lesbians* (Vancouver: Press Gang, 1991), 220.

55. Catharine R. Stimpson, "Nancy Reagan Wears a Hat: Feminism and its Cultural Consensus," in *Where the Meanings Are: Feminism and Cultural Space* (New York: Methuen, 1988), 184.

56. *Ibid.*, 189.

57. Sarah Schulman, *The Sophie Horowitz Story* (Tallahassee, FL: Naiad Press, 1984), 84.

58. *Ibid.*, 44.

59. *Ibid.*, 107–109.

60. *Ibid.*, 157.

61. *Ibid.*, 80–81.

62. Sarah Schulman, "When We Were Very Young: Radical Jewish Women on the Lower East Side, 1879–1919," in Melanie Kaye/Kantrowitz and Irena Klepfisz, eds., *The Tribe of Dina: A Jewish Women's Anthology* (Montpelier, VT: Sinister Wisdom Books, 1986), 232–253.

63. Paula Hyman, "Neighborhood Women and Consumer Protest," *American Jewish History* 70 (1981): 96–99, quoted in Schulman, "When We Were Very Young," 249.

64. Quoted in Arlene Stein, "The Year of the Lustful Lesbian," in Arlene Stein, ed., *Sisters, Sexperts, Queers: Beyond the Lesbian Nation* (New York: Plume, 1993), 18.

65. Schulman, *The Sophie Horowitz Story*, 1.

66. Schulman, *Girls, Visions and Everything*, 16.

67. Lois Weaver, quoted in Jill Dolan, "The Dynamics of Desire: Sexuality and Gender in Pornography and Performance," in *The Feminist Spectator as Critic* (Ann Arbor: University of Michigan Press, 1988), 68.

68. Dolan, "The Dynamics of Desire," 68.

69. Kate Davy, "Reading Past the Heterosexual Imperative: Dress Suits to Hire," *TDR* (Spring 1989): 153–170.

70. Sue-Ellen Case," Toward a Butch-Femme Aesthetic," in Henry Abelove, Michèle Aina Barale, and David M. Halperin, eds., *The Lesbian and Gay Studies Reader*, 294.

71. Schulman, *Girls, Visions and Everything*, 120.

72. Jack Kerouac, *On the Road* (New York: Viking Penguin, 1991).

73. Schulman, *Girls, Visions and Everything*, 59–60.

74. *Ibid.*, 144–145.

75. *Ibid.*, 164.

76. *Ibid.*, 103.

77. *Ibid.*, 137.

78. *Ibid.*, 178.

79. Sarah Schulman, *After Delores* (New York: New American Library, 1989).

80. Bonnie Zimmerman, *The Safe Sea of Women: Lesbian Fiction 1969-1989* (Boston: Beacon Press, 1990), 212.

81. *Ibid.*,, 212.

82. Schulman, *After Delores*, 152.

83. *Ibid.*, 30.

84. Slavoj Zizek, *Looking Awry: An Introduction to Jacques Lacan Through Popular Culture* (Cambridge, MA: MIT Press, 1991), 62–63.

85. Schulman, *After Delores*, 153.

86. *Ibid.*, 17.

87. Sarah Schulman, *People in Trouble* (New York: New American Library, 1991).

88. Munt, "Somewhere over the Rainbow…', 48–49.

89. Schulman, *People in Trouble*, 113.

90. *Ibid.*, 113.

91. Loewenstein, "Troubled Times," 220.

92. *Ibid.*, 220.

93. *Ibid.*, 223.

94. Schulman, *People in Trouble*, 147.

95. *Ibid.*, 142.

96. *Ibid.*, 186.

97. *Ibid.*, 188.

98. *Ibid.*, 227.

99. *Ibid.*, 228.

100. J. Laplanche and J-B Pontalis, *The Language of Psychoanalysis,* trans. Donald Nicholson-Smith (London: Karnac, 1988), 194.

101. Sigmund Freud and Josef Breuer, *Studies on Hysteria,* trans. James Strachey and Alix Strachey (New York: Penguin, 1991), 74.

102. Schulman, *Empathy,* 12.

103. *Ibid.*, 6.

104. *Ibid.*, 157.

105. Heinz Kohut, "Introspection, Empathy, and Psychoanalysis," *Journal of the American Psychoanalytical Association* 7 (1959): 459–483.

106. Schulman, *Empathy,* 6.

107. Laplanche and Pontalis, *The Language of Psychoanalysis,* 206.

108. Schulman, *Empathy,* 158-159.

109. *Ibid.*, 159.

110. *Ibid.*, 162.

111. *Ibid.*, 179.

112. *Ibid.*,179.

113. *Ibid.*, 182.

114. Lowenstein, "Troubled Times," 222.

115. Munt, "Somewhere over the Rainbow…," 47.

116. Schulman, *Empathy,* 146.

117. Joan Nestle, "Butch-Femme Relationships: Sexual Courage in the 1950s," in *A Restricted Country*, 106.

CHAPTER 6. Que(e)rying Pedagogy: Teaching the Un/popular Cultures

1. A neologism coined by a gay psychologist on analogy with other psychological terms for irrational feelings, "homophobia" from the outset consigns and confines its analytic scope to the commonsensical and intrapsychic world

of understanding of what many now refer to in a telling shorthand as the "'phobe." "'Phobe" also erases gender specificity. Attempts by some lesbian writers to inscribe the gender specific "lesbophobia" into discussions of homophobia have met with little success. Only lesbians seem to know or use the term. Although the usual speculation is that "lesbophobia" is an unlovely word, verbal ugliness seems less likely the cause of its unpopularity than general inability to imagine the targets of such mistreatment.

2. Mary Bryson and Suzanne de Castell, "Queer Pedagogy: Praxis Makes Im/Perfect," in Mary Bryson and Suzanne de Castell, eds., *Radical Interventions: Identity, Politics, and Differences in Educational Praxis* (Albany, NY: State University New York Press, forthcoming).

3. Deborah P. Britzman, "Is There a Queer Pedagogy? Or, Stop Reading Straight," *Educational Theory* 45 (Spring 1995): 152.

4. Michael Warner, "From Queer to Eternity: An Army of Theorists Cannot Fail," *Village Voice Literary Supplement* (June 1992): 19.

5. See my "Addressing Heterosexism in Women's Studies Classrooms," in Debra Shogan, ed., *A Reader in Feminist Ethics* (Toronto: Scholars Press, 1992), 449–465.

6. Charles Russell, *Poets, Prophets, and Revolutionaries: The Literary Avant-Garde from Rimbaud to Postmodernism* (New York: Oxford University Press, 1985), 16.

7. Heather Zwicker, "Queer Readings" (paper presented at the 1994 Learned Societies Confrence, Lesbian and Gay Studies, Calgary, Alberta), 1.

8. See Carolyn Gammon, "Lesbian Studies Emerging in Canada," in Henry L. Minton, ed., *Gay and Lesbian Studies Issue,* special issue of *Journal of Homosexuality* 24 (1992): 137–160.

9. See Allison Berg, Jean Kowaleski, Caroline Le Guin, Ellen Weinauer and Eric A. Wolfe, "Breaking the Silence: Sexual Preference in the Composition Classroom," in Linda Garber, ed., *Tilting the Tower: Lesbians Teaching Queer Subjects* (New York: Routledge, 1994), 108–116.

10. Sarah Schulman, *The Sophie Horowitz Story* (Tallahassee, FL: Naiad Press, 1984), 66.

11. Ed Cohen, "Who Are 'We'? Gay 'Identity' as Political (E)motion: (A Theoretical Rumination)," in Diana Fuss, ed., *inside/out: Lesbian Theories, Gay Theories* (New York: Routledge, 1991), 81.

12. Deborah P. Britzman, "Decentering Discourses in Teacher Education: Or, The Unleashing of Unpopular Things," *Boston University Journal of Education* 173 (1991): 63–65.

13. Richard D. Mohr, "Gay Studies in the Big Ten: A Survivor's Manual," in *Gays/Justice: A Study of Ethics, Society, and Law* (New York: Columbia University Press, 1988), 277–292.

14. Richard D. Mohr, "The Ethics of Students and the Teaching of Ethics: A Lecturing," in *Gays/Justice: A Study of Ethics, Society, and Law*, 293.

15. Mohr, "Gay Studies in the Big Ten," 291–292.

16. Mohr, "The Ethics of Students and the Teachings of Ethics: A Lecturing," 300.

17. Mohr, "Gay Studies in the Big Ten," 280.

18. *Ibid.*, 281.

19. *Ibid.*, 290.

20. *Ibid.*

21. Linda Garber, ed., *Tilting the Tower: Lesbians Teaching Queer Subjects* (New York: Routledge, 1994).

22. Henry L. Minton, ed., *Gay and Lesbian Studies Issue*, special issue of *Journal of Homosexuality* 24 (1992).

23. Warner, "From Queer to Eternity: An Army of Theorists Cannot Fail," 18.

24. Garber, *Tilting the Tower*; Kathy Obear, "Opening Doors to Understanding and Acceptance: A Facilitator's Guide to Presenting Workshops on Lesbian and Gay Issues" (Amherst, MA: The Human Advantage, n.d.).

25. Jeffrey Escoffier, "Generations and Paradigms: Mainstreams in Lesbian and Gay Studies," *Journal of Homosexuality* 24 (1992): 7–26

26. Thomas Yingling, "Sexual Preference/Cultural Reference: The Predicament of Gay Culture Studies," *American Literary History* 3 (Spring 1991): 184–197.

27. Jacquelyn N. Zita, "Lesbian and Gay Studies: Yet Another Unhappy Marriage?," in Linda Garber, ed., *Tilting the Tower: Lesbians Teaching Queer Subjects*, 258–276.

28. Eve Kosofsky Sedgwick, *Epistemology of the Closet* (Berkeley: University of California Press, 1990); Britzman, "Is There a Queer Pedagogy? Or, Stop Reading Straight."

29. Sedgwick learned this from Shoshana Felman, *Jacques Lacan and the Adventure of Insight: Psychoanalysis in Contemporary Culture* (Cambridge: Harvard University Press, 1987), and Felman, "Psychoanalysis and Education: Teaching Terminable and Interminable," *Yale French Studies* 63 (1982): 21–44.

Felman learned it from Lacan. In "Is There a Queer Pedagogy? Or, Stop Reading Straight," Britzman draws out the implications from all of the above.

30. Marilyn Frye, "A Lesbian Perspective on Women's Studies," in Margaret Cruikshank, ed., *Lesbian Studies: Present and Future* (Old Westbury, NY: The Feminist Press, 1982), 194–197; Gail B. Griffin, *Calling: Essays on Teaching in the Mother Tongue* (Pasadena, CA: Trilogy, 1992); and Martindale, "Addressing Heterosexism in Women's Studies Classrooms."

31. That contradictory refrain appears in many of the responses which were collected and most usefully included in the Study Committee on the Status of Lesbians and Gay Men, "From Invisibility to Inclusion: Opening the Doors for Lesbians and Gay Men at the University of Michigan," June 1991.

32. Sarah Chinn, "Queering the Profession, or Just Professionalizing Queers?," in Linda Garber, ed., *Tilting the Tower: Lesbians Teaching Queer Subjects*, 243.

33. Sedgwick, *Epistemology of the Closet*, 13, 15, 27; Britzman, "Is There a Queer Pedagogy? Or, Stop Reading Straight."

34. Felman, *Jacques Lacan and the Adventure of Insight*, 59.

35. Berg et al., "Breaking the Silence: Sexual Preference in the Composition Classroom," 108–116.

36. *Ibid.*, 110.

37. *Ibid.*, 111.

38. *Ibid.*, 112.

39. See note 31.

40. Felman, *Jacques Lacan and the Adventure of Insight*, 78–80; Sedgwick, *Epistemology of the Closet*, 4–8.

41. Martindale, "Addressing Heterosexism in Women's Studies Classrooms," 459.

42. Griffin, *Calling: Essays on Teaching in the Mother Tongue*, 179.

43. *Ibid.*, 179.

44. *Ibid.*, 180.

45. *Ibid.*, 180.

46. *Ibid.*, 181.

47. Cherríe Moraga and Gloria Anzaldúa, eds., *This Bridge Called My Back: Writings By Radical Women of Color* (Watertown, MA: Persephone Press, 1981).

48. Lacan quoted in Felman, *Jacques Lacan and the Adventure of Insight*, 55.

49. Michael Warner, "Introduction," *Fear of a Queer Planet: Queer Politics and Social Theory* (Minneapolis: University of Minnesota Press, 1993), xix.

50. Joan W. Scott, "Multiculturalism and the Politics of Identity," *October* (Summer 1992): 14.

51. James Clifford, "Introduction: Partial Truths," in James Clifford and George Marcus, eds., *Writing Culture: The Poetics and Politics of Ethnography* (Berkeley: University of California Press, 1986), 12.

52. Shoshana Felman and Dori Laub, *Testimony: Crises of Witnessing in Literature, Psychoanalysis, and History* (New York: Routledge, 1992), 5.

53. Felman, *Jacques Lacan and the Adventure of Insight*, 79; quoting Lacan, 83.

54. Lacan quoted in Felman, *Jacques Lacan and the Adventure of Insight*, 82.

55. Scott, "Multiculturalism and the Politics of Identity," 14.

56. Lisa M. Walker, "How to Recognize a Lesbian: The Cultural Politics of Looking Like What Your Are," *Signs* 18 (Summer 1993): 888.

57. Luce Iragaray, *Speculum of the Other Woman*, trans. Gillian Gill (Ithaca, NY: Cornell University Press, 1985), 171.

58. Lacan quoted in Felman, *Jacques Lacan and the Adventure of Insight*, 83–84.

BIBLIOGRAPHY

Abelove, Henry, Michèle Aina Barale, and David M. Halperin, eds. "Introduction." In *The Lesbian and Gay Studies Reader*. New York: Routledge, 1993.

Abraham, Julie. "A Case of Mistaken Identity?" *Women's Review of Books* (July 1994): 36–37.

Aislan, *Where's the Trough? And other Aislan Cartoons*. Toronto: McClelland and Stewart, 1985.

Alphabet Threat 3 (1993).

Anzaldúa, Gloria. *Borderlands/La Frontera: The New Mestiza*. San Francisco: Spinsters, 1987.

———. "To(o) Queer the Writer—Loca, escritora y chicana." In Betsy Warland, ed. *InVersions: Writing by Dykes, Queers & Lesbians*. Vancouver: Press Gang, 1991.

Asantewaa, Eva Yaa. "Sister to Brother: Women of Color on Coming Together with Men." Special Issue of *Outweek* 40 (April 4, 1990): 45–46.

Austin, S. Bryn with Pam Gregg. "A Freak Among Freaks: The 'Zine Scene." In Arlne Stein, ed. *Sisters, Sexperts, Queers: Beyond the Lesbian Nation*. New York: Plume, 1993.

Barr, Marleen. "Food for Postmodern Thought: Isak Dinesen's Female Artists as Precursors to Contemporary Feminist Fabulators." In Libby Falk Jones and Sarah Webster Goodwin, eds. *Feminism, Utopia, and Narrative*. Knoxville: University of Tennessee Press, 1990.

Bechdel, Alison. *Dykes To Watch Out For*. Ithaca, NY: Firebrand, 1986.

———. *More Dykes To Watch Out For*. Ithaca, NY: Firebrand, 1988.

———. *New, Improved! Dykes To Watch Out For*. Ithaca, NY: Firebrand, 1990.

———. *Dykes To Watch Out For: The Sequel*. Ithaca, NY: Firebrand, 1992.

———. *Spawn of Dykes To Watch Out For*. Ithaca, NY: Firebrand, 1993.

———. "Serial Monogamy." In Margaret Reynolds, ed. *The Penguin Book of Lesbian Short Stories*. London: Viking, 1993.

Belsey, Catherine. *Critical Practice*. London: Methuen, 1980.

Berg, Allison, Jean Kowaleski, Caroline Le Guin, Ellen Weinauer, and Eric A. Wolfe. "Breaking the Silence: Sexual Preference in the Composition Classroom." In Linda Garber, ed. *Tilting the Tower: Lesbians Teaching Queer Subjects*. New York: Routledge, 1994.

Berlant, Lauren and Elizabeth Freeman. "Queer Nationality." *boundary 2* (Spring 1992): 149–180.

Bernheimer, Charles and Claire Kahane, eds. *In Dora's Case: Freud—Hysteria—Feminism*. 2nd ed. New York: Columbia University Press, 1990.

Blankley, Elyse. "Return to Mytilene: Renee Vivien and the City of Women." In Susan Merrill Squier, ed. *Women Writers and the City: Essays in Feminist Literary Criticism*. Knoxville: University of Tennessee Press, 1984.

Boffin, Tessa and Jean Fraser, eds. *Stolen Glances: Lesbians Take Photographs*. London: Pandora, 1991.

Bordo, Susan. "Review Essay: Postmodern Subjects, Postmodern Bodies." *Feminist Studies* 18 (Spring 1992): 159–715.

Brodribb, Somer. *Nothing Mat(t)ers: A Feminist Critique of Postmodernism*. North Melbourne, Australia: Spinifex, 1992.

Britzman, Deborah P. "Decentering Discourses in Teacher Education: Or, The Unleashing of Unpopular Things." *Boston University Journal of Education* 173 (1991): 60–80.

———. "Structures of Feeling in Curriculum and Teaching." *Theory Into Practice* 31 (Summer 1992): 252–258.

———. "Is There a Queer Pedagogy? Or, Stop Reading Straight," *Educational Theory* 45 (Spring 1995): 151–166.

———. "Beyond Innocent Readings: Educational Ethnography as a Crisis of Representation." In William Pink and George Noblitt, eds. *The Future of the Sociology of Education*. New Jersey: Hampton Press, 1995.

Brossard, Nicole. *The Aerial Letter*. Translated by Marlene Wildeman. Toronto: The Women's Press, 1988.

———. *Lovhers*. Translated by Barbara Godard. Montreal: Guernica, 1986.

Brownworth, Victoria A. "Parochialism and Polarization: The Politics of Lesbian and Gay Reading." *Lambda Book Report* 3 (March/April 1993): 10–11.

Bryson, Mary and Suzanne de Castell. "Queer Pedagogy: Praxis Makes Im/Perfect." In Bryson and de Castell, ed. *Radical Interventions: Identity, Politics, and Differences in Educational Praxis.* Albany, N.Y.: State University of New York Press, 1995.

Burana, Lily, Roxxie, and Linnea Due, eds. *Dagger: On Butch Women.* San Francisco: Cleis Press, 1994.

Bürger, Peter. *Theory of the Avant-Garde.* Translated by Michael Shaw. Minneapolis: University of Minnesota Press, 1994.

Butler, Judith. *Gender Trouble: Feminism and the Subversion of Identity.* New York: Routledge, 1990.

———, "Discussion." *October* (Summer 1992): 108–120.

———. *Bodies That Matter: On the Discursive Limits of "Sex".* New York: Routledge, 1993.

Califia, Pat. *Macho Sluts.* Boston: Alyson, 1988.

Case, Sue-Ellen. "Tracking the Vampire." *differences* 3 (Summer 1991): 1–20.

Case, Sue-Ellen. "Toward a Butch-Femme Aesthetic." In Henry Abelove, Michèle Aina Barale, and David M. Halpern, eds. *The Lesbian and Gay Studies Reader.* New York: Routledge, 1993. First published in *Discourse* 11 (1988/89): 55–71.

———. ed. *Performing Feminisms: Feminist Critical Theory and Theatre.* Baltimore: Johns Hopkins University Press, 1990.

Castle, Terry. "Sylvia Townsend Warner and the Counterplot of Lesbian Fiction." *Critical Practice* 4 (1990): 213–235.

———. *The Apparitional Lesbian: Female Homosexuality and Modern Culture.* New York: Columbia University Press, 1993.

Chauncey, George Jr. "Christian Brotherhood or Sexual Perversion? Homosexual Identities and the Construction of Sexual Boundaries in the World War 1 Era." In Martin Bauml Duberman, Martha Vicinus, and George Chauncey, Jr., eds. *Hidden From History: Reclaiming the Gay and Lesbian Past.* New York: New American Library, 1989.

Chinn, Sarah. "Queering the Profession, or Just Professionalizing Queers?" In Linda Garber, ed. *Tilting the Tower: Lesbians Teaching Queer Subjects.* New York: Routledge, 1994.

Christian, Barbara, Ann Du Cille, Sharon Marcus, Elaine Marks, Nancy K. Miller, Sylvia Schafer, and Joan W. Scott. "Conference Call." *differences* 2 (Fall 1990): 52–108.

Chua, Lawrence. "We Ought To Be in Pictures." *Village Voice Literary Supplement* (June 1992): 25.

Clark, Danae. "Commodity Lesbianism." In Henry Abelard, Michèle Aina Barale and David M. Halperin, eds. *The Lesbian and Gay Studies Reader.* New York: Routledge, 1993.

Clark, Suzanne. *Sentimental Modernism: Women Writers and the Revolution of the World.* Bloomington: Indiana University Press, 1991.

Clifford, James. "Introduction: Partial Truths." In James Clifford and George Marcus, eds. *Writing Culture: The Poetics and Politics of Ethnography.* Berkeley: University of California Press, 1986.

Cohen, Ed. "Who Are 'We'? Gay 'Identity' as Political (E)motion: (A Theoretical Rumination)." In Diana Fuss, ed. *inside/out: Lesbian Theories, Gay Theories.* New York: Routledge, 1991.

Corinne, Tee. "Comics By Women." *Country Women Magazine* 29 (1977): 25–27.

Cotnoir, Louise, Lise Guevremont, Claude Beausoleil, and Hugues Corriveau. "Interview with Nicole Brossard on *Picture Theory.*" Translated by Luise von Flotow-Evans. *Canadian Fiction Magazine* 47 (1983): 122–135.

Creet, Julia. "Daughter of the Movement: The Psychodynamics of Lesbian S/M Fantasy." *differences* 3 (Summer 1991): 135–159.

Culler, Jonathan. *On Deconstruction: Theory and Criticism after Structuralism.* Ithaca, New York: Cornell University Press, 1982.

Davy, Kate. "Constructing the Spectator: Reception, Context, and Address in Lesbian Performance." *Performing Arts Journal* 29 (1986): 43–52.

———. "Reading Past the Heterosexual Imperative: Dress Suits to Hire." *TDR* (Spring 1989): 153–170.

DeJean, Joan. *Fictions of Sappho 1546–1937.* Chicago: University of Chicago Press, 1989.

Delany, Samuel R. "Street Talk/Straight Talk." *differences* 3 (Summer 1991): 21–38.

de Certeau, Michel. *The Practice of Everyday Life.* Translated by Steven F. Rendall. Berkeley: University of California Press, 1984.

de Lauretis, Teresa, ed. *Feminist Studies/Critical Studies.* Bloomington: Indiana University Press, 1986.

———. *Technologies of Gender: Essays on Theory, Film, and Fiction.* Bloomington: Indiana University Press, 1987.

———. "Sexual Indifference and Lesbian Representation." *Theatre Journal* 40 (1988): 155–177.

———. "Eccentric Subjects: Feminist Theory and Historical Consciousness." *Feminist Studies* 16 (1990): 115–150.

———. "Upping the Anti (sic) in Feminist Theory." In Marianne Hirsch and Evelyn Fox Keller, eds. *Conflicts in Feminism*. New York: Routledge, 1990.

———. "Film and the Visible." In Bad Object-Choices, ed. *How Do I Look: Queer Film and Video*. Seattle: Bay Press, 1991.

———. "Queer Theory: Lesbian and Gay Sexualities An Introduction." In Theresa de Lauretis, ed. *Queer Theory*, special issue of *differences* 3 (Summer 1991): iii–xviii.

———. *The Practice of Love: Lesbian Sexuality and Perverse Desire*. Bloomington: Indiana University Press, 1994.

de Man, Paul. *Blindness and Insight: Essays in the Rhetoric of Contemporary Criticism*. New York: Oxford University Press, 1971.

———. "The Resistance to Theory." *The Resistance to Theory*. Minneapolis: University of Minnesota Press, 1986.

Derrida, Jacques. "Limited Inc." *Glyph* 2 (1977): 162–254.

Derrida, Jacques and Marie-Françoise Plissart. "Right of Inspection." *Art & Text* 32 (Autumn 1989): 20–97.

DeSalvo, Louise A. "Every Woman Is an Island: Vita Sackville-West, the Image of the City, and the Pastoral Idyll." In Susan Merrill Squier, ed. *Women Writers and the City: Essays in Feminist Literary Criticism*. Knoxville: University of Tennessee Press, 1984..

DiMassa, Diane. *Hothead Paisan* Issue 1 (February 1991), Issue 2 (May 1991), Issue 5 (February 1992). New Haven, CT: Giant Ass Publishing.

———. *Hothead Paisan: Homicidal Lesbian Terrorist*. Pittsburgh: Cleis Press, 1993.

Doan, Laura, ed. *The Lesbian Postmodern*. New York: Columbia University Press, 1994.

Dolan, Jill. "The Dynamics of Desire: Sexuality and Gender in Pornography and Performance." *Theatre Journal* (May 1987): 156–174.

———. "Breaking the Code: Musings on Lesbian Sexuality and the Performer." *Modern Drama* 32 (March 1989): 146–158.

———. "'Lesbian' Subjectivity in Realism: Dragging at the Margins of Structure and Ideology." In Sue-Ellen Case, ed. *Performing Feminisms: Feminist*

Critical Theory and Theatre. Baltimore: Johns Hopkins University Press, 1990.

———. "In Defense of the Discourse: Materialist Feminism, Postmodernism, Poststructuralism…and Theory." *TDR* (Fall 1989): 58–71.

Duggan, Lisa. "Scholars and Sense." *Village Voice Literary Supplement* (June 1992): 27.

Edelman, Lee. *Homographesis: Essays in Gay Literary and Cultural Theory.* New York: Routledge, 1994.

Engelbrecht, Penelope. "'Lifting Belly Is a Language': The Postmodern Lesbian Subject." *Feminist Studies* 16 (Spring 1990): 85–114.

Escoffier, Jeffrey. "Generations and Paradigms: Mainstreams in Lesbian and Gay Studies." *Journal of Homosexuality* 24 (1992): 7–26.

Faderman, Lillian. *Surpassing the Love of Men: Romantic Friendship and Love between Women from the Renaissance to the Present.* New York: William Morrow, 1981.

———. *Odd Girls and Twilight Lovers: A History of Lesbian Life in Twentieth-Century America.* New York: Columbia University Press, 1991.

Felman, Shoshana. "Psychoanalysis and Education: Teaching Terminable and Interminable." *Yale French Studies* 63 (1982): 21–44.

———. *Jacques Lacan and the Adventure of Insight: Psychoanalysis in Contemporary Culture.* Cambridge: Harvard University Press, 1987.

———. and Dori Laub. *Testimony: Crises of Witnessing in Literature, Psychoanalysis, and History.* New York: Routledge, 1992.

Ferguson, Ann. "Is There a Lesbian Culture?" In Jeffner Allen, ed. *Lesbian Philosophies and Cultures.* Albany, NY: State University of New York Press, 1990.

———. "Patriarchy, Sexual Identity, and the Sexual Revolution," in "Viewpoint" by Ann Ferguson, Jacquelyn N. Zita, and Kathryn Pyne Addelson, "On 'Compulsory Heterosexuality and Lesbian Existence': Defining the Issues," *Signs* 7 (Autumn 1981): 158–172.

Findlay, Heather. "Freud's 'Fetishism' and the Lesbian Dildo Debates." *Feminist Studies* 18 (Fall 1992): 563–579.

Fisher, Roger and William Ury. *Getting to Yes: Negotiating Agreement Without Giving In.* London: Penguin, 1981.

Foucault, Michel. "The Subject and Power." In Brian Wallis, ed. *Art After Modernism: Rethinking Representation.* New York: Museum of Contemporary Art, 1984.

Freud, Sigmund and Josef Breuer. *Studies on Hysteria*. Translated by James Strachey and Alix Strachey. New York: Penguin, 1991.

Frye, Marilyn. "A Lesbian Perspective on Women's Studies." In Margaret Cruikshank, ed. *Lesbian Studies: Present and Future*. Old Westbury, NY: The Feminist Press, 1982.

———. *The Politics of Reality: Essays in Feminist Theory*. Trumansburg, NY: The Crossing Press, 1983.

———. "Some Reflections on Separatism and Power." In Sarah Hoagland and Julia Penelope, eds. *For Lesbians Only: A Separatist Anthology*. London: Onlywomen Press, 1988.

Fuss, Diana. *Essentially Speaking: Feminism, Nature and Difference*. New York: Routledge, 1989.

———. ed. *inside/out: Lesbian Theories, Gay Theories*. New York: Routledge, 1991.

Gagnier, Regenia. "Between Women: A Cross-Class Analysis of Status and Anarchic Humor." *Women's Studies* 15 (1988): 136–148.

Gallop, Jane. *Reading Lacan*. Ithaca, New York: Cornell University Press, 1985.

———. *Thinking Through the Body*. New York: Columbia University Press, 1988.

Gammon, Carolyn. "Lesbian Studies Emerging in Canada." In Henry L. Minton, ed., *Gay and Lesbian Studies Issue*, special issue of *Journal of Homosexuality* 24 (1992): 137–160.

Garber, Linda, ed. *Tilting the Tower: Lesbians Teaching Queer Subjects*. New York: Routledge, 1994.

Grace, Sherrill. "Quest for the Peaceable Kingdom: Urban/Rural Codes in Roy, Laurence, and Atwood." In Susan Merrill Squier, ed. *Women Writers and the City: Essays in Feminist Literary Criticism*. Knoxville: University of Tennessee Press, 1984.

Grahn, Judy. *Another Mother Tongue: Gay Words, Gay Worlds*. Boston: Beacon Press, 1984.

Griffin, Gabriele, ed. *Outwrite: Lesbianism and Popular Culture*. London: Pluto Press, 1993.

Griffin, Gail B. *Calling: Essays on Teaching in the Mother Tongue*. Pasadena, CA: Trilogy, 1992.

Grimard-Leduc, Micheline. "The Mind-Drifting Islands." In Sarah Hoagland and Julia Penelope, eds. *For Lesbians Only: A Separatist Anthology*. London: Onlywomen Press, 1988.

Gubar, Susan. "Sapphistries." *Signs* 10 (Autumn 1984): 43–62.

Halberstam, Judith. F2M: The Making of Female Masculinity." In Laura Doan, ed. *The Lesbian Postmodern*. New York: Columbia University Press, 1994.

Harris, Bertha. "The More Profound Nationality of their Lesbianism: Lesbian Society in Paris in the 1920s." In Phyllis Birkby, Bertha Harris, Jill Johnston, Esther Newton, and Jane O'Wyatt, eds. *Amazon Expedition: A Lesbian Feminist Anthology*. Albion, CA: Times Change, 1973.

———. "What We Mean to Say: Notes Toward Defining the Nature of Lesbian Literature." *Heresies* (Fall 1977): 5–8.

Hart, Ellen Louise. "Literacy and the Lesbian/Gay Learner." In Caroline Sidaway, M. Eugenia Rosa, Ellen Louise Hart, Sarah-Hope Parmenter, and Anza Stein, eds. *The Lesbian in Front of the Classroom: Writings by Lesbian Teachers*. Santa Cruz, CA: HerBooks, 1988.

Hart, Lynda. *Fatal Women: Lesbian Sexuality and the Mark of Aggression*. Princeton: Princeton University Press, 1994.

Hennegan, Alison. "On Becoming a Lesbian Reader." In Susannah Radstone, ed. *Sweet Dreams: Sexuality, Gender and Popular Fiction*. London: Lawrence & Wishart, 1988.

Henriques, Julian, Wendy Hollway, Cathy Urwin, Couze Venn, and Valerie Walkerdine, eds. *Changing the Subject: Psychology, Social Regulation and Subjectivity*. London: Methuen, 1984.

Hite, Molly. *The Other Side of the Story: Structures and Strategies of Contemporary Feminist Narrative*. Ithaca, NY: Cornell University Press, 1989.

Hoagland, Sarah Lucia and Julia Penelope, eds. *For Lesbians Only: A Separatist Anthology*. London: Onlywomen Press, 1988.

Hough, Robert. "Seizing Books: Degrading Customs." *The Globe and Mail*, 12 February 1994: D1, D5.

Hunt, Margaret. "A Fem's Own Story: An Interview with Joan Nestle." In Christian McEwen and Sue O'Sullivan, eds. *Out the Other Side: Contemporary Lesbian Writing*. London: Virago Press, 1988.

Hutcheon, Linda. *The Politics of Postmodernism*. New York: Routledge, 1989.

Huyssen, Andreas. *After the Great Divide*. Bloomington: Indiana University Press, 1986.

Inge, M. Thomas. *Comics as Culture*. Jackson, MS: University Press of Mississippi, 1990.

Irigaray, Luce. *Speculum of the Other Woman*. Translated by Gillian Gill. Ithaca, NY: Cornell University Press, 1985.

Iser, Wolfgang. *The Act of Reading: A Theory of Aesthetic Response*. Baltimore: Johns Hopkins University Press, 1978.

Jameson, Fredric. "On 'Cultural Studies,'" *Social Text* 34 (1993): 17–52.

———. *The Political Unconscious: Narrative as a Socially Symbolic Act*. Ithaca, NY: Cornell University Press, 1981.

———. *Postmodernism Or, The Cultural Logic of Late Capitalism*. Durham, NC: Duke University Press, 1992.

Jay, Karla and Joanne Glasgow, eds. *Lesbian Texts and Contexts: Radical Revisions*. New York: New York University Press, 1990.

Jeffreys, Sheila. "Butch and Femme: Then and Now." In Lesbian History Group, ed. *Not a Passing Phase: Reclaiming Lesbians in History 1840–1985*. London: The Women's Press, 1989.

———. *The Lesbian Heresy: A Feminist Perspective on the Lesbian Sexual Revolution*. North Melbourne, Australia: Spinifex, 1993.

Jenkins, III, Henry. "Star Trek Rerun, Reread, Rewritten: Fan Writing as Textual Poaching." *Critical Studies in Mass Communication* 5 (1988): 85–107.

Johnston, Jill. *Lesbian Nation: The Feminist Solution*. New York: Simon and Schuster, 1973.

Juno, Andrea and V. Vale. *Angry Women*. San Francisco: Re/Search Publications, 1991.

Kennard, Jean E. "Ourself behind Ourself: A Theory for Lesbian Readers." In Elizabeth A. Flynn and Patrocinio P. Schweickart, eds. *Gender and Reading: Essays on Readers, Texts, and Contexts*. Baltimore: Johns Hopkins University Press, 1986.

Kennedy, Elizabeth L. and Madeline D. Davis. *Boots of Leather, Slippers of Gold: The History of a Lesbian Community*. New York: Routledge, 1993.

Kennedy, Pagan. "P.C. Comics." *The Nation* (19 March 1990): 386–389.

King, Katie. "The Situation of Lesbianism as Feminism's Magical Sign: Contests for Meaning and the U.S. Women's Movement, 1968–1972." *Communications* 9 (1986): 65–91.

———. "Producing Sex, Theory, and Culture: Gay/Straight Remappings in Contemporary Feminism." In Marianne Hirsch and Evelyn Fox, eds. *Conflicts in Feminism*. New York: Routledge, 1990.

———. "Audre Lorde's Lacquered Layerings: The Lesbian Bar as a Site of Literary Production." In Sally Munt, ed. *New Lesbian Criticism: Literary and Cultural Readings*. New York: Columbia University Press, 1992

Kohut, Heinz. "Introspection, Empathy, and Psychoanalysis." *Journal of the American Psychoanalytical Association* 7 (1959): 459–483.

Kristeva, Julia. "Postmodernism?" In Harry R. Garvin, ed. *Romanticism, Modernism, Postmodernism, Bucknell Review.* Lewisberg, PA: Bucknell University Press, 1980.

Laplanche, J. and J-B Pontalis. *The Language of Psychoanalysis.* Translated by Donald Nicholson-Smith. London: Karnac, 1988.

Lentz, Kirsten Marthe. "The Popular Pleasures of Female Revenge (Or Rage Bursting in a Blaze of Gunfire)." *Cultural Studies* 7 (October 1993): 374–405.

Lippard Lucy. *Get the Message?: A Decade of Art for Social Change.* New York: Dutton, 1984.

Loewenstein, Andrea Freud. "Troubled Times: Interview with Sarah Schulman." In Betsy Warland, ed. *InVersions: Writing by Dykes, Queers & Lesbians.* Vancouver: Press Gang, 1991.

Lorde, Audre. *Zami: A New Spelling of My Name.* Freedom, CA.: The Crossing Press, 1983.

———. *Sister Outsider.* Trumansburg, NY: The Crossing Press, 1984.

Loulan, JoAnn. *The Lesbian Erotic Dance: Butch Femme Androgyny and Other Rhythms.* San Francisco: Spinsters, 1990.

MacFarquahar, Larissa. "Putting the Camp Back into Campus." *Lingua Franca* (Sept./Oct. 1993): 6–7.

Maggenti, Maria. "Wandering Through Herland." In Arlene Stein, ed. *Sisters, Sexperts, Queers: Beyond the Lesbian Nation.* New York: Plume, 1993. An earlier version appeared in a special issue of *Outweek* 40 (April 4, 1990): 42–43.

Marks, Elaine. "Lesbian Intertextuality." In George Stambolian and Elaine Marks, eds. *Homosexualities and French Literature: Cultural Contexts/Critical Texts.* Ithaca, NY: Cornell University Press, 1979.

———. "'Sappho 1900': Imaginary Renee Viviens and the Rear of the Belle Epoque." *Yale French Studies* 7 (1988): 175–189.

Marshall, Donald G. *Contemporary Critical Theory: A Selective Bibliography.* New York: Modern Language Association, 1993.

Martin, Biddy. "Lesbian Identity and Autobiographical Difference[s]." In Bella Brodzki and Celeste Schenke, eds. *Life/Lines: Theorizing Women's Autobiographies.* Ithaca, NY: Cornell University Press, 1988.

———. "Sexual Practice and Changing Lesbian Identities." In Michèle Barrett and Anne Phillips, eds. *Destabilizing Theory: Contemporary Feminist Debates*. Stanford: Stanford University Press, 1992.

Martin, Biddy and Chandra Talpede Mohanty. "Feminist Politics: What's Home Got to Do with It?" In Teresa de Lauretis, ed. *Feminist Studies/Critical Studies*. Bloomington: Indiana University Press, 1986.

Martin, Wendy. "Another View of the 'City Upon the Hill': The Prophetic Vision of Adrienne Rich." In Susan Merrill Squier, ed. *Women Writers and the City: Essays in Feminist Literary Criticism*. Knoxville: University of Tennessee Press, 1984.

Martindale, Kathleen. "Addressing Heterosexism in Women's Studies Classrooms." In Debra Shogan, ed. *A Reader In Feminist Ethics*. Toronto: Scholars Press, 1992.

Martindale, Kathleen and Martha Saunders. "Realizing Love and Justice: Lesbian Ethics in the Upper and Lower Case." *Hypatia* (Fall 1992): 148–171

Meese, Elizabeth A. *(Ex)Tensions: Re-Figuring Feminist Criticism*. Urbana: University of Illinois Press, 1990.

———. "Theorizing Lesbian: Writing—A Love Letter." In *Lesbian Texts and Contexts: Radical Revisions*. New York: New York University Press, 1990.

———. *(Sem)erotics: Theorizing Lesbian: Writing*. New York: Columbia University Press, 1992.

Meigs, Mary. "Falling Between the Cracks." In Betsy Warland, ed. *InVersions: Writings by Dykes, Queers and Lesbians*. Vancouver: Press Gang, 1991.

Merck, Mandy. "The Amazons of Ancient Athens." *Perversions: Deviant Readings*. London: Virago Press, 1993.

"Michael Coren's Diary." *Frank,* 7 July 1994, n.p.

Miller, Nancy K. "Changing the Subject: Authorship, Reading, and the Reader." In Teresa de Lauretis, ed. *Feminist Studies/Critical Studies*. Bloomington: Indiana University Press, 1986.

Minton, Henry L., ed. "Gay and Lesbian Studies Issue." Special issue of *Journal of Homosexuality* 24 (1992).

Miss Spentyouth. *Judy!* 1 (Spring Fever, 1993).

Mohr, Richard D. "Gay Studies in the Big Ten: A Survivor's Manual." *Gays/Justice: A Study of Ethics, Society, and Law*. New York: Columbia University Press, 1988.

———. "The Ethics of Students and the Teaching of Ethics: A Lecturing." *Gays/Justice: A Study of Ethics, Society, and Law.* New York: Columbia University Press, 1988.

Moraga, Cherríe and Gloria Anzaldúa, eds. *This Bridge Called My Back: Writings By Radical Women of Color.* Watertown, MA: Persephone, 1981.

Morris, Tom. "Life's a pimp." *The Guardian,* 19 April 1994, 10.

Munk, Erika. "Brainchild of a Lesser God." *Village Voice,* 11 October 1988, 103–104.

Munt, Sally. "'Somewhere over the Rainbow…': Postmodernism and the Fiction of Sarah Schulman." In Sally Munt, ed. *New Lesbian Criticism: Literary and Cultural Readings.* New York: Columbia University Press, 1992.

Nestle, Joan. "The Fem Question." In Carole S. Vance, ed. *Pleasure and Danger: Exploring Female Sexuality.* New York: Routledge, 1984.

———. "Butch-Femme Relationships: Sexual Courage in the 1950s." In *A Restricted Country.* Ithaca, NY: Firebrand Books, 1987.

———. *A Restricted Country.* Ithaca, NY: Firebrand, 1987.

———. *The Persistent Desire: A Femme-Butch Reader.* Boston: Alyson Publications, 1992.

Nicholson, Linda J. ed. *Feminism/Postmodernism.* New York: Routledge, 1990.

Obear, Kathy. "Opening Doors to Understanding and Acceptance: A Facilitator's Guide to Presenting Workshops on Lesbian and Gay Issues." Amherst, MA: The Human Advantage, n.d.

Omosupe, Ekua. "Black/Lesbian/Bulldagger." *differences* 3 (Summer 1991): 101–111.

Ontario Federation of Students Research Department and Rory Crath and Peter Regier. "The Campus Closet: Institutional Homophobia in Ontario Post-Secondary Education." Toronto, Ontario, Canada, 1991.

Paglia, Camille. *Sexual Personae: Art and Decadence From Nefertiti to Emily Dickinson.* New York: Vintage, 1990.

Penley, Constance. "Feminism, Psychoanalysis, and the Study of Popular Culture." In Lawrence Grossberg, Cary Nelson, and Paula A. Treichler, eds. *Cultural Studies.* New York: Routledge, 1992.

Pérez, Emma. "Irigaray's Female Symbolic in the Making of Chicana Lesbian Sitios y Lenguas (Sites and Discourses)." In Laura Doan, ed. *The Lesbian Postmodern.* New York: Columbia University Press, 1994.

Perkins, Stephen. "Subspace Zines: International Zine Show." *Alternative Press Review* (Winter 1994): 22.

Powers, Ann. "Queer in the Streets, Straight in the Sheets." *Village Voice*, 29 June 1993, 24, 30–31.

Pratt, Minnie Bruce. *Rebellion: Essays 1980-1991*. Ithaca, NY: Firebrand Books, 1991.

President's Select Committee for Lesbian and Gay Concerns, Rutgers University. "In Every Classroom." New Brunswick, NJ, 1989.

Radhakrishnan, R. "Ethnic Identity and Post-Structuralist Difference." *Cultural Critique* 6 (1987): 199–220.

———. "Negotiating Subject Positions in an Uneven World." In Linda Kaufman, ed. *Feminism and Institutions*. London: Basil Blackwell, 1989.

———. "The Changing Subject and the Politics of Theory." *differences* 2 (1990): 126–152.

Radicalesbians. "The Woman-Identified Woman." In Anne Koedt, Ellen Levine, and Anita Rapone, eds. *Radical Feminism*. New York: Quadrangle, 1973.

Rand, Erica. "We Girls Can Do Anything, Right Barbie? Lesbian Consumption in Postmodern Circulation." In Laura Doan, ed. *The Lesbian Postmodern*. New York: Columbia University Press, 1994.

Raymond, Janice G. "Putting the Politics Back Into Lesbianism." *Women's Studies International Forum* 12 (1989): 149–156.

Reich, June L. "Genderfuck: The Law of the Dildo." *Discourse* 1 (Fall 1992): 112–127.

Reynolds, Margaret, ed. *The Penguin Book of Lesbian Short Stories*. Toronto: Viking, 1993.

Rich, Adrienne. "Compulsory Heterosexuality and Lesbian Existence." In Henry Abelove, Michèle Aina Barale, and David M. Halperin, eds. *The Lesbian and Gay Studies Reader* New York: Routledge, 1993.

Rich, B. Ruby. "Feminism and Sexuality in the 1980s." *Feminist Studies* 12 (1986): 525–561.

Robson, Ruthann. "Embodiment(s): The Possibilities of Lesbian Legal Theory in Bodies Problematized by Postmodernisms and Feminisms." *Law and Sexuality: A Review of Lesbian and Gay Legal Issues* 2 (1992): 37–80.

Roof, Judith. *A Lure of Knowledge: Lesbian Sexuality and Theory*. New York: Columbia University Press, 1991.

———. "Lesbians and Lyotard: Legitimation and the Politics of the Name." In Laura Doan, ed. *The Lesbian Postmodern*. New York: Columbia University Press, 1994.

Rooney, Ellen. *Seductive Reasoning: Pluralism as the Problematic of Contemporary Literary Theory*. Ithaca, NY: Cornell University Press, 1989.

Ross, Andrew. "New Age Technoculture." In Lawrence Grossberg, Cary Nelson, and Paula Treichler, eds. *Cultural Studies*. New York: Routledge, 1992.

Ross, Andrew. *No Respect: Intellectuals & Popular Culture*. New York: Routledge, 1989.

Roy, Camille. "Speaking in Tongues." In Arlene Stein, ed. *Sisters, Sexperts, Queers: Beyond the Lesbian Nation*. New York: Plume, 1993.

Rubin, Gayle. "The Traffic in Women: Notes on the 'Political Economy' of Sex." In Rayna R. Reiter, ed. *Toward an Anthropology of Women*. New York: Monthly Review, 1975.

———. "Thinking Sex: Notes for a Radical Theory of the Politics of Sexuality." In Carole S. Vance, ed. *Pleasure and Danger: Exploring Female Sexuality*. New York: Routledge, 1984.

Russell, Charles. *Poets, Prophets, and Revolutionaries: The Literary Avant-Garde From Rimbaud to Postmodernism*. New York: Oxford University Press, 1985.

Saegert, Susan. "Masculine Cities and Feminine Suburbs: Polarized Ideas, Contradictory Realities." *Signs* 5 Supplement (1980): S96–111.

Schulman, Sarah. *The Sophie Horowitz Story*. Tallahassee, FL: Naiad Press, 1984.

———. *Girls, Visions and Everything*. Seattle: Seal Press, 1986.

———. "When We Were Very Young: Radical Jewish Women on the Lower East Side, 1879–1919." In Melanie Kaye/Kantrowitz and Irena Klepfisz, eds. *The Tribe of Dina: A Jewish Women's Anthology*. Montpelier, VT: Sinister Wisdom Books, 1986.

———. *After Delores*. New York: New American Library, 1989.

———. *People in Trouble*. New York: New American Library, 1991.

———. *Empathy*. New York: Dutton, 1992.

———. *My American History: Lesbian and Gay Life During the Reagan/Bush Years*. New York: Routledge, 1994.

———. "Questions." *Lambda Book Report* 4 (July/August 1994): 49.

Scott, Joan W. "Multiculturalism and the Politics of Identity." *October* (Summer 1992): 12–19.

Sedgwick, Eve Kosofsky. *Between Men: English Literature and Male Homosocial Desire*. New York: Columbia University Press, 1985.

———. "A Poem Is Being Written." *Representations* 17 (1987): 110–143.

———. *Epistemology of the Closet*. Berkeley: University of California Press, 1990.

———. "Gender Criticism." In Stephen Greenblatt and Giles Gunn, eds. *Redrawing the Boundaries: The Transformation of English and American Literary Studies*. New York: Modern Language Association, 1992.

Seidman, Steven. "Identity and Politics in a 'Postmodern' Gay Culture: Some Historical and Conceptual Notes." In Michael Warner, ed. *Fear of a Queer Planet: Queer Politics and Social Theory*. Minneapolis: University of Minnesota Press, 1993.

Shockley, Ann Allen. "A Meeting of the Sapphic Daughters." *Sinister Wisdom* 9 (Spring 1979): 54–59.

Silverman, Kaja. *The Subject of Semiotics*. New York: Oxford University Press, 1983.

Smith, Paul. *Discerning the Subject*. Minneapolis: University of Minnesota Press, 1988.

Solanis, Valerie. "Excerpts from the SCUM (Society for Cutting Up Men) Manifesto." In Robin Morgan, ed. *Sisterhood Is Powerful*. New York: Vintage, 1970.

Solomon, Alisa. "Queer Culture: A Celebration—and a Critique." *Village Voice*, 21 June 1994, 3–4, 33.

Spivak, Gayatri Chakravorty. "Feminism and Deconstruction, Again: Negotiations." In *Outside in the Teaching Machine*. New York: Routledge, 1993.

Squier, Susan Merrill, ed. *Women Writers and the City: Essays in Feminist Literary Criticism*. Knoxville: University of Tennessee Press, 1984.

Stambolian, George and Elaine Marks. *Homosexualities and French Literature*. Ithaca, NY: Cornell University Press, 1979.

Steedman, Carolyn. *Landscape for a Good Woman*. New Brunswick, NJ: Rutgers University Press, 1987.

Stein, Arlene. "Sisters and Queers: The Decentering of Lesbian Feminism." *Socialist Review* 22 (1992): 33–55.

———. ed. *Sisters, Sexperts, Queers: Beyond the Lesbian Nation.* New York: Plume, 1993.

———. "The Year of the Lustful Lesbian." In Arlene Stein, ed. *Sisters, Sexperts, Queers: Beyond the Lesbian Nation.* New York: Plume, 1993.

Stimpson, Catharine R. "Nancy Reagan Wears a Hat: Feminism and its Cultural Consensus." In *Where the Meanings Are: Feminism and Cultural Spaces.* New York: Methuen, 1988.

———. "Zero Degree Deviancy: the Lesbian Novel in English." In *Where the Meanings Are: Feminism and Cultural Spaces.* New York: Methuen, 1988.

———. "Afterword: Lesbian Studies in the 1990s." In Karla Jay and Joanne Glasgow, eds. *Lesbian Texts and Contexts: Radical Revisions.* New York: Columbia University Press, 1990.

Storey, John. *An Introductory Guide to Cultural Theory and Popular Culture.* Athens, GA: University of Georgia Press, 1993.

Study Committee on the Status of Lesbians and Gay Men. "From Invisibility to Inclusion: Opening the Doors for Lesbians and Gay Men at the University of Michigan," June 1991.

Swindells, Julia. "Liberating the Subject? Autobiography and 'Women's History': A Reading of the Diaries of Hannah Cullwick." In Personal Narratives Group, ed. *Interpreting Women's Lives: Feminist Theory.* Bloomington: Indiana University Press, 1989.

Tuna, Bess. "Hothead Paisan: Our Favorite Lesbian Terrorist interviewed by Bess Tuna on KBRAT (plus a real interview with Diane and Stacey, artist and publisher) by Fish." *Brat Attack* 3 (1993): 26–33.

Venn, Couze. "The Subject of Psychology." In Julian Henriques, Wendy Hollway, Cathy Urwin, Couze Venn, and Valerie Walkerdine, eds. *Changing the Subject: Psychology, Social Regulation and Subjectivity.* London: Methuen, 1984.

Viegener, Matias. "There's Trouble in That Body: Queer Fanzines, Sexual Identity and Censorship." *Fiction International* 22 (1992): 123–136.

Walton, Jean. "Sandra Bernhard: Lesbian Postmodern or Modern Postlesbian." In Laura Doan, ed., *The Lesbian Postmodern.* New York: Columbia University Press, 1994.

Walker, Lisa M. "How to Recognize a Lesbian: The Cultural Politics of Looking Like What You Are." *Signs* 18 (Summer 1993): 866–890.

Warland, Betsy, ed. *InVersions: Writings by Dykes, Queers and Lesbians.* Vancouver: Press Gang, 1991.

Warner, Michael. "From Queer to Eternity: An Army of Theorists Cannot Fail." *Village Voice Literary Supplement* (June 1992): 18–19.

———. "Introduction." In Michael Warner, ed. *Fear of a Queer Planet: Queer Politics and Social Theory*. Minneapolis: University of Minnesota Press, 1993.

———. ed. *Fear of a Queer Planet*. Minneapolis: University of Minnesota Press, 1993.

Waugh, Patricia. *Feminine Fictions: Revisiting the Postmodern*. New York: Routledge, 1989.

Weedon, Chris. *Feminist Practice and Poststructuralist Theory*. Oxford: Basil Blackwell, 1987.

Weeks, Jeffrey. *Sexuality and Its Discontents*. London: Routledge, 1985.

West, Cornel. "The New Cultural Politics of Difference." In Russell Ferguson, Martha Gever, Trinh T. Minh-ha, and Cornel West, eds. *Out There: Marginalization and Contemporary Cultures*. New York: New Museum of Contemporary Art, 1990.

Whatling, Clare. "Reading Awry: Joan Nestle and the Recontextualization of Heterosexuality." In Joseph Bristow, ed. *Sexual Sameness: Textual Differences in Lesbian and Gay Writing*. New York: Routledge, 1992.

Wheeler, Elizabeth. "Bulldozing the Subject." *Postmodern Culture* (May 1991): 5–17.

White, Patricia. "Female Spectator, Lesbian Specter: The Haunting." In Diana Fuss, ed. *inside/out: Lesbian Theories, Gay Theories*. New York: Routledge, 1991.

Wiegman, Robin. "Introduction: Mapping the Lesbian Postmodern." In Laura Doan, ed. *The Lesbian Postmodern*. New York: Columbia University Press, 1994.

Williams, Raymond. *Keywords*. London: Flamingo, 1983.

Wilson, Elizabeth. "Forbidden Love." In *Hidden Agendas: Theory, Politics, and Experience in the Women's Movement*. London: Tavistock, 1986.

Wittig, Monique. *The Lesbian Body*. Translated by David Le Vay. New York: Bard, 1976.

———. and Sande Zeig. *Lesbian Peoples: Material for a Dictionary*. New York: Avon, 1978.

———. "Paradigm." In George Stambolian and Elaine Marks, eds. *Homosexualities and French Literature*. Ithaca, NY: Cornell University Press, 1979.

———. *The Straight Mind and Other Essays*. Boston: Beacon Press, 1992.

———. "The Point of View: Universal or Particular?" In *The Straight Mind and Other Essays*. Boston: Beacon, 1992.

———. "The Mark of Gender." In *The Straight Mind and Other Essays*. Boston: Beacon, 1992.

Yingling, Thomas. "Sexual Preference/Cultural Reference: The Predicament of Gay Culture Studies." *American Literary History* 3 (Spring 1991): 184–197.

Zimmerman, Bonnie. *The Safe Sea of Women: Lesbian Fiction 1969–1989*. Boston: Beacon Press, 1990.

———. "Lesbians Like This and That: Some Notes on Lesbian Criticism for the Nineties." In Sally Munt, ed. *New Lesbian Criticism: Literary and Cultural Readings*. New York: Columbia University Press, 1992.

Zita, Jacquelyn N. "Lesbian and Gay Studies: Yet Another Unhappy Marriage?" In Linda Garber, ed. *Tilting the Tower: Lesbians Teaching Queer Subjects*. New York: Routledge, 1994.

Zizek, Slavoj. *Looking Awry: An Introduction to Jacques Lacan through Popular Culture*. Cambridge, MA: MIT Press, 1991.

Zwicker, Heather. "Queer Readings." Paper presented at the 1994 Learned Societies Conference, Lesbian and Gay Studies, Calgary, Alberta, 1994.

INDEX

AIDS fiction, 105, 107, 127–133
Abelove, Henry, Michèle Aina Barale, and David M. Halperin, eds.: *The Lesbian and Gay Studies Reader*, 50, 53, 137–138
Academic feminism, 11
Acker, Kathy, 65
ACT UP, 135
agency, 88–90
Althusser, Louis, 83, 87, 88
American Gulf War, 132–134
Anderson, Benedict, 16
Angry Women, 55
Anzaldúa, Gloria: 26, 29, 49, 93; *Borderlands/La Frontera*, 93; and Cherríe Moraga, *This Bridge Called My Back*, 86, 153
Asantewa, Eva Yaa, 71
autobiography: *A Restricted Country* as, 80; lesbian, 89–90; sexuality and, 98; and subjectivity, 96–101; working-class, 93, 96 (*see also* life writing)
avant-garde: and censorship, 59–60; and lesbian avant-garde, 57; and lesbian-feminism, 10; as substitute for politics, 136; neo-avant-garde, 76; theorists of, 76

Bad Attitude, 61 (*see also* lesbian sex magazines; pornography, lesbian sex practices)
Barnard College 1982 "The Scholar and The Feminist IX" Conference, 5–8, 81, 119; and the sex wars, 5 (*see also* sex wars)
Barney, Natalie, 40
Barthes, Roland, 88–89, 114
Bechdel, Alison, 25, 27, 57, 58, 62–63, 64, 66, 67, 68, 69, 70, 71, 72, 75, 77; as postmodern cartoonist, 30; and race, 31; *Dykes To Watch Out For*, 30-31, 55–76
Bereano, Nancy, 59, 94 (*see also* lesbian publishers; gay and lesbian publishers)
Berg, Allison, Jean Kowaleski, Caroline Le Guin, Ellen Weinauer and Eric A. Wolfe: "Breaking the Silence: Sexual Preference in the Composition Classroom," 148–149
Berlant, Lauren and Elizabeth Freeman, 107–108
Bernhard, Sandra, 20
Bimbox, 61 (*see also* zines)
bisexuality: and *Empathy*, 131; and *People In Trouble*, 129
Bobbitt, Lorena, 65–66
Bordo, Susan, 27
Borghi, Liana, 82
Brat Attack, 62 (*see also* zines)
Bright, Susie, 90
Britzman, Deborah P., 138
Brontë, Charlotte, 120
Brossard, Nicole, 49, 74, 106, 108–109, 112–113
Bryson, Mary and Suzanne de Castell, 137–138

Burroughs, William, 65
butch-femme, 6–7, 29; and class, 40, 81; and desire, 83; and film, 45–46; and identity, 83; and Joan Nestle, 30; and lesbian feminism, 136; and lesbian sexual practices, 78; and low culture/high theory, 80; and oral history, 40; and race, 40; and reading, 40–46; and representation, 78; and Sarah Schulman, 131; and the sex wars, 81; as centering lesbian sexuality, 90; as lesbian camp, 123; as performativity, 22; 77–101; as reading subject positions, 78; femme invisibility, 101; lesbian-feminism as, 80, 100; the representation of, 41–46; the semiotic codes of, 79
Butler, Judith, 12, 21, 25–26, 49, 70, 107–108; and *Judy!*, 29, 33–34, 51–54; as post-gay theorist, 28; *Bodies That Matter*, 52; *Gender Trouble*, 22–23, 24, 26, 27, 94
Bürger, Peter, 61, 76

Califia, Pat, 81, 89
cartoons: as coming out narratives, 30; and lesbian comic strips, 30; (*see also* comic books; zines; queer zines)
Case, Sue-Ellen, 10, 26, 44, 48, 72–74; "Toward a Butch-Femme Aesthetic," 84, 86, 101, 123 (*see also* performance theorists; lesbian theatre)
Castle, Terry, 35, 49, 54, 104–105, 107; *The Apparitional Lesbian*, 47–48
censorship: and *Hothead Paisan*, 59–60
Center for Lesbian and Gay Studies at the City University of New York, 146; and Joan Nestle, 83
Chauncey, George: "Christian Brotherhood or Sexual Perversion? Homosexual Identities and the Construction of Sexual Boundaries in the World War I Era," 43

citational practices, 109; lesbian absence/presence in, 42, 46–54; and butch-femme, 41–46; and *Judy!*, 51–54; and lesbian theory, 16, 44; and queer theory, 47, 48; and race, 87; and the displacement of the lesbian subject, 14–19, 46–54; and the failure of, 50; and transference, 52–54; the politics of, 16, 40
city-island, the, 103, 116–117; and the Sapphic model, 111–113; in lesbian fiction, 106; Lesbos as, 107 (*see also* lesbian literary tradition)
Clark, Danae, 15
Cohen, Ed, 141, 148
Color Purple, The, 69, 156
Combrowicz, Witold, 36
comic books, 60; and anger, 60; and queer zines, 57; and realism, 60; and the avant-garde, 69; and women's bookstores, 60; and women's sexuality, 57; as a sight of lesbian representation, 66–69 (*see also* cartoons; queer zines; zines)
compulsory heterosexuality, 4, 5, 22, 48, 49 (*see also* lesbian continuum; Rich, Adrienne)
Corinne, Tee, 60
Creet, Julia: "Daughter of the Movement: The Psychodynamics of Lesbian S/M Fantasy," 50
cross-dressing, as performativity, 22
Culler, Jonathon, 36
cultural feminism, 7–8; and lesbian essentialists, 8, 110; and the anti-urban politics of, 119 (*see also* lesbian-feminism)
cultural materialism, 43, 110; and definitions of culture, 14–19; and sexual identity, 22–23
cultural studies: and humanist pedagogies, 138; and lesbian-feminism, 16; and lesbian postmodernism, 16
culture: and definitional anxiety of, 17; and feminism, 10; and gender, 15; and lesbian theory, 14; and

lesbian-feminism, 10; and politics, 17; and race; 15; and the sex wars, 10; definitions of, 13–19; feminist, 3; high, 18–19; lesbian un/popular, 13–19; lesbian, 8, 10; popular, 17, 19; problems of, 15; the teaching of, 159

Daly, Mary, 57, 70
Davy, Kate, 73, 123 (*see also* performance theorists; lesbian theatre)
De Certeau, Michel, 35–36, 51
De Lauretis, Teresa, 10, 21, 22, 24, 26, 44, 49, 73, 123; "Film and the Visible," 45–47; "Sexual Indifference and Lesbian Representation," 23, 45–47, 84–85, 86–87; *Technologies of Gender*, 90; *The Practice of Love*, 47, 73
De Man, Paul, *The Resistance to Theory*, 33, 36, 37–38
Dead Jacqueline Susann Quarterly, 52
DeJean, Joan, 106, 112
Delany, Samuel, 78
Derrida, Jacques, 49, 75, 88, 92
Desert Hearts, 69
detective fiction, 14, 119, 120–122, 126; *The Sophie Horowitz Story* as parody of, 120
Diamond, Neil, 85
DiMassa, Diane, 27, 57, 58, 59, 60, 62, 63-64, 65, 66, 68, 70, 71, 72, 75; *Hothead Paisan*, 30-31, 55–76
Doan, Laura, ed.: *The Lesbian Postmodern*, 1, 20
Dolan, Jill, 73–74, 123 (*see also* performance theorists; lesbian theatre)
Douglas, Mary, 16
drag: as performativity, 22; lesbian, 85
Duberman, Martin, 146
Dykes To Watch Out For, 55–76; and anger, 57; and butch-femme, 63; and feminist popular culture, 57; and film, 69–70; and Firebrand, 59; and heterosexuality, 68–69; and humor, 67; and its readers, 67, 72; and lesbian and gay publishing, 59; and lesbian representation, 57; and lesbian sexual practices, 71; and lesbian sexual-political practices, 56; and lesbian-feminist culture, 68–69; and popular culture, 69–70; and race, 62; and realism, 72; and representation, 63; and s/m, 63; and sexual (in)difference, 69–70, 72; and sexuality, 57; and spectatorial communities, 63; and spectatorship, 58; and the lesbian-feminist vanguard, 58; and the politics of looking, 58; and the politics of naming, 58; and whiteness, 62–63; as femme comic, 56; as lesbocentric, 58; as multiracial, 63; as narrative, 71; as postmodern, 68–69; as serial novel, 68–69; insemination, pregnancy, and childbirth in, 71

Edelman, Lee: *Homographesis*, 47–48
empathy, 130–134
Engelbrecht, Penelope: "'Lifting Belly is a Language': The Postmodern Lesbian Subject," 1
essentialism, 8; and anti-essentialism, 82, 89, 116; and epistemology, 66; and ethnicity, 17; and lesbian writing, 116; and reading practices, 90; as nature/culture controversy, 17, 82; the impasse over, 17, 84; the refusal of, 90; vs constructionism, 8

Faderman, Lillian, 7–9, 44, 101, 107, 108, 117–118; *Odd Girls and Twilight Lovers*, 7, 35, 42; *Surpassing the Love of Men*, 42
fantasy: and butch-femme sexuality, 46
Felman, Shoshana: *Jacques Lacan and the Adventure of Insight*, 33, 36; and Dori Laub, *Testimony*, 137; 150, 156
feminism: 10; and culture, 3; and

heterosexuality, 5; and lesbian sex radicals, 7; and postmodernism, 10; and poststructuralism, 10; and sexuality, 9; and the gay/straight split, 10, 22; butch-femme as the subject of, 83–86
feminist cultural consensus, the, 4, 119
feminist cultural wars, 10
feminist postmodernism: and lesbian postmodernism, 20
Ferguson, Ann: "Patriarchy, Sexual Identity and the Sexual Revolution," 4–5
Fisher, Roger and William Ury: *Getting to Yes*, 92–93
For Lesbians Only, 107
Foucault, Michel, 8, 49, 87, 116
Freire, Paolo, 142
Freud, Sigmund, 15, 36, 47, 156; "A Case of Homosexuality in a Woman," 130–134; and *Empathy*, 130–134
Frye, Marilyn, 11, 108; "Lesbian 'Sex'," 44
Fuss, Diana, 25–26, 49, 70; *Essentially Speaking*, 26; *inside/out*, 26

Gagnier, Regenia: "Between Women: A Cross-Class Analysis of Status and Anarchic Humor," 67–68
Gallop, Jane, 36, 85
Garber, Linda: *Tilting the Tower*, 53, 144
Gates Jr., Henry Louis, 17
Gay Games IV, the Cultural Festival of, 16
gay and lesbian publishing, the cultural politics of, 37
gender: as performativity, 51; and writing, 106
genre: and postmodernism, 89; fiction and its postmodern deconstruction, 25; romance novels and, 119; mixed, 86; transgression, 96 (*see also* autobiography; detective fiction)

Goffman, Irving, 16
Goldberg, Whoopi, 69
Gordon, Bette, 67
Grahn, Judy: 26, 44, 108; *Another Mother Tongue*, 115–117
Griffin, Gail B.: *Calling*, 151–153, 156–157,
Grossberg, Lawrence, Cary Nelson and Paula Treichler: *Cultural Studies*, 15
Guardian, 18
Gubar, Susan, 106, 112

Halberstam, Judith, 48
Harris, Bertha, 11–12, 114, 115
Hart, Lynda: *Fatal Women*, 58
heterosexuality: and Adrienne Rich, 3–4
historiography: feminist, 37, 101
history, 100; butch-femme as lesbian, 77–101, 110
Holy Titclamps: 62 (*see also* lesbian sex magazines; pornography; lesbian sex practices)
hooks, bell, 55
Hothead Paisan: 55–76; and anger, 57; and Canada Customs, 59; and Catholicism, 64; and censorship, 59–60; and feminist politics, 60; and generational tensions in, 70; and heterosexuality, 70; and its readership, 59; and lesbian diversity, 63; and lesbian representation, 57; and lesbian theory, 70; and lesbian-feminism, 59, 65–66, 70; and paranoid fantasies, 65–66; and *SCUM Manifesto*, 70; and sex 'n violence, 65–66; and sexuality, 57; and the leatherdyke zinescene, 64; and the severed penis, 65–66; and weapons, 65–66; and whiteness, 63; as avant-garde, 55–76; as butch zine, 56; as counter-discourse, 70; as feminist popular culture, 57; as poetic quest, 65–66; as postmodern,

57; as queerzine, 56; as revenge fantasy, 59–60; in relation to men, 59; spirituality in, 64–66; the formal innovations of, 57
Hughes, Holly, 85, 123
Huyssen, Andreas, 76
hysteria: and *Empathy*, 130–134

identity, identification, and, 35, 37, 130–134, 144
Inge, Thomas: *Comics as Culture*, 57
Iser, Wolfgang: *The Act of Reading*, 36

Jameson, Frederic, 15–16, 17, 100
jazz, 13
Jeffreys, Sheila: *Not a Passing Phase*, 42
Johnson, Barbara, 49
Johnston, Jill, 24, 107
Journal of Homosexuality, The, 144
Judy!: and *Judith Butler*, 29, 51–54; as fanzine, 51–54; as manifesto, 53

Kelly, Mary, 120
Kennedy, Elizabeth L. and Madeline D. Davis: *Boots of Leather, Slippers of Gold*, 39–45
Kerouac, Jack: *On the Road*, 124–125
King, Katie, 3, 49, 78, 82, 90; "Producing Sex, Theory, and Culture: Gay/Straight Remappings in Contemporary Feminism," 21; "The Situation of Lesbianism as Feminism's Magical Sign," 39–41
Kristeva, Julia, 51, 76

Lacan, Jacques, 36, 47, 87, 88, 153, 157, 159
Lambda Book Report, 34, 35, 58, 122
language: and sexuality, 43–46; and the resistance to theory, 37
Laplanche, J. and J-B Pontalis: *The Language of Psychoanalysis*, 32, 59
Leduc, Violette: *La Bartarde*, 85
Lesbian and Gay Studies Newsletter (MLA), 53

Lesbian Avengers, The, 103
Lesbian Herstory Archives, 98
lesbian and gay publishers: Firebrand, 59, 94; Naiad Press, 119, 122; Seal Press, 119 (*see also* lesbian publishers)
lesbian and gay studies, 1, 2, 11, 12, 22, 25–26; and antihomophobic pedagogy, 31; and canonicity, 33–34, 45; and feminist pedagogy, 25; and minoritizing discourse, 32; 33–34; and pedagogy, 147; and queer pedagogy, 25; and queer theory, 31, 33–34; and reading practices, 32; and women's studies, 31; as postidentitarian, 116; the academic institutionalization of, 28, 33–34, 37, 137; without a queer pedagogy, 31
lesbian bar cultures: 1940s and 1950s, 43–46
lesbian chic, 2, 18, 104, 127
lesbian continuum, the, 3, 5, 13, 42, 48 (*see also* compulsory heterosexuality; Rich, Adrienne)
lesbian culture, 40, 127; and opera, 54; the insularity of, 106; the scarcity model of, 54
lesbian film: and butch-femme, 45–46; and spectatorial communities, 45–46
lesbian identity: and authenticity, 41, 81; and gay men, 50; and generational conflict, 49, 50; and lesbian-feminism, 11–12; and literature, 11–12; and politics, 103; and whiteness, 11–12; as "not-women," 12, 84 (*see also* Wittig, Monique); as ontology, 11; as resexualized, 86–90; as the effect of reading practices, 28–29, 33–54
lesbian literary tradition, 104–119, 122; and anti-realism, 108; and the Amazonian model, 113–117; Anglo-American, 113–117;

Francophone lesbian literary tradition, 111; Romantic friendship model, 117–119; Sapphic model, 106, 111–113; Sarah Schulman, and the, 136; the symbolic geographies of, 106–109; three models of, 106, 109–111 (*see also* city-island, the; urbanity)

lesbian postmodernism, 1–2, 11–12, 19–24, 121; and cultural activity, 19–24; and feminism, 2, 20; and graphic art, 25–32; and its erasure of feminism, 20–21, 25; and lesbian autobiography, 25–32; and lesbian culture, 24; and lesbian erotica, 24; and lesbian fiction, 25–32; and lesbian identity, 19–24; and lesbian sexual practices, 19–24; and lesbian subjectivity, 25-32; and lesbian-feminism, 1–2, 19–24; and reading practices, 25–32; and realism, 127; and representation, 25–32; and the politics of desire, 25–32; and the technologies of, 24; and the written texts of, 24; and urbanity, 105; as avant-garde, 24; as ethico-political crisis, 24; as fashion, 24; as performative, 24; as the rewriting of lesbian-feminism, 25–32; as undertheorized, 26; as un/popular culture, 14, 24; blindspots of, 26; Sarah Schulman and, 135–136; the critiques of, 11–12

lesbian publishing: Firebrand Books, 59; Naiad Press, 68 (*see also* gay and lesbian publishing)

lesbian reader response, 35; and reading pleasure, 35

lesbian romance novels: *Empathy* as parody of, 134; and realism, 134

lesbian separatism, 106–109, 119; and the masculine city, 117; lesbian culture as, 105; Sarah Schulman as anti-separatist novelist, 108; the insularity of, 106

lesbian sex magazines: and feminism, 61–62; and lesbian sex radicals 7; and sexual practices, 61–62; and the crisis in representation, 62; and the feminist cultural consensus, 62; and the sex wars, 62; and their readership, 61–62

lesbian sexual practices, 135; and the sex wars, 29; s/m, 29

lesbian sexuality: and Freud, 133

lesbian studies: and humanist pedagogies, 138; and women's studies, 9

lesbian subjectivity, 23; and male writers, 112; and representation, 23; and the politics of naming, 23

lesbian theatre, 123, 127; and performance theorists, 123–125; and realism, 86–87; theories of, 84–86

lesbian theory, 4, 11–12, 33–54; and female sexuality, 9, 21; and feminism, 21; and identity and identification, 37; and lesbian-feminism, 33–54; and paper lesbians, 29, 33–54; and politics, 21; and postmodernism, 10–11; and poststructuralism, 26, 38; and psychoanalysis, 26; and race, 21; and lesbian reading practices, 28, 33–54; and sexual minorities, 21; and sexuality, 80–86; and subjectivity, 84; and the female/feminist/lesbian subject, 83–86; and the feminist cultural wars, 10–11; and the gay/straight split, 10, 21; and the sex wars, 10–11, 21; and theoretical divas, 37; and transference, 52–54; and women's studies, 26–27; as disciplinary shift, 37–39; as fiction, 86; as interdisciplinary, 37–39; as postmodernist, 37–39; construction and reception of, 36–37, 33–54; performance, film and theatre, 84–86; resistance to, 37–38; the anxieties of, 37; the pleasures of, 37; the postmodern turn toward, 36; the resistance to, 26–28

lesbian writing, 136; and essentialism,

116; and realism, 114; and romanticism, 114; and the realist-escape model, 114; and the romantic friendship model, 117–119; antiurbanity in, 117; the city as metaphor in, 105, 116

lesbian-feminism, 1–12; and generational conflict, 120; and genre fiction, 105; and heterosexuality, 71; and lesbian chic, 2; and lesbian postmodernism, 1–2, 14, 19–24; and lesbian sex cultures, 61; and pleasure, 61; and queer zines, 61; and reading practices, 38, 68; and realism, 55; and representation, 50; and sexual morality, 8; and the avant-garde, 1–2; and the desexualization of lesbianism, 4, 8; the vanguardism of, 4, 24; and the sex wars, 1–12; and violence, 58, 63; as butch-femme, 136; the anti-urban politics of, 105, 119; the culture of, 13, 49

Lesbian: and the politics of naming, 11–12; as feminism's magical sign, 12; as ontology, 104; performativity, 12; as the transcendental signifier, 9, 12; contests of meaning over, 5–7; the apparitional, 48; the etymology of, 11–12

lesbianism: and female socialization, 8, 9; and feminism, 2; and gender, 9; and heterosexual feminism, 8; and heterosexual feminists, 10; and postmodernism, 5; and representational politics, 8; as severed from feminism, 20; as vanguardism, 5; the desexualization of, 4

lesbians: and aesthetics, 49; and compulsory heterosexuality, 3, 5; and cultural practices, 10; and ethnicity, 17; and gay men, 1, 3, 14; and generational conflict, 2; and history, 6; and identity, 5, 11; and modernism, 4; and politics, 49; and representation, 10; and s/m, 8; and sexuality, 5; and style, 10; and the avant-garde, 2, 11; and the gay movement, 18; and the myth of origins, 2; and vampires, 48; as critics, 36; as intellectuals, 7, 14, 20, 38, 105, 120, Freud's theory of, 130; as sexual outlaws, 2; invisibility of, 18; or woman-identification, 4; the legitimation of, 2–3

life writing, 29 (*see also* genre; autobiography)

Lingua Franca, 53

Lippard, Lucy, 75

lipstick lesbians, 18

Lorde, Audre: 26, 29, 44, 49, 82, 93, 154; *Sister Outsider*, 86; *Zami*, 86–87, 90, 95

Loulan, JoAnn: *The Erotic Dance*, 77

Lynch, Michael, 146

MacFarquahar, Larissa, 53

Madonna, 89, 131

Maggenti, Maria, 71

male lesbians, 18

manifestos, 4, 86; and race, 87; and women's studies, 87; "Compulsory Heterosexuality and Lesbian Existence" as, 4; *Judy!* as, 53; lesbian-feminist, 49; *SCUM Manifesto*, 70

Marks, Elaine, 26, 49, 85, 106, 111–114

Marshall, Donald G.: *Contemporary Critical Theory*, 51

Martin, Biddy, 25–26, 44, 49; "Lesbian Identity and Autobiographical Difference[s]," 89–90; "Sexual Practice and Changing Lesbian Identities," 90, 98

Martin, Wendy, 118

Marx, Karl, 127, 136

Marxism: and culture, 15, 97, 136

McLaughlin, Sheila, 45-46

Meese, Elizabeth, 10, 49, 73; "Theorizing Lesbian: Writing—A Love Letter," 85–86, 92

men, 134

Merck, Mandy: *Perversions*, 110–111, 115, 116
meta-fiction: and realism, 104
minoritizing discourse, 22; and pedagogy, 139, 145, 149
Minton, Henry, L., 144
minority studies: and humanist pedagogies, 138
Miss Spentyouth: *Judy!*, 52–54 (*see also* Butler, Judith)
modernism: lesbian, 14; Adrienne Rich and lesbian, 4; and lesbian-feminism, 19
Mohanty, Chandra, 26
Mohr, Richard: "Gay Studies in the Big Ten: A Survivor's Manual," 142–144; "The Ethics of Students and the Teaching of Ethics: A Lecturing," 142–144, 148, 156–157
Moraga, Cherríe, 29, 49, 93; and Gloria Anzaldúa, *This Bridge Called My Back*, 86, 153
multiculturalism, 17
Munt, Sally: "'Somewhere over the rainbow ...': Postmodernism and the Fiction of Sarah Schulman," 104, 135–136
myth of origins, a, 2, 3, 110; and reading, 39

Near, Holly, 13
Nestle, Joan, 6, 25, 26, 27, 30, 44, 78, 79, 80, 81, 82, 83, 88, 89, 90, 93, 94, 95, 96, 97, 98, 99, 100, 101, 136; and fragmented subjectivity, 82; and gender, 83; and history, 82; and lesbian visibility, 82; *A Restricted Country*, 29–30, 77–101; as femme, 77–101; *The Persistent Desire*, 29
Nicholson, Linda J.: *Feminism/Postmodernism*, 20

O'Keeffe, Georgia, 120
Omosupe, Ekua, 109
On Our Backs, 61 (*see also* lesbian sex magazines; pornography; lesbian sex practices)
On the Road: and *Girls, Visions and Everything*, 124–125
opera, 13
Outlook, 71

Pagalia, Camille, 15–16
paper lesbians: and reading, 33–54; as anti-intellectualism, 36; as theory, 36–37
parody: and sexual identity, 22
Parting Glances, 156
pedagogy: and gay and lesbian studies, 147; and homophobia, 137; and poststructuralism, 137, 144, 152; and psychoanalysis, 138; and reading practices, 152, 153; and safety, 150; and sexuality, 145; and the production of ignorance, 150; and universalizing approaches to, 139, 145, 149; anti-racism and, 138, 153–154; antihomophobic, 147; canonicity and, 140; as theory of teaching, 145; critical, 145; feminist, 145; humanist assumptions of traditional, 138, 150; minoritizing approaches to, 139, 145, 149; pederastic, 53; queer, 137–159; trauma and, 32, 138, 141, 149, 156; un/popular culture and, 31–32, 137–159
performance theorists, 73–75
performativity, 22; and lesbian identity, 80–86
Pérez, Emma, 49
Phranc, 85
Plato: "Apology," 144
politics: and aesthetic activism, 129; and aesthetics, 20; and lesbian postmodernism, 20; and sex, 20; and the avant-garde, 20
popular culture, 1–2, 11; lesbian, 11
pornography, 24; lesbian, 7, 135; lesbians in heterosexual, 18

post-colonialism: and lesbian writing, 109
postmodern lesbian theory, 21–23
postmodernism, 12; and lesbian subjectivity, 80–86; and lesbian-feminism, 19; and Marxism, 136; and metanarratives, 20; and Sarah Schulman, 104, 131; and the sex wars, 104; *Dykes To Watch Out For*, as, 76; feminism and, 12; *Hothead Paisan* as, 76; lesbian, 19
poststructuralism: and anti-poststructuralism, 39; and ethnography, 39, 44; and historiography, 44; and lesbian representation, 45–46; modernist reading practices, 39; and mythoethnography, 110; and pedagogy, 137–159
Pratt, Minnie Bruce, 26, 98
psychoanalysis: and *Empathy*, 130–134; and feminist literary and film criticism, 46; and lesbian sexuality, 47; and pedagogy, 138; and poststructuralism, 46
Pynchon, Thomas, 65

Queer Nation, 30
Queer Sites Conference (Toronto, 1993), The, 36
queer theory, 11, 22–23; and generational models of, 53; and lesbian theory, 47; and pedagogy, 137–159, 148; and Sarah Schulman, 104; and the ghosting of the lesbian subject, 47–48; and the teaching of culture, 159; the academic institutionalization of, 23, 45
queer zines, 58; and anger, 57; and form, 61–62; and sexuality, 57; and women's comics, 57; as lesbian avant-garde, 61–62; as manifestos, 61–62 (*see also* cartoons; comic books; queer zines)

race, 7, 17; American Judaism, 120–122; and Asian-American lesbians, 63, 64; and citational practices, 87; and Euramerican lesbianism, 26; and fantasy, 46; and First Nations Peoples, 64; and *Hothead Paisan*, 63; and lesbian identity, 86; and lesbian sexuality, 46, 154; and pedagogy, 138, 153–154; and postmodern lesbian culture, 26; and the sex wars, 119–120; and whiteness, 11–12, 26; Black civil rights movement, 143; Judaism in Joan Nestle, 95–96; *Stonewall*, as Amerocentric signifier, 109; white lesbian culture, 11–12, 26, 109; whiteness and *Dykes To Watch Out For*, 62–63
Raymond, Janice G., 6; "Putting the Politics Back Into Lesbianism," 99, 101
reading practices, 26, 32; and butch-femme, 40, 77–101; and desire, 35; and essentialism, 90; and ethnography, 39; and genre fictions, 35; and identity formation, 28–29, 33–54; and lesbian and gay bookstores, 33; and lesbian modernism, 39; and lesbian subjectivity, 33–54; and lesbian theory, 33–39; and lesbian visibility, 45; and lesbian-feminism, 36, 40; and misreading, 40; and pedagogy, 152, 153; and postmodernism, 120; and realism, 40; and sexuality, 33–54, 78; and the displacement of the lesbian subject, 46–54; and the formation of lesbian communities, 28–29, 33–54, 40; and the sex wars, 10, 33–54; and transference, 52–54; anti-poststructuralist, 39; as contested site, 40; as fanship, 54; critical and theoretical works and, 35; feminist approaches to, 36; humanist approaches to, 36; in relation to knowledge production, 35; Lacanian approaches to, 36; les-

bian, 28-29, 35, 39; models of, 33-34; the politics of, 41

representation, 26, 129; and desire, 67-68; and lesbian cultural practices, 50; and politics, 8; and poststructuralism, 45-46; and reading practices, 153; and realism, 66-69; and sexuality, 104; and spectatorial communities, 84-86; comics as, 66-69; cultural politics of, 119; lesbian theatre and, 73-75; lesbian, 45; the crisis in, 45-46

resistance: and agency, 88-90; and negotiating subjectivity, 90-94; and subjectivity, 88-90

Rich, Adrienne: as lesbian theory, 4; "Compulsory Heterosexuality and Lesbian Existence," 2-5, 8, 27, 40, 42, 44, 48, 49, 118, 120, 152, as manifesto of lesbian modernism, 5

Rich, Ruby B.: "Feminism and Sexuality in the 1980s," 1, 10

romantic friendship, 42, 99

Roof, Judith: *A Lure of Knowledge*, 26, 47-48, 49

Roy, Camille, 18

Rubin, Gayle: "The Traffic in Women," 9, 49; "Thinking Sex: Notes for a Radical Theory of the Politics of Sexuality," 8-10

Rule, Jane: *Desert of the Heart*, 151

Russell, Charles, 19, 68, 75-76

Said, Edward: *Orientalism*, 156

Sandoval, Chela, 78

Sanger, William W., 99

Sappho, 28, 40, 42, 105, 106, 109, 110, 111, 112, 136

Schulman, Sarah, 25, 27, 37, 56, 103-136; *After Delores*, 125-127; and lesbian sex, 104; and lesbian-feminist writing, 104; and the sex wars, 104; as anti-separatist novelist, 108; as lesbian writer, 134-136; as postmodernist, 104; as universal writer, 134-136; *Empathy*, 103, 130-134, 135, 136; *Girls, Visions and Everything*, 122-125, and Kerouac's *On the Road*, 124-125; *My American History*, 103; *People In Trouble*, 127-130, 132-133, 135; *The Sophie Horowitz Story*, 120-122, 140-141;*When We Were Very Young*, 121

Sedgwick, Eve Kosofsky: as post-gay theorist, 28, 31; *Between Men*, 47; 51, 52; *Epistemology of the Closet*, 21-23, 47, 145, 149, 150

Segrest, Mab, 98

sex trade workers: and lesbian culture, 99-100, 122

sex wars, the, 1-12, 104; and Joan Nestle, 81; and postmodernism, 104; and poststructuralism, 104, 135; and race, 7, 119-120; and Sarah Schulman, 123; and the repressive feminist mother, 50

sex/gender system, 9-10

sexology, 41; and lesbian identity, 41-42, 117

sexual (in)difference, 73; and butch-femme, 84-86; and de Lauretis, 22-23, 45-46; and hom(m)osexuality, 45-46, 73, 85; and representation, 45-46

sexual practices: and the city, 119

sexuality, 7; and feminism, 9; and gender, 9, 23; and identity, 5, 147; and knowledge, 147; and lesbian pornography, 7; and lesbian public sex, 7; and lesbian s/m, 7; and lesbian subcultures, 78; and lesbian textuality, 40, 151; and lesbians, 7, 9, 80-90, 104; and pedagogy, 145, 147; and politics, 78; and race, 154; and representation, 46; and sexual minorities, 8, 9; and theory, 9; history of, 8, 9

She Must Be Seeing Things, 45-46

Shockley, Ann: "A Meeting of the Sapphic Daughters," 115

Smith, Patti, 127

Smith, Paul: *Discerning the Subject*, 87–89, 97, 100
Solanis, Valerie: *SCUM (Society for Cutting Up Men) Manifesto*, 70–71
Solomon, Alisa, 16–17
spectator, the lesbian, 73–75
spirituality: and politics, 64–66
Spivak, Gayatri, "Feminism and Deconstruction, Again: Negotiations," 92
Split Britches, 74
Squier, Susan Merrill, ed.: *Women Writers and the City*, 118, 120
Star Trek, 52
Steedman, Carolyn: *Landscape for a Good Woman*, 93, 96-98
Stein, Arlene: "Sisters and Queers: The Decentering of Lesbian Feminism," 1–2; *Sisters, Sexperts, Queers: Beyond the Lesbian Nation*, 2
Stein, Gertrude, 28, 40, 42, 106, 120
Stimpson, Catharine R., 69, 114–115; "Nancy Reagan Wears a Hat: Feminism and Its Cultural Consensus," 1, 4, 10, 26, 49, 119–120; "Zero Degree Deviancy," 122
Stonewall: as Amerocentric signifier, 109; the twenty-fifth anniversary of, 16–17
Storey, John: *An Introductory Guide to Cultural Theory and Popular Culture*, 13
subject positions: and agency, 88–90; and Althusser, 87; and feminist theory, 83–86; and Foucault, 87; and history, 89; and Lacan, 87; and sexuality, 98; and the avant garde, 84; anthologies and, 86; fragmented, 82; historicizing, 94; lesbian, 26, 80–86; the negotiation of, 30, 90–94; the political consequences of, 94
Swindells, Julia, 96–98

Taste of Latex, 62 (*see also* lesbian sex magazines; pornography; lesbian sex practices)

Toronto Centre for Lesbian and Gay Studies, 146
transsexuality: as performativity, 22; Female-to-Male, 24
trauma: and pedagogy, 138, 141, 149–150, 156; and queer pedagogy, 32

un/popular culture, 13; *Dykes To Watch Out For*, as, 76; *Hothead Paisan* as, 76; lesbian postmodernism as, 11–12; lesbian-feminism as, 1–2; the two developments in, 31; the making of, 13–19; the reception of, 29–30; the teaching of, 31–32, 137–159
universalizing discourse, 22, 47, 104; and pedagogy, 139, 145, 149; and the ghosting of the lesbian subject, 47
urbanity: and lesbian postmodernism, 105; and lesbian separatism, 118; and masculinity, 117; anti-urbanity, 117; as the site of the lesbian literary quest, 125; lesbian-feminist alienation from, 118 (*see also* lesbian literary history)

Vance, Carole, ed.: *Pleasure and Danger*, 8
Venn, Couze, 93
Village Voice, 16
Vivien, Renee, 116

Walker, Alice: *The Color Purple*, 69, 151–152, 156–157
Walker, Lisa M.: "How to Recognize a Lesbian: The Cultural Politics of Looking Like What You Are," 158
Warner, Michael, 12; *Fear of a Queer Planet*, 155, 159; "From Queer to Eternity: An Army of Theorists Cannot Fail," 138–141, 144
Waugh, Patricia: *Feminine Fictions*, 88
Weeks, Jeffrey, 141
Weldon, Fay, 103

West, Cornel, 94
Whatling, Clare: "Reading Awry: Joan Nestle and the Recontextualization of Heterosexuality," 82
White, Patricia: "Female Spectator, Lesbian Specter: The Haunting," 13
Wilde, Oscar, 65
Williams, Raymond: *Keywords*, 14–15, 17
Wittig, Monique, 12, 44, 49, 84, 85, 105, 106, 108–110, 112, 113, 114; and Sande Zeig, *Lesbian Peoples*, 110–111
Wollstonecraft, Mary, 154
women's music, 13
women's studies, 2; and humanist pedagogies, 138; lesbian theory ignored in, 27, 37
WOW Cafe, 73–75, 123–125; and spectatorial communities, 123; Schulman's "Kitsch-Inn" as parody of, 123
Wuornos, Aileen, 58

Zimmerman, Bonnie: *The Safe Sea of Women*, 38–42, 45, 125
zines, 52–54, 59, 61; as gendered, 56; Decentralized World-Wide Networker Congress Subspace International Zine Show 1992, The, 61–62; editors, 61 (*see also* cartoons; comic books; queer zines)